CA$H IN
ON THE COMING
REAL ESTATE
CRASH

How to Protect Yourself from Losses Now, and **Turn a Profit** After the Bubble Bursts

David J. Decker and George G. Sheldon

WILEY

John Wiley & Sons, Inc.

Published by John Wiley & Sons, Inc., Hoboken, New Jersey.
Published simultaneously in Canada.

For general information on our other products and services or for technical support, please contact our Customer Care Department within the United States at (800) 762-2974, outside the United States at (317) 572-3993 or fax (317) 572-4002.

Wiley also publishes its books in a variety of electronic formats. Some content that appears in print may not be available in electronic books. For more information about Wiley products, visit our web site at www.wiley.com.

Library of Congress Cataloging-in-Publication Data:

Decker, David J., 1962-
   Cash in on the coming real estate crash : how to protect yourself from losses now, and turn a profit after the bubble bursts / David J. Decker and George G. Sheldon.
      p.   cm.
   Includes bibliographical references (p.   ).
   ISBN-13: 978-0-471-79100-3 (pbk.)
   ISBN-10: 0-471-79100-8 (pbk.)
      1. Real estate investment—United States.   2. Financial crises—United States.   I. Sheldon, George.   II. Title.
   HD255.D443   2006
   332.63'24—dc22

                                              2005034271

Printed in the United States of America.

10 9 8 7 6 5 4 3 2 1

For my mom and dad, Pete and Roger.
I may be the only son lucky enough to have a mom named Pete.
Thanks for everything.

—Dave

ABOUT THE AUTHORS

DAVID J. DECKER is a full-time real estate investor and broker. After buying his first real estate investment property at age 23, he has gone on to acquire hundreds of apartment units and other commercial properties. He continues to assist clients in reaching their investment goals. He lives with his wife Bobbi and their two children in the suburbs of Milwaukee, Wisconsin. You can learn more about Dave by visiting his web site at www.davidjdecker.com.

GEORGE G. SHELDON is the author of 20 books and a consultant on business-related topics. He is a member of the American Society of Journalists and Authors and served as a newspaper correspondent for five years, publishing more than 1,000 articles. He has worked as an editorial consultant, technical editor, and publishing consultant. George enjoys looking for real estate properties for investment. You can learn more about him by visiting his web site at www.georgesheldon.com.

CONTENTS

Acknowledgments   xi

PART ONE THE COMING REAL ESTATE BUST

INTRODUCTION

How to Make Real Estate Buying or Selling Decisions
When a Crash May Be Imminent   3

CHAPTER 1

Do You Have a False Sense of Security? Why You Should
Be Preparing for a Crash—Even If It Never Comes   7

CHAPTER 2

What Caused the Real Estate Bubble, What Could
Trigger a Crash, and Why the Crash Will Be
Regional, Not National   17

CHAPTER 3

History Lessons from Previous Real Estate Bubbles:
Who Lost and Who Came Through Stronger   41

PART TWO DEFENSIVE STRATEGIES: HOW TO PROTECT YOURSELF AND AVOID LOSSES

CHAPTER 4

How to Assess the Likelihood of a Crash in Your
Neighborhood   55

CHAPTER 5

Should You Sell Now?   89

CHAPTER 6

Should You Buy Now?   107

CHAPTER 7

Cash Flow Action Plan for Homeowners (So You
Aren't Forced to Sell When the Market Is Down)   125

CHAPTER 8

Cash Flow Action Plan for the Investor: Make Sure
You Can Hold Your Property through a Down Cycle   141

CHAPTER 9

Don't Put All Your Real Estate Eggs in One Basket:
Hedging and Balancing Your Portfolio   153

**PART THREE   How to Profit When
the Crash Happens**

CHAPTER 10

Life After the Bust: How Homeowners, Investors,
Landlords, Lenders, and the National Economy
Will React—and How to Profit   165

CHAPTER 11

Signs of Spring: When to Start Buying After a Crash   175

CHAPTER 12

Creative Financing When No One Wants to Lend:
Describing the Conditions That Are Likely to Prevail
Under Illiquid Lending Policies   183

CHAPTER 13

The Best Way to Time the Market Rebound:
Use Options   197

CHAPTER 14

Profiting from Short Sales and Buying Preforeclosure   211

CHAPTER 15

Buying at the Auction   223

CHAPTER 16

How to Buy REOs   231

CHAPTER 17

The Most Overvalued and Undervalued Markets
in the United States   239

Appendix A   247

Appendix B   264

Notes   268

Index   270

ACKNOWLEDGMENTS

Writing a book is a team effort and would not have been possible without the brilliant efforts of our agent, Bob Diforio, and all of the hardworking people at John Wiley & Sons, including Senior Editor Richard Narramore, Assistant Editor Emily Conway, and Senior Production Editor Linda Indig.

PART ONE

THE COMING REAL ESTATE BUST

How to Make Real Estate Buying or Selling Decisions When a Crash May Be Imminent

Making money in real estate is simple. Buy low, hold the property for years, sell high. While you own it, make improvements, adding value to your property. Pay your taxes on your profits, and live happily ever after.

Don't have the money to invest in real estate? Not a problem. Use other people's money to finance your investment. Live in the real estate, maintain your property, allow your equity to build. Each year, you own a bigger chunk of your mortgaged property. As your share of the property increases, the bank's decreases.

That's the way it is supposed to work. That's the way it has been done for decades.

Until now.

Now you buy a property, wait a short time, and then sell the property for thousands more than you paid for it months ago. It's called flipping. You sell it to someone else, who is probably buying it to sell to someone else. The sky's the limit.

Or is it?

Your neighbor's home, so much like yours, just sold last year for double what you paid for your property. Maybe you should sell.

Or maybe you should buy one of the condos in Miami. The value keeps increasing, weekly. You agree today to purchase a property in 90 days, and before you close, you sell your purchase option to another investor, pocketing the profit.

What a great way to make some fast money.

Until you hear the pop.

When the real estate bubble bursts, your best-laid plans may crash with it. No one thinks it could happen to them, until it is too late.

Since mid-2003, a series of events have occurred that have precariously affected the United States real estate market. Any one occurrence would have had little effect on the overall market, but together, the stability of the market is questioned.

Consider these events:

$ The growing costs of the Iraq War became neverending. The U.S. government had spent more than $200 billion in the war effort.

$ The U.S. government's deficit spending grew the national debt from $6,783,231,062,743.62 to $7,929,627,702,504.17.[1] In two years, that is an increase of $1.146 trillion. Each U.S. citizen—from the newborn to the eldest—needs to pay $26,674 to pay off the debt.[2]

$ The Consumer Price Index increased 38.2 percent for energy. This increase is based on pre-Hurricane Katrina data.[3]

$ Hurricanes Katrina and Rita caused more than $300 billion of damage. Only about 20 percent of the storm damaged was insured. The U.S. taxpayers will be paying for the damage for years.

$ Mortgage rates were increasing in September and October 2005. By the end of October, mortgage rates had nudged over 6 percent, and mortgage applications had dropped off.[4]

Recognizing a real estate bubble is not easy. Prices of real estate rise, which is not necessarily out of the ordinary. As they keep rising, everyone is happy. It's only after they stop rising, or they decrease, that a real estate bubble can be diagnosed.

Real estate bubbles do not blanket the nation. Rather, bubbles are localized. Just because a bubble occurs in one section or region does not mean a bubble will occur in another.

Different factors can help predict the likelihood of local real estate bust. Loss of jobs, the local economy, rate of increase of prices, interest rates, and availability of housing are just some of the factors that can drive a real estate bust.

Common sense tells you when things get out of whack. On New Jersey's oceanfront, there are former motels being converted to condos. For $160,000, you can buy a 280-square-foot unit. Investors are gobbling them up. The questions stands: "How many people are willing to spend that much money for 280 square feet?"

Today, there is much media hype and speculation about the probability of a real estate bubble bust. It is true? Will it happen? If it is going to happen, where will it occur?

This book sifts fact from fiction so that you can see through the hype.

Cash In on the Coming Real Estate Crash reveals that the road ahead is ground already traveled. We have been there before. We are headed there again.

As has always been the case in history, some will heed the warnings and others will ignore them, casting their lot with fate.

Some of those who ignore the warnings will emerge from the crisis with their lives, their luck, and their fortunes intact. Others will become someone else's opportunity.

Some of those who heed the warnings will find themselves prepared for a storm that never comes. But even these will be better able to enjoy what for most is their largest nest egg—the homes they live in—worry free.

However, there may be those who will find this book to be their life preserver. Others will use it to build a fortune. Throughout history, when markets have whipsawed, fortunes have been made and lost.

The readers of this book will be prepared for whatever lies ahead. Let the journey begin.

CHAPTER 1

Do You Have a False Sense of Security? Why You Should Be Preparing for a Crash— Even If It Never Comes

In the early 1990s, Tom and Jill Hindy lived in a beautiful four-bedroom house near a tranquil bird sanctuary in the West Hills of Los Angeles. It had features that rivaled any home displayed in the glossy home decorating magazines, like sparkling black and white bathroom tile. At one point, the Hindy home would have fetched $300,000—far more than they paid for it. But of course, they had no plans to sell.

Those plans changed once Tom had lost his job. By that time, the Hindys had ample company in the unemployment line, and before long, their mortgage was $30,000 past due. It was time to sell, but their $250,000 asking price drew only yawns, not offers.

"We're not irresponsible people," Jill told a *Los Angeles Times Magazine* writer at the time. Tom, a skilled cabinetmaker, could find only irregular work. He drove daily to construction sites looking for work, where as many as 150 others would show up seeking employment. In better times, the competition for work was minimal.

After six months, Jill could not keep it inside any more. With the financial pressure increasing, she finally told several close friends of their plight. The Hindys were facing foreclosure.

Jill's revelation opened a floodgate of heartache. One of Jill's best friends admitted that she was actually in foreclosure. Amazingly, another couple admitted that they were not homeowners at all. They confessed to the lie that they had told everyone for years. It turns out they were only renting. Ironically, what was once a fact to be ashamed of became their saving grace. These tenants were spared from the real estate steamroller.[1]

Jill and Tom's story, with their friends' stories, illustrate what happens during a real estate crash. Their story, from the California real estate bubble of the late 1980s and early 1990s, shows what happens when the bubble bursts. Homes once worth more than $300,000 cannot be sold at a 20 percent discount.

Before the California real estate bust, millions of the state's residents had based their lavish lifestyles on the false belief that property values could only increase. Pre-bust, it was chic and in style to have a large home and a huge mortgage. It said something about the person.

Accounts of the run-up in prices before the bubble burst are eerily familiar. These were the good times. A new era had dawned. The normal ups and downs of the real estate cycle had been put out to pasture. By 1989, the local real estate market enjoyed 60 percent increases.

But the bust arrived with a vengeance. Nearly 300,000 Californians lost their jobs. While other portions of the country thrived, prosperity remained elusive in southern California. By 1992, the state had witnessed a 30 percent decline in housing starts. More than 20,000 licensed real estate agents simply vanished. The aerospace industry lost thousands of jobs, and its collapse rippled through the southern half of the Golden State.

Many who had bought before the boom, which had started in 1986, survived the paper losses to their property, and because they didn't have to sell, were able to hold on to their houses and investments. But tens of thousands did lose their homes, filed for bankruptcy, and lost years of their life's work. That happens when real estate goes bust.

The premise of *Cash In on the Coming Real Estate Crash* is that we have been experiencing market performance in real estate that is extraordinary. The result has been real estate price escalation far beyond historical averages. The simple fact is that just like a pot of boiling water, the status quo cannot be sustained. Either the water will be boiled off or it must be allowed to cool.

The question then becomes not will the good times end, but instead, *when* the good times end, how will they end, and what will it be like? Will there be a soft landing at a new price plateau or will there be a bloodbath of reversals?

These are life-changing questions. Most people have the largest part of their financial nest egg in their homes. Decisions about when to buy a home or when and how much to invest in real estate are the most important financial decisions you will make in a lifetime. *Cash In on the Coming Real Estate Crash* will help you make these critical decisions in light of the evidence that many local real estate markets are in a high-priced bubble that may soon burst. This book will help you decide whether you should buy a house or invest in real estate now, what you can do to protect yourself against a downturn in your local market, and how to profit from the crash when and if it comes.

Meet the Author: Dave Decker

I am not an economist or a statistician, although I've graphed more than a few supply and demand curves in my time. I bought my first investment property in 1986 when I was twenty-three. Fifteen months later I went into real estate full-time, working as an investment broker selling apartment buildings. Today I own and manage a portfolio of investment properties in the Midwest. This book is written from my perspective as a seasoned professional real estate investor. My goal is to blend careful research with the wisdom I've picked up from observing the ups and downs of the real estate market over many years. I wrote this book because I believe there are too many fast and loose games being played in real estate today. Soon enough, the music will stop playing and some people will be without a seat.

Don't get me wrong. Real estate is a great business. But over the long term, it's get rich slow, not get rich quick. You may have ridden the current real estate wave to easy money with your house or investment property. If so, congratulations. But don't let this make you complacent. Many property owners will wind up with less than they started with if they assume current market conditions will never change.

Here's an example. In 1988, many of my clients were selling apartment buildings they had bought in the late 1970s and early 1980s. Ten years later, owners were finally able to sell them again for what they had paid for them. Back in those days, many bought for tax shelter benefits, not for cash flow. So besides enjoying little or no capital gains, many of these owners suffered negative cash flow, too. When they were finally able to sell at near break-even prices, the money returned to them had been depreciated by a decade of high inflation.

Not every owner got out at break-even. I remember the painful phone conversation with an owner when I had to tell him how much cash he would need to bring to closing to *sell* his building.

While memories like this are seared into my consciousness, it seems that too many others have forgotten. Or maybe it's just a new crop of real estate investors who have never lived through a down cycle in real estate. I hope this book will help you avoid learning the hard way the lessons learned when real estate crashes.

You might be surprised to learn that I am bullish on real estate. I can't think of an industry offering more opportunities to the average man or woman, and it's fun. But the days of every idiot flipping condos are going to end. The opportunity now lies in making informed, long-term, value investment decisions and applying tried and tested real estate principles. This book explains how to get ready so that when and if a crash comes, you will be positioned to profit from it.

Present Conditions Will Not Last

Is there a real estate bubble? Before you can choose between real estate crash investing strategies, or even can know whether any of the strategies are applicable, we first have to look at current market circumstances and why they are extraordinary.

The experts have begun to weigh in:

"Although a 'bubble' in home prices for the nation as a whole does not appear likely, there does appear to be, at a minimum, signs of froth in some local markets where home prices seem to have risen to unsustainable levels," according to Alan Greenspan, then chairman of the Federal Reserve Board. On June 9, 2005, testifying before the Joint Economic Committee of the U.S. Congress he added, "The apparent froth in housing markets may have spilled over into mortgage markets."

By September 2005, even real estate cheerleaders were giving mixed messages:

"Lower-than-expected mortgage interest rates will push home sales to a fifth consecutive record in 2005. In fact, long-term interest rates look very favorable," David Lereah, the chief economist of the National Association of REALTORS® (NAR), said. (Realtors and real estate agents always are cheery about the real estate market. That's their job.)

"The simple fact is we still have more buyers than sellers in most of the country," said Lereah. "This supply–demand imbalance is continuing to put pressure on home prices, but we should get closer to equilibrium by the end of the year. . . . Obviously, there are some local bubbles, but I tend to think that with most of the bubbles, the air will come out slowly, rather than popping."

During the first week of September 2005, analysts were forecasting that U.S. housing sales will begin to decline from record levels by the end of the year and into 2006. The slowing sales pace was expected to end the supersized price gains many parts of the country have experienced.

Richard DeKaser, chief economist at National City Corporation in Cleveland, said he believed that 53 metropolitan areas, representing 31 percent of the country's housing market, were "extremely overvalued and confront a high risk of a future price correction."

What could the price correction look like? DeKaser said that over the past 20 years, 64 cities have seen home price declines of 10 percent or more over two years.

Many homeowners disagree and continue to be wildly optimistic about the real estate market. Twenty-four percent of recently surveyed homeowners said they expect annualized gains of 10 percent or more in the coming years. This survey by RBC Capital Markets, a subsidiary of RBC Financial Group, also suggests that real estate wealth gains are prompting homeowners to spend and borrow even more. However, that's not how the survey participants describe themselves: "Not only are most people expecting big real estate gains to continue, most people don't believe these gains have impacted their spending," according to RBC Capital Markets managing director of Equity Research, Scot Ciccarelli.

By a two to one ratio, individuals are more optimistic about their personal finances than they are for the national economy. "Not surprisingly, those that were the most optimistic about their personal financial situation were those in the upper income categories and those that had experienced the biggest real estate gains," according to RBC. An ostrich may hide its head in the sand, but U.S. homeowners are blinded by a pile of easy money home equity.

The Law of Averages

Historically, real estate prices march in lockstep with inflation. This is not a surprise, since most durable consumer goods prices also track closely to inflation. However, in the past several years, with inflation seemingly tamed at rates of between 2 percent and 3 percent, real estate has somehow managed to break free of any gravitational constraints with prices in some markets rising 100 percent or more.

This phenomenon will not continue. Real estate markets are governed by averages, too.

The stock market is relentless in its march toward average. Most well-paid, highly educated financial managers are unable to assemble consistently a stock portfolio that routinely outperforms the market. In fact, all markets are subject to the law of averages. Whether the index is the Standard & Poor's 500, the Dow Jones Industrial Average, or the average price of a single-family home, these indexes have well established historical norms.

Of course, market performance fluctuates dramatically. There are good years and bad years when a market outperforms or underperforms the historical norms. Sometimes market performance is so unusual, it becomes front page news. During the dot-com bubble, stock market performance was sufficiently unusual that it was front page news and on the tip of the tongue of the everyday person for years. Human-interest stories carried features about the freshly minted dot-com millionaires. When the markets crashed, the media checked in again with the where-are-they-now tales about *former* dot-com millionaires!

The stock market dominated media business coverage until it got pushed off the front pages by a better story. A story about real estate.

This latest media darling is really not a new story at all, just an old one recycled, which is not to fault the media for covering the boom in real estate. Results have been extraordinary. The subject is worthy of attention.

But since it is an old story, we should be able to discern the final chapters now. Whether the subject is athletics, education, or the markets, one thing we can always rely on is that extraordinary output is possible only through extraordinary input. Remove the extraordinary circumstances that produced the unusual results, and conditions will return to the ranks of the ordinary. Later chapters explain in more detail how this applies to the real estate bubble.

Many are still arguing about which factors propelled the dotcom stocks to new heights, but for our purposes, we can certainly conclude that they were extraordinary. We can conclude that they were extraordinary because the results were extraordinary. Analyzing the stock market is beyond the scope of this book, and the debate about what drove the stock market may go on forever, but the argument can revolve only around *which* extraordinary events fueled the boom and bust.

Because when it was all done, the law of averages still ruled the markets. A champion sprinter can complete a mile in less than four minutes. But how much longer can he go? Should we expect him to complete two miles in eight minutes? We know better. The extraordinary input can be sustained only for so long.

So it is with markets.

When prices fall, even the elite of the real estate industry can be caught in a crash. Gifted Donald Trump, the property tycoon, had achieved superstar notoriety for his flamboyant business style in the 1980s. He expanded into other businesses, including transportation. Then everything began to unravel.

By 1990, the effects of a recession left Trump unable to meet loan payments. He shored up his businesses with additional loans. He postponed interest payments. The increasing debt brought Trump to business bankruptcy, and the brink of personal bankruptcy. At the height of the crises, Donald Trump was more than $900 million in the red.

Bondholders and banks had lost hundreds of millions of dollars, but opted to restructure his debt to avoid the risk of losing even more by foreclosing. In other words, they had allowed Trump to get in so deep, they had to lend him more to keep him in business. They could not afford to allow him to go bankrupt.

It finally worked out for Trump. By 1994, he had eliminated most of his $900 million personal debt. Trump had reduced significantly his nearly $3.5 billion in business debt. While he was forced to relinquish the Trump Shuttle, he managed to retain Trump Tower and the control of his three casinos in Atlantic City. Remarkably, he fought his way back, and in typical Trump style, he wrote a book about it called *The Art of the Comeback*.

It may be easy to dismiss Donald Trump's troubles as the overreaching ambition of an attention-seeking tycoon, but in fact, Mr. Trump has plenty of company. The real estate landscape is littered with the corpses and the lost fortunes of many a real estate expert. Don't let it happen to you!

CHAPTER 2

What Caused the Real Estate Bubble, What Could Trigger a Crash, and Why the Crash Will Be Regional, Not National

Economists See a Bubble

Accroding to the Federal Deposit Insurance Corporation (FDIC), home prices nationwide have escalated about 50 percent nationally in the past five years. But in many local markets, the increases are far more dramatic and unsustainable. In Chico, California, homes appreciated 45 percent in value in 2004 alone. A recent report from National City Corporation in Cleveland claims that 31 percent of local housing markets are "extremely overvalued."[1] Other experts report that "the rampant growth of house prices over the past decade, the rising price of houses relative to rent and the astonishing gap in many cities between price and income are almost unprecedented in recent history. The last time things felt this way, in the late 1980s, real house prices subsequently dropped by one-third in cities like Boston and Los Angeles."[2]

In late 2005, then Federal Reserve chairman Alan Greenspan said publicly that some regions of the country may be seeing "unsustainable price gains" and that "house price increases have outstripped gains in income and rents in recent years."[3] As a result, he explained during an August 2005 symposium, "House turnover will decline from currently historic levels, while home price increases will slow, and prices could even decrease." Economists at Goldman Sachs suggested that U.S. housing in 2005 was overvalued by 10 percent. Comparing median home prices to median household income, the economists concluded, "This estimate is based on an average mortgage rate of about 6 percent, and we expect rates to rise."[4] New York's Lehman Brothers, Inc. has been quoted as saying that buyers are "taking interest only loans and other exotic loans in a desperate attempt to afford the house, and that's a sign the market is nearing the top."

Another economist commented, "I think we're at the peak now. . . . I think this is it, although the evidence we have at the moment is not entirely convincing."[5] According to Freddie Mac chief executive Richard Syron, the real estate crash may be limited to high-end urban areas around the United States, but the result will hurt the entire national economy, by dampening consumption.[6]

Of course, not every economist agrees that a bubble exists. In a recent report from the Office of Federal Housing Enterprise Oversight (OFHEO), "Largest U.S. House Price Increases in More Than 25 Years," OFHEO chief economist Patrick Lawler states that "there is no evidence here of prices topping out; on the contrary, house price inflation continues to accelerate, as some areas that have experienced relatively slow appreciation are picking up steam." However, the OFHEO report goes on to say that 30 of the 265 metropolitan areas had fourth-quarter price appreciation over 25 percent! Twenty-five states enjoyed double-digit price growth, including eight states with more than 20 percent increases. Fourteen metropolitan areas have appreciated over 100 percent in the past five years.[7]

Even real estate cheerleader and chief economist of the National Association of REALTORS® David Lereah admits that a rise in speculation, the high home price-to-income ratio, and the increased use of adjustable rate mortgages by buyers are problematic.

"The home price-to-income ratio is alarmingly high, especially in California, rising from 23 percent in 2003 to 32 percent in 2004." So far in 2005 risky adjustable rate mortgages have made up 40 percent of mortgage loans, when they should be around 25 percent. "The increase in the use of adjustable rate mortgages at a time when fixed mortgage rates are at historic lows is troubling."

Bubble evidence is everywhere. It can be found in the home prices and in the expert commentary. But you can also see it in the behavior of people around you. Today, everyone is talking about real estate the same way they did about dot-com stocks a few years ago. Economist Mark Schniepp described it this way: "Real estate talk is unabating. It's the number one topic of conversation these days everywhere you go," he said. "And that's dangerous."[8] Suddenly, the real estate marketplace is teeming with freshly minted millionaire real estate geniuses. Without prior meaningful experience, non-real estate professionals are making a killing flipping condos and other properties. In Venice, Florida, there are more real estate agents than there are properties available for sale. In some markets, subdivision lots and condominiums are sold by lottery because supply is not sufficient to meet demand. Buyers are literally lining up to bid. A typical real estate market just does not afford these kinds of opportunities.

CASE STUDY: MARKET EXUBERANCE

By David J. Decker

I've been a licensed real estate broker and owner of real estate specializing in commercial properties for nearly 20 years. The past several years have been like nothing I have ever experienced before. Locations where properties were once illiquid and hard to sell are now moving in days or weeks. These properties used to often require seller financing and other creative measures to sell them. Today they move quickly for cash.

A few months ago, I sold an apartment building to a stock-broker. I asked him for some investing advice. He told me to buy real estate.

Eighteen months before that, I sold an apartment building for $750,000. At first, the building failed to appraise. The appraisal report came back at an estimate of fair market value of only $700,000, and the deal fell apart. I didn't blame the appraiser for his opinion. I couldn't find any comparable sales to justify the higher value, either.

However, the same day the appraiser filed his report, I was able to bring in another buyer who would offer $750,000. We went to a different bank, hired a different appraiser, and closed the deal. Just for good measure, I sold the identical building next door for a little more a few weeks later. Since that time, these two buildings have sold again for even more money.

While inexperienced investors are standing in line to snap up any kind of investment property that may be available, tenants are getting in on the real estate boom, too. Any renter with two pennies to rub together who hasn't filed bankruptcy in the past six months seems to be able to qualify for a home loan. The result is the most difficult property management environment that I have ever experienced.

Conditions like these are unusual, and they won't last forever. The only question is whether the slowdown will be orderly and measured or marked by panics and crashes.

Understanding Real Estate Markets

To really understand a real estate market, and see through current hype, an understanding of real estate market ratios is essential.

When you read reports about increases in average home prices, those reports are probably referring to the *median home prices*. A median price is the point at which half of the prices are higher and half of the prices are lower. A median average is used instead of a pure mathematical average because sales at the extremes of the price range can skew the results. *Median incomes* work the same way.

There are plenty of reports today lamenting the divergence of median home prices from the median income. These reports are referring to the *price-to-income ratio*. These reports would be meaningful if interest rates were unchanged, but obviously interest rates have declined to historic lows. The result is that an individual earning the median income can afford a greater home price because lower interest rates translate to lower payments. Therefore, these reports can be misleading and the price-to-income ratio is of less value.

However, there are plenty of other reports and data that prove the cost of housing has been growing faster than incomes. Some of them have already been presented here. Remember the five-year, 50 percent increase reported by the FDIC. The OFHEO found 14 Metropolitan Statistical Areas (MSAs) with 100 percent or more growth over five years. Incomes in these areas have not kept pace. Price-to-income ratios are inconsistent with historical norms.

However, falling interest rates mitigate the impact of increased housing prices, which is to say the *housing debt-to-income* ratio is still reasonable in many areas. The housing debt-to-income ratio is the percentage of debt compared to disposable income. Most people buy their homes by borrowing the money they need to purchase the property. In the early 2000s, there has been a prolonged period of record low interest rates. This phenomenon has allowed homes to remain within reach of the median income even though prices have increased. So even though homeowners have larger housing debt than ever, their monthly mortgage payments have not grown correspondingly because of lower interest rates.

The Key Number for Property Owners to Watch: Housing Affordability Index

The National Association of REALTORS® (NAR) has developed a Housing Affordability Index (HAI) and publishes updates on this report monthly. The REALTORS® report demonstrates how affordable buying a home is. The HAI combines the median income with the median home price within the context of current home mortgage rates to compute an affordability quotient. A score of 100 means the median income can exactly afford the median home price. Scores over 100 indicate that housing is increasingly affordable.

The HAI is the most important index for any investor or homeowner to track. At this writing, the national HAI is well over 100, but it is falling as interest rates rise. Some regions of the country have an HAI that is perilously low, and interest rates are still rising there, too. All regions will see lower HAI numbers as interest rates increase. Chapter 4 goes into more detail about the HAI and how to find the HAI number for your region.

Why the Crash Will be Regional, Not National

The preceding data on affordability would make an excellent case against a real estate bubble-bust. After all, thanks to low interest rates, housing prices are still affordable. Indeed, there has never been a nationwide real estate reversal in nominal prices since the Great Depression, and we don't see one happening now. But remember, the data presented were national statistics. There is no national real estate market. Real estate is a fiercely local business.

The nature of averages blunts the extremes. Returning to the FDIC report that measured a 50 percent increase in average home values over five years, remember that this period also included 14 MSAs that increased by 100 percent or more during the same time.

The graphs in Figures 2.1 through 2.5 illustrate the point.

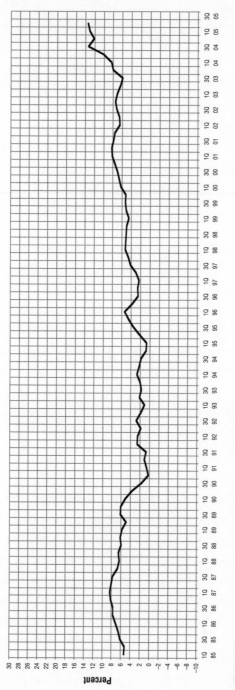

FIGURE 2.1   *Home Price Appreciation—U.S.A.*

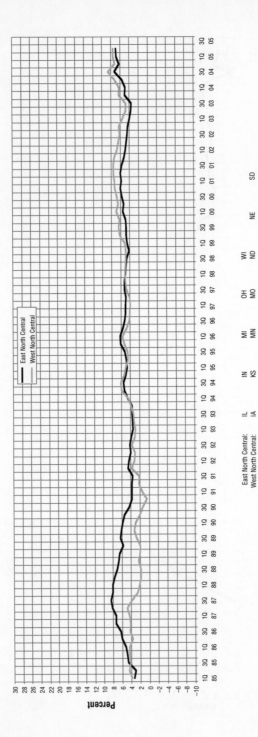

FIGURE 2.2   Home Price Appreciation—Midwest

24

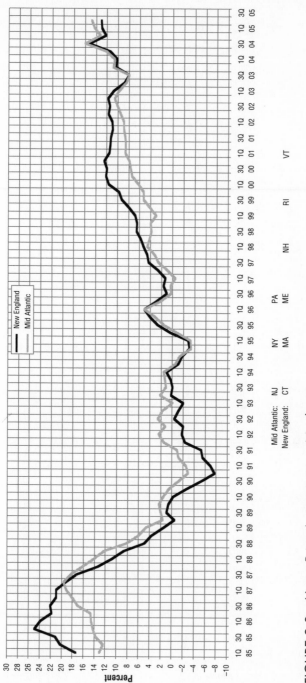

FIGURE 2.3 *Home Price Appreciation—Northeast*

Mid Atlantic: NJ   NY   PA
New England: CT   MA   ME   NH   RI   VT

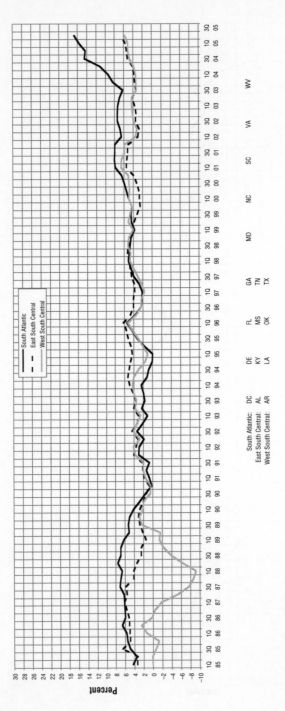

FIGURE 2.4 Home Price Appreciation—South

South Atlantic:	DC	DE	FL	GA	MD	NC	SC	VA	WV
East South Central:	AL	KY	MS	TN					
West South Central:	AR	LA	OK	TX					

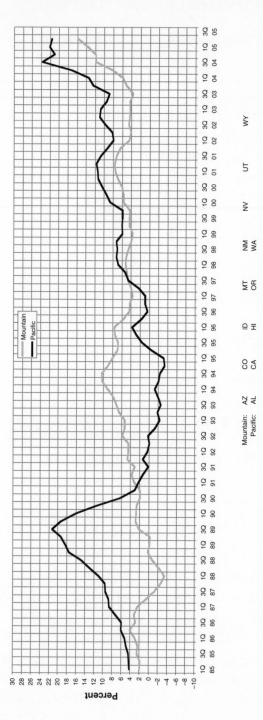

FIGURE 2.5 Home Price Appreciation—West

Figure 2.1 traces national appreciation rates since 1985. The chart reflects mostly pedestrian performance with a few interesting peaks and valleys until 2003 when the line leaps off the chart.

However, breaking down the country into four regions tells a different story. Clearly, we see from Figures 2.2 through 2.5, the South and Midwest were not invited to the same appreciation party. Figure 2.5 shows the West region making an eerie repeat of the experience from the early 1990s. There are signs of trouble in the Northeast as well.

Stated succinctly, some regions of the country are not poised for a bubble-bust because there is no bubble to bust. However, even this information must be presented with a caveat. The regional graphs are still averages. No doubt, some of these regions include Metropolitan Statistical Areas (MSAs) that have done well. For example, humble Racine, Wisconsin, in the heart of the lackluster Midwest, makes the cut of the top 100 fastest appreciating MSAs. A thorough understanding and application of the measures presented in Chapter 4 are essential to reaching any conclusion about your own local market.

Similarly, to conclude that an area is at the brink of disaster simply because home prices have recently spiked is also too simplistic. The common denominator to every past regional real estate crash has been economic calamity. When jobs disappear, real estate value disappears with them.

The Impact of Employment

That interest rates have a huge impact on real estate values is not a surprise, but an equally important factor is employment. You would be unlikely to be able to take advantage of historically low interest rates to make a home purchase if you are unemployed. Fortunately, recent unemployment rates have been favorable, hovering about 5 percent.

One can better understand the importance of employment and

economic vibrancy by studying the real estate market in Japan. The Japanese enjoy interest rates even lower than ours, but with a decade-long economic stagnation, real estate values have failed to respond.

Every real estate submarket is always vulnerable to regional recessions and unemployment. Therefore, even areas of the United States that have not experienced extraordinary price escalation could be impacted by deteriorating local economic conditions. Pertinent examples are the Pennsylvania steel towns that fell into decline when the steel mills closed. However, these cases would not be called bubble-busts because the calamities resulting from closing the mills were not preceded by a bubble.

What will make regional layoffs and plant closings the topic of national news coverage will be whenever reversals strike the same areas that have been experiencing a real estate bubble. Layoffs and business failures are nothing new. The extraordinary input in this case is the combination of an ordinary business cycle retraction with a vulnerable, inflated real estate market. Instead of price stagnation or general malaise, the result of the employment losses in the bubble regions could be blood in the streets.

Exactly where a wave of unemployment is likely to strike is difficult to predict. There is nothing about a real estate bubble itself that makes a local economy more susceptible to unemployment or other business failures. However, a real estate bubble-bust could pour fuel onto the cauldron of economic reversal, creating a vicious circle leading to still more job losses and real estate equity bloodletting.

To summarize, the real estate industry has performed like an elite track star. With low interest rates and full employment serving as the wind behind her back, our star has made record time. Beyond the next bend, however, the road is less certain. The wind could change or a pothole could cause a fall. Other causes of economic calamity that could serve as a pin to the real estate bubble are the subjects of the next section.

What Caused the Bubble

Real estate responds to low interest rates like a hungry dog to food. If a little is good, more must be better. Low interest rates are the magic elixir that brings a smile to the faces of both buyers and sellers.

Two pricing mechanisms, real return and inflation premium, determine interest rates. With inflation at historic lows, interest rates have declined accordingly. However, low inflation alone cannot explain current interest rate pricing. Real returns have bowed to market pressure as more lenders rush to grab a piece of the market. The influx of competition has resulted in a hyper-segmented market full of creative new loan programs being hawked to even sub-par credit applicants, as we shall see. The bottom line is that interest rates are priced based on the extraordinary convergence of both low inflation and reduced real returns.

Home buyers are most concerned about one thing: the size of the monthly payment. The historically low interest rates of recent years have served as a huge pay raise to middle America. Able to qualify for a much larger mortgage on the same income, Americans were suddenly capable of buying more housing. And middle America went shopping. Real estate values have taken off as a result.

To say that lower interest rates will propel real estate values is an obvious statement. But there have been other factors at work adding more fuel to the real estate fire.

Low, stable interest rates are usually a boon to the stock market as well, but not this time. Instead of delivering on a boom, dot-com stocks went bust. The rest of the market has been flat.

For years, investors have been faced with choosing between lackluster savings rates and a stock market treading water. Real estate has become the only game in town. But even this observation does not completely describe the situation.

Interest rates are not only low, but money is easy to borrow. Normally conservative lenders are throwing money around like drunken sailors on shore leave. Sub-par credit applicants can find a wide range of borrowing opportunities for a home purchase. Adjustable rate mortgages (ARMs) are readily available to help qualify a prospective homeowner who would otherwise never be able to borrow. Interest only loans are a similar salve for the borrower reaching to afford today's inflated real estate prices.

Case Study: Easy Money Absurdity

By David J. Decker

Not long ago, a loan officer from a bank where I have some loans stopped by my office to discuss further business opportunities. That lenders are going to the offices of the borrowers is telling by itself. The loan officer wanted to discuss converting one of my apartment buildings to condominiums.

My banker started the conversation by telling me that my current tenants could buy their apartments with a monthly payment that would be less than half of the rent they were paying me. I was incredulous. I was aware that interest rates were low, but I couldn't understand how these rates could slice my tenants' rent payments in half.

The lender went on to explain that using a new loan program, the tenants could buy their units under a borrowing scheme where payments were so low, they were not enough to pay the interest on the loan. Therefore, the debt would grow with time.

I was again incredulous. "You are hanging these people out to dry" was my response. The low payments might seem nice today, but unless current appreciation rates continue, the condominium owner will soon owe more than the property is worth. My conservative banker friend assured me I had nothing to worry about. "What do you care? You've got your money," he said.

I was amazed for the third time. It didn't make sense to me that a smart businessperson would make a loan under such

foolish circumstances. Then it dawned on me. The crazy reverse amortization loans would just be sold on the mortgage
secondary market. I would get my money, the bank would collect some fees for making a few loans, and the taxpayers will
get to bail out Freddie Mac when too many homeowners like
my former tenants bail out of these foolish programs.

I never did the deal. In the words of George Ross, co-star of
the television show *The Apprentice*, right-hand man to Donald
Trump, and veteran of hundreds of multimillion-dollar real estate
transactions, "Just because a lender is willing to give you the
money doesn't mean you should take it." Sage advice indeed.

With the economy thundering along at full employment (unemployment rates of 5 percent or less), there are more Americans
than ever able to participate in the housing boom, which would explain why home ownership has grown to an all-time high of 70 percent of all households.

Just as a champion Olympic sprinter is the extraordinary convergence of genetics, training, coaching, and discipline, so, too, is
this real estate market the extraordinary convergence of low inflation, low real returns on interest rates, easy money, weak alternative
investments, and full employment.

The question becomes, How long can this happy confluence
of circumstances be maintained? How long can the sprinter keep
sprinting?

What Could Trigger the Crash

Having an understanding of the factors that pump air into the bubble helps to understand how this situation could become unraveled,
leading to a decline. If the unraveling occurs fast enough, the result
will be a crash.

Interestingly, many of the factors leading to the bubble are interrelated. One obvious example is inflation and interest rates. Regardless, we are dependent on all the factors continuing their extraordinary performance to continue the boom. Conversely, any failures could have a domino effect.

The crash factors that we explore in this section include inflation, interest rates, liquidity, investment alternatives, and employment.

Inflation Part I: Market Pressures

The balanced federal government budgets of the 1990s combined with consistent productivity gains have resulted in stable, low inflation. Unfortunately, balanced federal budgets are a distant memory. More storm clouds are on the horizon for inflation.

Both Chicago Federal Reserve president Michael Moskow and Federal Reserve Bank of Kansas City president Thomas Hoenig spoke at separate events in late September 2005. Their message was clear. The Federal Reserve remained concerned that inflation pressures were building, and the central bank will push interest rates higher to keep inflation at bay.

"We feel it's necessary to reduce accommodation," Moskow said when speaking to reporters after a speech. *Accommodation* refers to the strategy of using low interest rates to stimulate economic growth. Moskow added that inflation has risen to the high end of a "comfort zone of price stability," echoing comments made in other recent speeches. "It's a situation we have to monitor on a regular basis very carefully."

Hoenig said consumer prices have already risen significantly because of the higher energy costs, while unit labor costs are rising and economic capacity is being absorbed. "When you see all three coming together, you must be alert," said Hoenig, speaking at a Kansas City Fed forum in Clinton, Oklahoma. "The mission of the Fed is to be sensitive to these pressures."

Inflation Part II: Rising Energy Prices

During 2005, the cost of a gallon of gasoline increased dramatically. In September 2003, Americans were paying, on average, around $1.60 per gallon. The following year, the price had risen to $1.90. But in September 2005, U.S. motorists dug deeper than ever before into their pockets to pay more than $3.00 a gallon for gasoline. Following Hurricane Katrina, gasoline prices spiked to record highs. Although the increases were short-lived, gas was costing $3.50 to $5.00 per gallon for a few days. Motorists were relieved when the price fell back to the $2.75 range.

Because of the rising costs of crude oil and our dependence on energy, gasoline prices will remain high and not return to 2003–2004 price levels. While Americans may adjust to paying more per gallon for gas, it takes a bigger bite out of their budgets. Paying $35 to $65 for a tank of gas stings and trickles down throughout the economy. Home delivery of products costs more. Pizza shops added a $1.00 to $2.00 surcharge to deliver an order. Florists increased their prices, or added a delivery surcharge. Small businesses have begun turning down free upgrades offered to them by auto rental companies. Rather than accepting larger, gas-guzzling cars, business travelers are choosing smaller, economy models.

Because of the higher cost of energy, it costs more to produce and deliver goods and services. The impact on consumer goods, from pizzas to flowers, will be widespread. Eating out costs more, from driving to the restaurant to the price of the meal. Groceries cost more. Even taxes will increase, because it costs more to heat government buildings and to fuel police cars and school buses. Already there are reports of some school districts experimenting with a four-day schedule to reduce fuel costs.

Not good news for a consumer driven economy.

How Higher Energy Costs Affect Real Estate Markets.   The effects of paying more for energy will ripple through the economy. Energy is such a fundamental building block of our economy that everything will cost more, because everyone is paying more for energy, either directly or indirectly. Luxurious housing will always appeal to the masses, but fewer will be able to afford it. Modest, safe housing will be more in demand. Job losses in some sectors may be likely. Certainly, sectors like tourism will be impacted by lower available discretionary funds and higher fuel costs.

Businesses and individuals will look for ways to cut costs and eliminate unnecessary expenses. People who have only marginally qualified for loans using nontraditional financing will find themselves in particular trouble as belt-tightening becomes necessary.

As the effects of higher energy costs grip the economy, more localized busts are likely to occur. Everyone will be affected by the higher costs of energy.

The repercussions are already being felt. By late September 2005, the American Bankers Association (ABA) noted an increase in delinquent payments on personal loans, auto loans, home equity loans, and lines of credit. A key reason for the increase in the delinquencies, according to the ABA, was the strain of higher gas prices.

Inflation Part III: The Impact of Hurricanes Katrina and Rita

Of course, we have our friends Katrina and Rita and their devastation of the Gulf Coast oil refineries to thank in part for the current increase in gasoline prices.

By mid-September 2005, estimates of damage were set at $200 billion. However, it appears that deficit spending is the strategy the politicians will use to pay for the rebuilding of the Gulf Coast.

The Katrina disaster occurred during the war on terrorism. Because of spending nearly $200 billion thus far—directly and indirectly—on the Iraq War, the bulge in the government deficit is headed for another healthy dose of red ink. With these two major expenses—probably topping $400 billion—the federal treasury will vacuum funds available for borrowing, placing the government in competition with other users of borrowed money, like real estate owners and investors. Economists call this phenomenon "crowding out." The man on the street calls it "higher interest rates."

Yet some people think the storm damage and subsequent reconstruction is good for the economy. The effect of the extensive storm damage is that it will help some people involved in reconstruction, hurt many others for a long time, and transfer wealth. It will help some sectors of the economy and hurt other sectors, but the overall effect will be negative.

Interest Rates

We have already observed the impact of inflation on interest rates. That increasing inflation causes increasing interest rates is a concept understood by everyone. Not surprisingly, in response to inflationary pressure, the Federal Reserve Bank (the Fed) initiated a policy of raising the prime rate. Then chairman Greenspan's remarks, both before and after Hurricanes Katrina and Rita, indicated that the policy of increasing interest rates would remain. By mid-September 2005, the Fed had raised rates by a quarter-percentage point at each of its past 11 policy-making meetings, taking the federal funds rate to 3.75 percent from a decades-low 1 percent in June 2004.

From all indications, the Fed's policy of increasing interest rates to contain inflation remains steadfast. These increased interest rates will, sooner or later, affect the housing industry. When mortgage rates increase, the affordability of housing will decline with the ability to buy houses.

According to Goldman Sachs, a 1-percentage-point rise in mortgage rates would reduce the fair market value of home prices by 8 percent. As mortgage rates rise, it requires a larger down payment to qualify for the loan. It also means that higher priced houses are less affordable to a larger number of potential buyers. The continued affordability of housing may be placed in jeopardy. If mortgage rates rise, how affordable will a home remain? Consumers have already been resorting to ARMs and interest-only loans to afford present housing prices. A large increase in interest rates will be like an anvil on the camel's back.

Liquidity

Liquidity refers to the ability to obtain financing, regardless of the rate of interest. You have already read about the variety of mortgage programs that define the ease of obtaining financing in the current market. It's hard to imagine money being easier to obtain.

If the economy hits some rough spots, maxed-out homeowners will start to have trouble. Already the ABA has reported an increase in default rates related to higher fuel costs. If defaults surge, additional stresses will be placed on the already embattled mortgage secondary markets, particularly Freddie Mac.

We have been here before. In the 1980s, real estate was booming with no end in sight. Real estate limited partnerships designed to take advantage of generous depreciation allowances flourished. Never mind that these partnerships made no economic sense; in the upside down world of 1980s real estate, the goal was to produce losses for wealthy investors seeking shelter from income taxes. But as the government giveth, so it taketh away.

In 1987, new tax legislation took effect, eliminating key lucrative real estate tax loopholes just as the spot price of oil was crashing. The resulting real estate crash was so severe, an entire segment of the banking industry, the savings and loans, perished under the weight of foreclosures. A government bailout of the FSLIC (the savings and loan equivalent of the FDIC) had to be engineered to make good on customer deposits in failed institutions. The FSLIC disappeared along with the savings and loan industry.

One of the outcomes of the savings and loan crisis in the 1980s was tighter lending practices designed to eliminate the abuses that had contributed to the bust. The lesson is likely to be repeated now.

One day soon, the lending community may awaken to the reality that interest only and reverse amortization loans do not constitute conservative lending practice. Even the prevalence of ARM loans may be brought into question. When financial institutions wake up to these practices, lending parameters will tighten and borrowed money will be harder to get.

Herein lies the domino effect. As inflation causes interest rates to rise, prices that could only be sustained by access to easy-money, no interest loans will begin to weaken. Heavily leveraged home-owners will find their homes no longer worth the debt against them. Foreclosure will result. As foreclosures increase, lending practices will tighten.

Investment Alternatives

Real estate has been the hottest investing game in town for years. Low interest rates have punished savers. The stock market has logged only lackluster performance. Part of real estate's stellar performance can be attributed to simple matters of supply and demand. Dollars earmarked for investment have sought out the only investment class currently yielding a meaningful return.

However, changing market conditions will rearrange the landscape of investment opportunities. A marketplace where real estate is the only hope of obtaining a fair return is extraordinary and cannot be sustained.

For one thing, higher interest rates will attract money away from real estate and back to savings. If the stock market comes back to life, investment dollars that might have been committed to real estate in the past will be siphoned off for other opportunities.

Employment = Nitroglycerin

The most accurate description of the present real estate market is that it is a powder keg waiting to explode. Real estate is vulnerable. This description is a useful prediction because it allows for the possibility of there being no crash at all. After all, powder kegs that are carefully handled do not explode. However, if present real estate conditions represent a powder keg, then employment is the nitroglycerin.

We already stated that it would be impossible to take advantage of low interest rates if you were unemployed. In fact, unemployment quickly reduces every other factor to trivia.

Any real estate market, no matter how sound, will collapse in the face of sufficient unemployment. The opposite is also true. Even vulnerable real estate markets can avoid a crash so long as employment remains strong. That is another reason we are not predicting a national real estate crisis.

The employment factor will get interesting if any bubble markets are afflicted with a wave of job losses. Consider a theoretical situation. Meet our hypothetical homeowner couple Tom and Jill Homeowner. Tom loses his job. The couple falls behind in their mortgage payments. They need to sell.

Unfortunately, Tom is not the only one out of work. Not only is there more competition for work, there's more competition for buyers in the real estate market as the unemployed increasingly seek to bail out of their homes.

Tragically, bowing to inflationary pressure, interest rates have increased. The same household income just won't buy as much house as it used to. Additionally, the crazy low down payment and interest only loan programs have all disappeared, removing subprime borrowers and other applicants from contention in the home purchasing arena.

Tom and Jill Homeowner would love to just slash their price

and put an end to the nightmare, but they already have their home priced at what they owe. Foreclosure looms.

Sounds familiar? This example was deliberately crafted to remind you of the real-life story of Tom and Jill Hindy that you encountered in Chapter 1. There is ample history of real estate bubbles ending in a crash that should serve as sufficient warning to every homeowner and real estate investor.

CHAPTER 3

HISTORY LESSONS FROM PREVIOUS REAL ESTATE BUBBLES: WHO LOST AND WHO CAME THROUGH STRONGER

The Titans of Tragedy

Whether you are convinced that a real estate bubble exists, or a bust may occur, there are lessons to be learned from the past. Consider William Zeckendorf, the immensely successful New York City developer of the 1950s who went bust in the rising interest rates of 1965.

"Zeckendorf engaged in a real-life game of Monopoly involving some of the most prestigious properties in the United States, including the United Nations site, the Chrysler Building and the Chase Manhattan Plaza in Manhattan and Denver's Mile High Center."[1] William Zeckendorf has been described as "overenthusiastic, overzealous, over-everything." He had an insatiable appetite for the big real estate deal. Active in developing properties after World War II, Zeckendorf became a flamboyant real estate developer.

Under his leadership, Webb & Knapp, based in Manhattan, built $3 billion worth of commercial projects in 20 years. Zeckendorf became the embodiment of glamorous real estate deal making, which included developing Roosevelt Airfield (where Charles

Lindbergh began his transatlantic flight), to acquiring the land for the United Nations, to building the University of Long Island.

Zeckendorf's most remembered and best deal was putting together the land where the United Nations stands today. Turtle Bay was a wooded hollow on the eastern slope of Manhattan. In the early 1800s, Turtle Bay became developed with streets, tenements, warehouses, and wharfs. Following the Civil War, the owners of many of the buildings converted them into smelly slaughterhouses, cattle pens, and meat packaging plants. Eight decades later, they still operated at full capacity. The area was a visual cesspool and septic tank. The foul odor stained the air of the surrounding neighborhoods.

"On days when the wind blew from the east, the smells from the slaughterhouses reached to Third Avenue and beyond. This is why the section of Tudor City backing on First Avenue has no windows," William Zeckendorf penned in his memoir.

Zeckendorf was able to acquire the land at $17 a square foot, a bargain at the time. Just blocks away, land was sold for $300 a square foot.

In 1965, the overextended Zeckendorf lost it all. The bubble had burst. His companies were forced into bankruptcy. When he died in 1976, the 71-year-old Zeckendorf was broke. Many have concluded that his biggest mistake in business was that he could not see failure. He only envisioned the upside, and overleveraged. He never planned an exit strategy for any of his investments.

Following World War I, the 1920s were a period of prosperity so unrivaled that the decade gained the moniker the Roaring Twenties. The nation's economy was changing from farming and rural living to industrialization and urban living. Americans were busy working in new factories, and those jobs produced incomes that allowed the purchase of automobiles and other previously unheard-of consumer goods. Middle-class Americans enjoyed new advantages from their employment, including paid vacations and other fringe benefits.

The stock market was rising. Investors were becoming wealthy.

Florida was becoming a hot spot for those northerners who tired of the cold weather.

With easy credit, anyone could invest in sunny Florida, and it made sense to do so. Florida had become the playground for the rich and famous. People drove there and vacationed there. Tourism was booming. Land prices and real estate started to appreciate.

A $1,500 investment turned into $300,000 within a year. By 1922, the *Miami Herald* had become the heaviest newspaper in the world owing to the weight of the real estate advertisements. Illegal casinos and drinking parlors flourished in Miami.

Those northerners pumped money into the sure thing of Florida real estate. The prices snowballed. Everyone enjoyed the ride, watching their money double, triple. Land was developed. New, rolling golf courses were built. Mansions were constructed, complete with lavish lawns and extravagant swimming pools. Land close to the waterfront was the most desirable. Then it happened.

Pop.

By 1925, prices were so far out-of-whack that real estate was no longer affordable. New investors stopped coming. Old investors wanted out and started to sell. Panic set in. When the bubble popped, the local market crashed. Prices fell as everyone wanted out. Heavily indebted investors wanted out even faster to avoid bankruptcy.

The next year, things worsened. An unnamed hurricane (they were not named back in those days) smashed into southern Florida. Winds over 125 mph ravaged Florida in September 1926 and converted much of Palm Beach County into swamplands. After the devastating monster storm, a gigantic tidal wave crashed onto the towns of Moore Haven and Belle Glade. More than 13,000 homes were destroyed. The death toll of 415 was staggering.

The Mediterranean fruit fly arrived, and obliterated the state's large citrus industry. It took years for Florida to recover fully, even though for the rest of the country, 1926 to 1929 was highly prosperous. When the stock market crashed in 1929, it had little effect on Florida. The Great Depression had arrived early in the Sunshine State with the real estate crash of 1925.

More recently, the Reichmann family firm of Olympia & York repeated the story of the seemingly unsinkable, meeting their demise in titanic proportions. The Reichmann family had escaped Nazi-occupied Hungary and had fled to Morocco during World War II. As turbulence erupted from Morocco's effort to gain independence from France in the 1950s, the Reichmanns fled again, this time to Canada.

In Canada, the Reichmanns proceeded to build an astonishing real estate empire. They built the World Financial Center in New York, First Canadian Place in Toronto, and Canary Wharf, an enormous mixed-use project in London. The business community regarded the Reichmanns as smart, highly ethical, and prudent. They were generous philanthropists as well.

By 1991, the Reichmann family was listed by *Fortune* magazine as the fourth richest family worldwide. The *Wall Street Journal* regarded their flagship company, Olympia & York, as "too big to fail." But fail they did. The Reichmanns and Olympia & York, caught in a market downturn, found themselves shipwrecked on the docks of the Canary Wharf development.

The Reichmanns would go on to redeem themselves, partnering with brilliant real estate wizard George Soros. Doing business as Reichmann International, the Reichmanns have once again repeated their past successes.

On October 19, 1987, now better known as Black Monday, the stock market lost 22 percent of its value. Reversals of this magnitude are often called a crash even if they play out over several weeks. But Black Monday set a new standard as an abrupt, ugly crash.

Real estate is not traded at one main exchange, like stocks, bonds, or commodities. Accordingly, there is no way to find a 22 percent loss in one day in real estate anywhere in our nation's history. There has never been a 22 percent loss of real estate value in one week, or even one month. That's probably because real estate does not work the same way as the stock market.

Today, with the click of a computer button, stocks can be sold. Values can be determined within seconds. However, real estate still takes time to sell. There are no instant valuations.

In fact, when real estate bubbles burst, it can take several years for the value to bottom out in most markets. When the air goes out of a real estate bubble, it can be more like a slow leak from a bald tire than a blowout. Consider the real estate crash of the late 1980s.

In the 1980s, California enjoyed a spirited real estate market. When it crashed in the late 1980s, property values fell. The Office of Federal Housing Enterprise Oversight (OFHEO), part of the U.S. Department of Housing and Urban Development (HUD), tracks home values. It developed an index to determine market trends. Had you bought a house for $260,000 in 1990 in Los Angeles, and it tracked the OFHEO index closely, six years later you would have been able to sell it for only about $200,000. Although California's real estate prices have trended upwards over the past several years, the OFHEO index is sobering. Los Angeles real estate rose more than 25 percent just in 2004, but showed signs of a cooldown in the second half of 2005.

Following Black Monday in New York City in 1987, housing prices fell 6 percent between the end of 1989 and the end of 1990. The major real estate run-up ended with the stock market crash, and a bubble burst. It took a while for the real estate market to bottom out. Wall Street jobs were gone—about 30,000 of them by 1990. By 1993, the prices of homes in the New York metropolitan area were 11 percent below their levels in 1989.

Home prices remained flat for the next decade. Then they took off again, heading into record pricing. In the third quarter of 2005, the market was reported cooling.

"In Manhattan, the average sales price fell almost 13 percent in the third quarter from the second quarter. The amount of time it took to sell a home was also up 30.4 percent over the same period."[2]

Dallas-area home prices climbed in the early 1980s but crashed in 1986. In a perfect example of where local economic conditions lead to a housing bust, oil prices dipped and took the local housing prices down, too. Following a decade-long oil boom, home builders and buyers became too comfortable with the local economy. The price of sweet Texas crude oil peaked in March of 1981 at $35 a barrel. Then it fell. In 1986, Texas crude had collapsed to just $9 a barrel.

Housing prices in Texas remained high for a while. But when the oil business had soured, the reality of job losses sank in. Home values dropped 10 percent and kept falling. By the end of the 1980s, all the real estate gains of the past decade had been given back. Prices for real estate remained low for years. The Dallas-Plano-Irving real estate market has since recovered but has not enjoyed the dramatic increases other Sunbelt cities have in this recent real estate boom.

In the 1988 presidential election, Massachusetts Governor Michael Dukakis touted the so-called Massachusetts Miracle. Running against then Vice President George H.W. Bush, Governor Dukakis attempted to take credit for the state's economic boom, but things were starting to unravel.

The state had been hit hard by deindustrialization in the 1970s because traditional textile and shoe industries were taking a beating from competition in the South and in the Third World. By 1975, Massachusetts manufacturing employment had dropped 16 percent below its 1967 level. The state's unemployment rate hit 11.2 percent, far above the national average.

Then in the early 1980s, Massachusetts saw economic growth. The new growth was heavily centered in high-tech industries and financial services within Boston and in its suburbs along the Route 128 highway. As technology advanced and computers became more powerful, business moved from IBM mainframes to minicomputers made by firms like Digital Equipment and Wang Laboratories. The high-tech boom created demand for software from local companies like Lotus. Massachusetts-based Raytheon, manufacturer of the Scud-busting Patriot antimissile system, received hefty orders from the Pentagon.

From 1983 to 1987, real estate values doubled. Wages for skilled trade workers shot up. The rising costs made New England's manufacturing sector increasingly uncompetitive. Wages peaked in 1984 and then declined. Speculation by real estate investors fueled a fevered building frenzy. The building boom created jobs for architects, developers, builders, tradesmen, bankers, construction workers, real estate agents, and lawyers. Hundreds of new buildings were erected to serve the state's expanding economy.

The region's growth was slowing by 1986, and construction of new commercial buildings and residences had become the state's primary source of fuel for the economic engine. By 1989, lenders stopped making loans, tightening credit, and cutting off the ability for investors to buy property and develop. The state slid into a tough recession, months before other parts of the country. From 1987 to 1990, 27,000 people lost their jobs.

In Boston, the housing prices skyrocketed to new record highs in 1987. And then, there was a pop. The bubble had burst.

Real estate began a steep slide in 1990, setting prices back to where they had been in 1985. The losses were about 20 percent of the market value. It took years for the market to recover. The Massachusetts Miracle fueled the state's real estate bust.

CASE STUDY: HOW FAR THE MIGHTY MAY FALL

By David J. Decker

I remember as a rookie in the real estate business marveling at the exploits of Frank Crivello, local developer extraordinaire. It seemed like everything Frank touched turned to gold. He was young, not much older than I.

As I sat at my back row desk of my employer's real estate sweatshop reading the front page exploits of another Crivello success, one of the old-timers in the office walked past and commented, "I remember when Oliver Plunkett was the golden boy on the front page of the paper. Six months later he was bankrupt."

Sure enough, six months later Frank Crivello was indicted on various criminal charges. In 1994, he pled guilty to three charges related to lying to banks to obtain financing. His troubles were so deep he took one of the largest local law firms down with him when he crashed.

Slow but steady may not sell as many newspapers, but sometimes it's better to stay out of the limelight.

Learning from the Past

It is important to examine the past as you move forward in today's real estate market. There are plenty of examples from which to learn. From Donald's Trump's restructuring of his businesses in the past decade to Japan's painful real estate bust, there is plenty of evidence that busts can and do happen.

But you can learn from the past. It can help you better understand today's volatile regional real estate markets. And considering past lessons, you can become a better investor in real estate, whether for your personal residence or investing for rental income or increased property value.

Here are some important points to remember about previous real estate bubbles and busts:

$ Real estate markets are local or regional; there has never been a countrywide bust since the Great Depression.

$ When a real estate bubble pops, it takes time for it to be noticed or to affect others in the market. In other words, the air flows out of the bubble slowly.

$ Overzealous investors inflate prices by speculative buying.

$ Investors will sell property quicker than homeowners when panic rules the market. This results in more properties on the market, further lowering prices.

$ It takes months, and even years, before a real estate market that has reversed itself hits the bottom and levels out.

$ The national average prices of new homes quoted by the media mean little in your local market.

$ Real estate booms often end in periods of market stagnation, correction, or reversal.

$ Real estate markets do not directly affect other distant markets; what is happening in the Youngstown, Ohio, real estate market has no effect on the Portland, Oregon, market.

$ Interest rates can affect all real estate markets, because interest rates rise on a nationwide basis.

$ The housing market is affected by supply and demand. The more supply, the more negative pressure is placed on prices, keeping them lower. When the supply is constricted in the face of increasing demand, prices rise.

$ Unemployment affects real estate values. When unemployment rises, local real estate markets stagnate, or reverse.

$ Low unemployment (or high employment) fuels an expansion of real estate values.

$ Nationwide statistics may have little to do with your local real estate market. Just because national real estate averages are up or down does not mean your market will or is doing the same thing.

$ Overextending (leveraging) is dangerous in volatile real estate markets.

$ People in any financial situation can be hurt during a real estate bust.

Applying History to Uncharted Territory

In 2005, the U.S. real estate markets moved into uncharted territory like never before. By October of that year, the following had occurred:

$ The U.S. government continued its war against terrorism and the deployment of troops in Iraq. The price tag was more than $200 billion, and rising each month.

$ The defense of the U.S. homeland against terrorism cost taxpayers more than ever.

$ Three huge hurricanes (Katrina, Rita, and Wilma) struck the Gulf Coast, causing substantial damage. While there were at least $40 billion of insured losses, estimates of $200 billion in damage were caused by the storms. Congress appropriated $62 billion in emergency relief and will be spending far more on the recovery and rebuilding effort.

$ A worldwide energy crunch occurred before Hurricanes Katrina and Rita smashed ashore. Gasoline rose to more than $2.50 a gallon before the storms, making U.S. consumers dig deeper into their pockets to find extra cash to fill the gas tank. On Labor Day weekend, just a few days after Hurricane Katrina had struck, gas skyrocketed to $3.50 a gallon (and in many places more).

$ Unemployment began to rise after the storms.

$ Natural gas and fuel oil rose 40 percent to 50 percent above price levels of the previous heating season.

$ Real estate markets in major areas continued to cool.

$ Between 60 percent and 85 percent of the new condos being sold in Miami were being bought by investors.

$ Interest rates were rising, slowing the housing markets. The Fed continued to push interest rates higher, in an attempt to fight or curtail inflation. As a result, real estate markets were slowing.

$ To pay for staggering expenditures, Congress chose to borrow more money rather than cut spending. The deficit grew larger.

There has never been another time in history like the year 2005. Over the past four years, half the jobs created by the economy were in the housing industry and related support businesses.

"Over the past four years, consumer spending and residential construction have together accounted for 90 percent of the total growth in GDP. And over two-fifths of all private sector jobs created since 2001 have been in housing-related sectors, such as construction, real estate and mortgage broking," *The Economist* reported.

Those jobs could disappear as bubbles pop and the effects on the local housing markets are felt.

PART TWO

DEFENSIVE STRATEGIES: HOW TO PROTECT YOURSELF AND AVOID LOSSES

CHAPTER 4

How to Assess the Likelihood of a Crash in Your Neighborhood

R eal estate is a local business. As we shall see, there are national trends and national factors that affect real estate. However, it is possible for some regions of the United States to experience rapid growth while other areas remain flat. Similarly, reversals are not visited on every area simultaneously. There has never been a national real estate decline since the Great Depression. Nevertheless, there have been regional declines, some of them severe. How to assess the health of your area both now and in the future is the subject of this chapter.

Supply and Demand in Real Estate

Real estate is subject to the laws of supply and demand like any other market. The concepts are easily understood. If the supply of real estate remains constant but demand increases, then prices will rise. Therefore, in order to understand the mechanics of the real estate market, you should understand the components of supply and demand that drive the market.

Components of Demand in Real Estate

There are four components of demand in real estate: employment, interest rates, income, and households.

Employment.   Job growth is the most important factor driving the demand for real estate. When the economy is expanding, more jobs are created. The additional workers will need a place to live, work, and shop. Thus employment growth drives every real estate sector, including residential, office, industrial, and retail.

The manner in which jobs are added to the economy trends toward slow and steady. Occasionally, you will read about a company expanding and adding a larger number of jobs, but typically jobs are added to the economy in small increments by smaller businesses.

Jobs can be lost more dramatically when a large business fails or closes a factory. Jobs are usually lost more quickly than they are added.

Interest Rates.   Since most real estate is purchased with borrowed money, interest rates have a vital, direct impact on demand.

Income.   Working hand in hand with employment growth is the median household income. Real inflation adjusted growth in income drives demand for real estate. As each household has more income, more money is available for every kind of consumer expenditure, including housing. Income growth also drives every sector of real estate.

Income growth and employment growth together give a good snapshot of the health of the local economy. The addition of many high paying jobs translates to a boom. If the jobs added are lower on the pay scale, the economic benefits are less and the boom more mild.

Lately, some forecasters have argued the divergence of median home prices and median incomes as evidence of a real estate bubble. This thinking is flawed because low interest rates give incomes greater buying power. The Housing Affordability Index is the better measure, taking into account median home prices, median incomes, and mortgage interest rates.

Households.   Household growth also drives demand in a local economy. The impact to residential real estate would be obvious, but all sectors again benefit. Note that the correct component is household growth, not population growth. Change in family size means that population growth will not impact household growth as directly.

The trend in this country is toward smaller family size. Therefore, household growth typically leads population growth slightly.

Components of Supply in Real Estate

There are two components of supply in real estate: existing stock and new construction.

Existing Stock of Real Estate.   At first, it may not be obvious how the existing stock of real estate impacts supply, but it does. The existing stock of real estate impacts the supply of real estate by virtue of being in a constant state of decline. Some of the existing stock is lost every year.

Like everything else, real estate wears out, sometimes to the point where the property is no longer useful and must be bulldozed. More often, real estate becomes obsolete. If the existing structure cannot be adapted to a new use, it will be torn down. Existing real estate is lost to redevelopment, storm water management, new infrastructure (large public works like highways and stadiums), and more.

New Construction.   New construction is the only positive source of supply in real estate. The process of development can take years to bring new real estate to fruition. In other words, supply cannot always react quickly to changes in demand.

New construction usually costs more every year, placing an additional constraint on the ability of new construction to supply a market.

The Interaction of Supply and Demand in Real Estate

Usually, changes in the components of supply and demand in real estate are slow and plodding. Jobs, income, and households are added in a predictable, steady manner. Even modest growth in employment, income, and households results in a healthy real estate market because even if new construction is sufficient to supply the demand, the cost of new construction is typically always increasing. Therefore, upward price pressure is exerted on the value of existing real estate in this market.

The supply of real estate is not as capable of responding to rapid, dramatic shifts in demand. For example, notwithstanding the steady trickle of real estate lost every year, the existing stock of real estate is fixed. Should demand suddenly fall, supply cannot be removed from the marketplace, so prices fall.

In cases of rapid growth in demand, new construction may lag behind demand. Even if construction is able to keep pace, the cost of the new real estate will be higher, resulting in upward price pressure in existing real estate.

There are leading indicators of price changes when real estate markets are turning direction. These leading indicators are the average days on the market (DOM) for selling a home, the months of inventory of unsold houses, and mortgage applications. When DOM and months of inventory are lengthening or if the number of applications is declining, this signals a market cooldown (or further plunging).

The Impact of Interest Rates

Borrowed money is the lifeblood of real estate. Interest rates additionally incorporate the impact of inflation, rendering interest rates as one of the most important factors in forecasting real estate values.

A reduction in interest rates has an impact similar to that of an increase in income. As the cost of a mortgage falls, consumers are able to afford to buy more real estate with the same income just as if they had experienced a pay increase and mortgage costs had remained fixed.

Declining interest rates do not benefit every sector of the real estate industry. As rates fall, home ownership becomes a more affordable reality for an increasing number of tenants. The result is increasing vacancy and declining rents in rental housing. This is exactly the circumstance experienced today in many local markets.

The Impact of Liquidity

Liquidity describes the ease and availability of obtaining capital for buying or investing in real estate. There are a number of factors impacting liquidity. All financial markets compete for capital. Real estate competes with the stock market, which competes with commodities, and so on.

If a market is hot, that market may siphon capital from other markets as investors seek the highest possible return with the lowest possible risk. Right now, real estate is hot. Money that might have been invested in other markets at another time is today invested in real estate.

Another factor impacting liquidity is the ability to borrow money. In a tight lending environment, less funds are available to be borrowed and lending criteria are more stringent. The present environment might be better described as a loose or easy money environment. There is a plethora of mortgage plans available for even sub-prime credit borrowers.

The Interaction of Interest Rates and Liquidity

We have already seen how present market conditions include low interest rates and easy credit. The result has been like pouring gasoline on the fire of real estate appreciation.

Interest rates and liquidity are two trends in real estate that are national instead of local. Interest rates and availability of credit are about the same in Iowa as they are in California.

Even though the trends are national, not every local market has experienced the same result. Not surprisingly, some areas have outperformed others. Some regions have escalated in price to the point that even with historically low interest rates, it is increasingly difficult to afford the median priced home on the median household income.

Assessing the Future of Your Neighborhood

A number of additional factors will determine how the nature of supply and demand will play out in various regions. These factors include past real estate cycles, current employment conditions, the existence of price bubbles in a market, home sales, leading indicators, the Housing Affordability Index (HAI), interest rates, and the availability of new construction.

Past Real Estate Cycles

Fortunately, most areas of the United States do not experience a boom and bust type of real estate cycle. However, some parts of the country do regularly experience rapid expansions followed by substantial reversals. These boom and bust markets congregate on either coast and in the South. The middle of the country is more stable.

Data service First American Real Estate Solutions studied 116 real estate markets and concluded that most of them experienced steady regular price increases. There were 30 markets that experienced boom and bust cycles, and these markets were congregated mostly in the Northeast, Florida, and California.

Current Employment Conditions

The more diversified the local economy, the less possibility that failure in one industry will provoke a real estate crash. The opposite is also true. The more dependent a region is on one sector, the greater the probability of a crash if that industry fails.

The examples are rampant and obvious. There are the Pennsylvania steel towns and the places like Flint, Michigan, that fell on hard times because of competition in automobiles. The southern California real estate crash of the early 1990s was due in part to job losses in the defense industry.

The Existence of Price Bubbles

The more hot air that has been pumped into the bubble in an area, the greater the chance that the bubble may pop, causing a real estate crash. Consider markets where appreciation has pushed values beyond what the median income can afford, even assuming historically low interest rates and easy credit. If interest rates increase, as they already have and will continue to do, these properties will become even less affordable. The inevitable consequence is downward pressure on prices.

If job growth and household growth remain strong, these factors may be able to blunt the impact of the interest rate pressure and values will at least hold. However, should one of these areas be afflicted with a reversal in employment, there may be blood in the streets.

Existing Home Sales, New Home Sales, and Condominium Sales

By tracking sales data of existing homes, new homes, and condominiums, you gain a sense of the market direction. Increasing sales is a sign of positive market momentum, while a plateau or decline in sales may indicate a turn in the market.

Leading Indicators: Days on the Market, Supply of Homes, Mortgage Applications

These indicators measure the health and direction of a local real estate market. When markets change direction, the first signs of change will be found in these indicators. Days on the market express the average time it takes to sell a home. The supply of homes expresses the time in months required to sell off the existing supply of homes at the present sales rate. Obviously, mortgage applications signal sales that are likely to take place.

Housing Affordability Index (HAI)

The National Association of REALTORS® reports a Housing Affordability Index that measures the ability of the median income to afford the median home price. A score of 100 means the median income is exactly sufficient to afford the median home price. Scores above 100 indicate greater ability to afford the median price of a home. This index incorporates present mortgage interest rates.

Interest Rates

Interest rates have a pivotal impact on the value and affordability of real estate. Real estate prices respond inversely to changes in interest rates. Currently, interest rates are at historical lows, but rising. Markets that are not straining the limits of affordability should be able to sustain some increases.

The Availability of New Construction

The easier a market is to supply, the better the chance the market will be oversupplied. One of the reasons the State of Florida tends to experience real estate booms and busts is that the area enjoys a year-around construction season, there is plenty of nonunion labor, and there is an abundance of land available for development.

Compiling the Data for Your Area

Projecting Employment and Income

Data for projecting employment and income vary by state. Go to the following web site to access links to each of the 50 states: http://www.projectionscentral.com/projections.asp?page=ProjSites.

Click on your state and search for data. Some links support data by county, others only for the entire state. All of the data are consistent in that each state is measuring employment projections for the years 2002 to 2012.

The federal Bureau of Labor Statistics (BLS) has also prepared a projection for the nation for the same time period, 2002 to 2012. Therefore, we can use the national projection as the benchmark for comparison to any other region of the country. The BLS projects a 14.8 percent increase in employment over the time period 2002 to 2012 and an annual growth rate of 1.4 percent.

If your region exceeds these benchmarks for employment growth, your area is better able to sustain past and future appreciation. If your region has experienced bubblelike growth but does not have a correspondingly positive forecast of employment growth, your area is more vulnerable.

Measuring the Bubble

Business failure is difficult to predict. However, there are estimates available for future job growth, household growth, income growth, and new construction. The amount of past appreciation is also known.

According to the FDIC, home prices have increased nationally by 50 percent in the past five years (2000 to 2005). This appreciation rate will serve as the benchmark for determining whether your region has experienced a bubble.

You can access data tables measuring home price appreciation in 379 Metropolitan Statistical Areas (MSAs) by visiting either of our web sites at davidjdecker.com or georgesheldon.com. Look up your MSA in the tables. If your area is not listed, choose the MSA that is closest or call your local tax assessing authority to get an estimate of the appreciation in your area for the last five years.

Using 50 percent appreciation over five years as the benchmark, assess the degree to which your region has experienced a bubble. Tables 4.2 and 4.3 illustrate the 20 MSAs that have experienced the most and the least appreciation.

Do not be fooled into thinking the top and bottom 20 MSAs represent the areas to avoid or the locations to find bargains. Such thinking is too simplistic.

The less appreciation your area has enjoyed, the less chance there is of a crash now. Of course, the opposite is also true. The greater the appreciation recently, the greater the chance of a crash.

Just because your area did not participate as vigorously in the appreciation of the past five years does not mean that you are immune from a bust anymore than strong appreciation ensures a crash now. Other factors must be considered, such as employment and income growth.

Projecting the Number of Households

The best available information for forecasting the number of households is the Census Bureau's statewide projections of population growth through the year 2025. These data are summarized by state in Table 4.4. The data suggest that most of the growth will occur

TABLE 4.1   U.S. Metropolitan Area Population Projections, Alphabetical

Metropolitan Area	2000	Rank	2010	Rank	2025	Rank	% Change 2000–2010
Altoona, PA MSA	129,100	222	128,600	231	127,400	239	-0.39%
Abilene, TX MSA	126,600	226	131,700	227	139,600	227	4.03%
Albany—Schenectady—Troy, NY MSA	875,600	56	882,100	58	900,900	62	0.74%
Albany, GA MSA	120,800	234	125,500	236	130,800	237	3.89%
Albuquerque, NM MSA	712,700	61	831,200	59	1,011,800	58	16.63%
Alexandria, LA MSA	126,300	227	120,800	239	111,400	253	-4.35%
Allentown—Bethlehem—Easton, PA MSA	638,000	65	655,600	69	689,900	70	2.76%
Amarillo, TX MSA	217,900	157	240,300	157	275,300	152	10.28%
Anchorage, AK MSA	260,300	138	299,500	135	358,600	132	15.06%
Anniston, AL MSA	112,200	245	109,100	253	105,100	259	-2.76%
Appleton—Oshkosh—Neenah, WI MSA	358,400	115	382,400	116	408,300	121	6.70%
Asheville, NC MSA	226,000	154	244,800	154	265,100	156	8.32%
Athens, GA MSA	153,400	195	168,900	194	186,400	196	10.10%
Atlanta, GA MSA	4,112,200	11	4,765,400	11	5,510,400	11	15.88%
Auburn—Opelika, AL MSA	115,100	240	138,600	220	168,200	201	20.42%
Augusta—Aiken, GA—SC MSA	477,400	86	514,400	89	558,000	91	7.75%
Austin—San Marcos, TX MSA	1,249,800	37	1,548,900	34	2,014,100	29	23.93%
Bakersfield, CA MSA	661,600	64	822,900	60	1,163,500	50	24.38%
Bangor, ME MSA	90,900	263	89,800	267	88,200	268	-1.21%
Barnstable—Yarmouth, MA MSA	162,600	188	183,300	183	222,400	174	12.73%
Baton Rouge, LA MSA	602,900	69	682,400	66	817,200	65	13.19%
Beaumont—Port Arthur, TX MSA	385,100	106	402,800	109	430,300	114	4.60%
Bellingham, WA MSA	166,800	185	197,400	175	241,400	166	18.35%
Benton Harbor, MI MSA	162,500	189	162,700	197	163,100	206	0.12%
Billings, MT MSA	129,400	221	142,200	217	154,400	213	9.89%
Biloxi—Gulfport—Pascagoula, MS MSA	364,000	113	393,900	111	426,600	115	8.21%
Binghamton, NY MSA	252,300	140	246,700	150	230,600	170	-2.22%
Birmingham, AL MSA	921,100	54	989,300	53	1,074,900	55	7.40%
Bismarck, ND MSA	94,700	260	122,400	237	159,700	211	29.25%
Bloomington—Normal, IL MSA	150,400	200	161,200	199	181,200	197	7.18%
Bloomington, IN MSA	120,600	235	126,300	235	131,400	236	4.73%

(Continued)

TABLE 4.1 (Continued)

Metropolitan Area	2000	Rank	2010	Rank	2025	Rank	% Change 2000–2010
Boise City, ID MSA	432,300	96	525,500	86	611,300	83	21.56%
Boston—Worcester—Lawrence, MA—NH—ME—CT CMSA	5,819,100	7	6,119,200	7	6,611,700	8	5.16%
Brownsville—Harlingen—San Benito, TX MSA	335,200	120	390,900	113	477,500	103	16.62%
Bryan—College Station, TX MSA	152,400	197	175,100	192	210,300	182	14.90%
Buffalo—Niagara Falls, NY MSA	1,170,100	42	1,161,200	46	1,135,900	52	-0.76%
Burlington, VT MSA	169,400	183	182,000	185	192,800	189	7.44%
Canton—Massillon, OH MSA	406,900	100	411,700	105	417,700	119	1.18%
Casper, WY MSA	66,500	275	76,400	275	87,500	270	14.89%
Cedar Rapids, IA MSA	191,700	170	202,100	172	213,400	181	5.43%
Champaign—Urbana, IL MSA	179,700	175	183,000	184	189,300	193	1.84%
Charleston—North Charleston, SC MSA	549,000	76	577,700	79	614,700	82	5.23%
Charleston, WV MSA	251,700	141	252,400	148	252,000	162	0.28%
Charlotte—Gastonia—Rock Hill, NC—SC MSA	1,499,300	33	1,696,800	31	1,923,000	30	13.17%
Charlottesville, VA MSA	159,600	191	179,800	186	207,100	185	12.66%
Chattanooga, TN—GA MSA	465,200	89	489,100	92	515,100	98	5.14%
Cheyenne, WY MSA	81,600	271	97,400	260	115,100	250	19.36%
Chicago—Gary—Kenosha, IL—IN—WI CMSA	9,157,500	3	9,630,300	3	10,297,400	4	5.16%
Chico—Paradise, CA MSA	203,200	164	231,900	160	292,600	145	14.12%
Cincinnati—Hamilton, OH—KY—IN CMSA	1,979,200	23	2,051,700	24	2,124,000	26	3.66%
Clarksville—Hopkinsville, TN—KY MSA	207,000	163	229,000	165	250,000	163	10.63%
Cleveland—Akron, OH CMSA	2,945,800	16	2,978,100	17	3,018,400	20	1.10%
Colorado Springs, CO MSA	516,900	80	576,200	80	642,300	77	11.47%
Columbia, MO MSA	135,500	217	151,100	208	170,100	200	11.51%
Columbia, SC MSA	536,700	79	593,300	77	666,600	75	10.55%
Columbus, GA—AL MSA	274,600	136	283,200	140	293,100	144	3.13%
Columbus, OH MSA	1,540,200	32	1,613,100	33	1,704,200	34	4.73%
Corpus Christi, TX MSA	380,800	108	403,700	108	439,300	108	6.01%
Corvallis, OR MSA	78,200	273	83,300	271	90,300	266	6.52%
Cumberland, MD—WV MSA	102,000	255	102,300	259	102,700	260	0.29%
Dallas—Fort Worth, TX CMSA	5,221,800	9	6,099,800	8	7,465,400	6	16.81%
Danville, VA MSA	110,200	249	111,200	251	112,600	252	0.91%

Davenport—Moline—Rock Island, IA—IL MSA	359,100	114	363,200	123	370,400	129	1.14%
Dayton—Springfield, OH MSA	950,600	52	950,300	54	950,000	59	-0.03%
Daytona Beach, FL MSA	493,200	82	562,800	81	670,200	74	14.11%
Decatur, AL MSA	145,700	207	157,900	202	173,100	199	8.22%
Decatur, IL MSA	114,700	242	113,400	250	111,100	254	-1.13%
Denver—Boulder—Greeley, CO CMSA	2,581,500	19	2,878,900	18	3,210,200	17	11.52%
Des Moines, IA MSA	456,000	90	484,800	93	515,600	97	6.32%
Detroit—Ann Arbor—Flint, MI CMSA	5,456,400	8	5,525,600	9	5,627,900	10	1.27%
Dothan, AL MSA	137,900	215	143,800	216	151,100	216	4.28%
Dover, DE MSA	126,700	225	133,200	225	139,400	229	5.13%
Dubuque, IA MSA	89,100	265	90,400	266	91,700	265	1.46%
Duluth—Superior, MN—WI MSA	243,800	146	246,000	151	248,500	165	0.90%
Eau Claire, WI MSA	148,300	203	154,300	204	160,800	208	4.05%
El Paso, TX MSA	679,600	63	744,900	63	846,300	63	9.61%
Elkhart—Goshen, IN MSA	182,800	172	196,000	176	207,800	184	7.22%
Elmira, NY MSA	91,100	262	89,200	268	83,700	272	-2.09%
Enid, OK MSA	57,100	276	58,800	276	60,300	276	1.73%
Erie, PA MSA	280,800	135	283,000	141	287,200	146	0.78%
Eugene—Springfield, OR MSA	323,000	123	351,200	126	389,300	125	8.73%
Evansville—Henderson, IN—KY MSA	296,200	131	304,600	134	312,100	140	2.84%
Fargo—Moorhead, ND—MN MSA	174,400	179	187,700	181	203,500	186	7.63%
Fayetteville—Springdale—Rogers, AR MSA	311,100	128	375,800	117	444,900	107	20.80%
Fayetteville, NC MSA	303,000	129	318,600	130	335,500	134	5.15%
Flagstaff, AZ—UT MSA	122,400	233	133,900	223	147,500	222	9.40%
Florence, AL MSA	143,000	208	152,700	205	165,000	203	6.78%
Florence, SC MSA	125,800	228	133,500	224	143,500	224	6.12%
Fort Collins—Loveland, CO MSA	251,500	142	283,800	139	319,800	137	12.84%
Fort Myers—Cape Coral, FL MSA	440,900	94	519,400	88	640,500	78	17.80%
Fort Pierce—Port St. Lucie, FL MSA	319,400	125	370,200	118	448,400	106	15.90%
Fort Smith, AR—OK MSA	207,300	162	231,400	162	263,800	158	11.63%
Fort Walton Beach, FL MSA	170,500	181	190,300	179	220,900	178	11.61%
Fort Wayne, IN MSA	502,100	81	524,900	87	545,200	92	4.54%
Fresno, CA MSA	922,500	53	1,150,300	47	1,631,400	37	24.69%
Gadsden, AL MSA	103,500	253	106,500	255	110,300	255	2.90%
Gainesville, FL MSA	218,000	156	245,000	153	286,600	148	12.39%
Glens Falls, NY MSA	124,300	230	127,000	234	134,700	234	2.17%
Goldsboro, NC MSA	113,300	243	118,100	244	123,300	242	4.24%
Grand Forks, ND—MN MSA	97,500	258	93,900	262	89,600	267	-3.69%
Grand Junction, CO MSA	116,300	239	127,700	233	140,400	225	9.80%

(Continued)

TABLE 4.1 (Continued)

Metropolitan Area	2000	Rank	2010	Rank	2025	Rank	% Change 2000–2010
Grand Rapids—Muskegon—Holland, MI MSA	1,088,500	47	1,127,200	48	1,184,500	48	3.56%
Great Falls, MT MSA	80,400	272	82,500	272	84,600	271	2.61%
Green Bay, WI MSA	226,800	153	244,600	155	263,900	157	7.85%
Greensboro—Winston-Salem—High Point, NC MSA	1,251,500	36	1,362,400	39	1,481,900	41	8.86%
Greenville—Spartanburg—Anderson, SC MSA	962,400	51	1,052,000	52	1,167,900	49	9.31%
Greenville, NC MSA	133,800	218	148,100	214	163,400	205	10.69%
Harrisburg—Lebanon—Carlisle, PA MSA	629,400	66	646,400	70	679,600	71	2.70%
Hartford, CT MSA	1,183,100	41	1,211,600	44	1,284,800	46	2.41%
Hattiesburg, MS MSA	111,700	246	119,200	242	127,400	239	6.71%
Hickory—Morganton—Lenoir, NC MSA	341,900	118	369,100	119	398,500	123	7.96%
Honolulu, HI MSA	876,200	55	947,100	55	1,082,900	54	8.09%
Houma, LA MSA	194,500	167	206,900	170	227,900	171	6.38%
Houston—Galveston—Brazoria, TX CMSA	4,669,600	10	5,365,200	10	6,447,100	9	14.90%
Huntington—Ashland, WV—KY—OH MSA	315,500	126	316,800	131	318,100	138	0.41%
Huntsville, AL MSA	342,400	117	383,900	115	436,100	111	12.12%
Indianapolis, IN MSA	1,607,500	28	1,720,100	30	1,820,800	31	7.00%
Iowa City, IA MSA	111,000	247	117,800	246	125,100	241	6.13%
Jackson, MI MSA	158,400	192	160,600	200	163,900	204	1.39%
Jackson, MS MSA	440,800	95	467,100	94	495,900	101	5.97%
Jackson, TN MSA	107,400	250	117,800	246	128,100	238	9.68%
Jacksonville, FL MSA	1,100,500	45	1,244,400	41	1,466,200	42	13.08%
Jacksonville, NC MSA	150,400	200	150,600	210	150,900	217	0.13%
Jamestown, NY MSA	139,800	213	138,800	219	135,900	233	-0.72%
Janesville—Beloit, WI MSA	152,300	198	159,400	201	167,100	202	4.66%
Johnson City—Kingsport—Bristol, TN—VA MSA	480,100	84	512,800	90	563,200	90	6.81%
Johnstown, PA MSA	232,600	152	229,100	164	222,200	175	-1.50%
Jonesboro, AR MSA	82,100	270	90,700	265	99,800	262	10.48%
Joplin, MO MSA	157,300	193	172,500	193	190,900	191	9.66%

Area							
Kalamazoo—Battle Creek, MI MSA	452,900	91	464,500	96	474,800	104	2.56%
Kansas City, MO—KS MSA	1,776,100	25	1,918,500	26	2,101,400	27	8.02%
Killeen—Temple, TX MSA	313,000	127	355,700	124	422,100	116	13.64%
Knoxville, TN MSA	687,200	62	751,000	62	813,700	66	9.28%
Kokomo, IN MSA	101,500	256	103,800	258	105,900	258	2.27%
La Crosse, WI—MN MSA	126,800	224	132,800	226	139,500	228	4.73%
Lafayette, IN MSA	182,800	172	193,400	177	202,800	187	5.80%
Lafayette, LA MSA	385,600	105	429,000	104	502,500	100	11.26%
Lake Charles, LA MSA	183,600	171	200,000	173	227,900	171	8.93%
Lakeland—Winter Haven, FL MSA	483,900	83	542,300	83	632,200	79	12.07%
Lancaster, PA MSA	470,700	88	490,300	91	528,600	94	4.16%
Lansing—East Lansing, MI MSA	447,700	92	451,600	100	457,300	105	0.87%
Laredo, TX MSA	193,100	168	237,500	158	306,500	141	22.99%
Las Cruces, NM MSA	174,700	177	212,200	168	269,500	155	21.47%
Las Vegas, NV—AZ MSA	1,563,300	31	1,890,500	27	2,253,400	25	20.93%
Lawrence, KS MSA	100,000	257	115,800	249	138,200	230	15.80%
Lawton, OK MSA	115,000	241	118,100	244	123,000	244	2.70%
Lewiston—Auburn, ME MSA	90,800	264	86,900	269	80,800	274	-4.30%
Lexington, KY MSA	479,200	85	528,400	85	586,700	89	10.27%
Lima, OH MSA	155,100	194	155,400	203	155,700	212	0.19%
Lincoln, NE MSA	250,300	144	278,100	142	312,600	139	11.11%
Little Rock—North Little Rock, AR MSA	583,800	73	629,500	71	678,300	72	7.83%
Longview—Marshall, TX MSA	208,800	161	219,900	167	237,200	168	5.32%
Los Angeles—Riverside—Orange County, CA CMSA	16,373,600	2	18,886,900	2	24,196,300	2	15.35%
Louisville, KY—IN MSA	1,025,600	49	1,063,200	51	1,096,700	53	3.67%
Lubbock, TX MSA	242,600	148	257,400	146	280,500	150	6.10%
Lynchburg, VA MSA	214,900	158	229,800	163	249,900	164	6.93%
Macon, GA MSA	322,500	124	340,500	127	360,900	130	5.58%
Madison, WI MSA	426,500	97	459,500	99	495,200	102	7.74%
Mansfield, OH MSA	175,800	176	176,500	191	177,300	198	0.40%
McAllen—Edinburg—Mission, TX MSA	569,500	74	707,300	65	921,600	60	24.20%
Medford—Ashland, OR MSA	181,300	174	205,900	171	239,000	167	13.57%
Melbourne—Titusville—Palm Bay, FL MSA	476,200	87	533,600	84	622,000	80	12.05%
Memphis, TN—AR—MS MSA	1,135,600	43	1,215,600	43	1,297,500	45	7.04%
Merced, CA MSA	210,600	160	254,400	147	347,100	133	20.80%
Miami—Fort Lauderdale, FL CMSA	3,876,400	12	4,384,200	12	5,167,100	12	13.10%
Milwaukee—Racine, WI CMSA	1,689,600	26	1,735,300	29	1,784,700	32	2.70%

(Continued)

TABLE 4.1 (Continued)

Metropolitan Area	2000	Rank	2010	Rank	2025	Rank	% Change 2000–2010
Minneapolis—St. Paul, MN—WI MSA	2,968,800	15	3,214,900	16	3,492,300	16	8.29%
Missoula, MT MSA	95,800	259	109,600	252	122,800	245	14.41%
Mobile, AL MSA	540,300	78	593,600	76	660,600	76	9.86%
Modesto, CA MSA	447,000	93	551,300	82	771,800	68	23.33%
Monroe, LA MSA	147,300	206	152,600	206	161,800	207	3.60%
Montgomery, AL MSA	333,100	121	367,200	122	410,100	120	10.24%
Muncie, IN MSA	118,800	238	118,200	243	117,900	249	-0.42%
Myrtle Beach, SC MSA	196,600	166	232,300	159	278,500	151	18.16%
Naples, FL MSA	251,400	143	325,100	128	438,800	109	29.32%
Nashville, TN MSA	1,231,300	38	1,386,400	37	1,538,800	39	12.60%
New London—Norwich, CT—RI MSA	293,600	132	296,600	136	304,400	143	1.02%
New Orleans, LA MSA	1,337,700	34	1,393,600	36	1,488,400	40	4.18%
New York—Northern New Jersey—Long Island, NY—NJ—CT—PA CMSA	21,199,900	1	22,140,500	1	24,319,900	1	4.44%
Norfolk—Virginia Beach—Newport News, VA—NC MSA	1,569,500	30	1,646,900	32	1,739,600	33	4.93%
Ocala, FL MSA	258,500	139	306,500	133	379,900	127	18.39%
Odessa—Midland, TX MSA	237,100	149	245,700	152	259,100	160	3.63%
Oklahoma City, OK MSA	1,083,300	48	1,194,800	45	1,368,900	43	10.29%
Omaha, NE—IA MSA	717,000	60	763,300	61	817,600	64	6.46%
Orlando, FL MSA	1,644,600	27	1,956,300	25	2,436,800	23	18.95%
Owensboro, KY MSA	91,500	261	95,500	263	95,000	264	2.30%
Panama City, FL MSA	148,200	204	164,000	196	188,300	195	10.66%
Parkersburg—Marietta, WV—OH MSA	151,200	199	152,000	207	152,900	215	0.53%
Pensacola, FL MSA	412,200	99	462,500	97	540,000	93	12.20%
Peoria—Pekin, IL MSA	347,400	116	351,500	125	359,300	131	1.18%
Philadelphia—Wilmington—Atlantic City, PA—NJ—DE—MD CMSA	6,188,500	6	6,362,400	6	6,680,300	7	2.81%
Phoenix—Mesa, AZ MSA	3,251,900	14	3,785,000	14	4,445,400	14	16.39%
Pine Bluff, AR MSA	84,300	268	83,500	270	82,700	273	-0.95%
Pittsburgh, PA MSA	2,358,700	21	2,343,900	22	2,314,900	24	-0.63%

Pittsfield, MA MSA	84,700	267	81,700	274	76,100	275	-3.54%
Pocatello, ID MSA	75,600	274	82,100	273	88,100	269	8.60%
Portland—Salem, OR—WA CMSA	2,265,200	22	2,621,500	21	3,122,900	19	15.73%
Portland, ME MSA	243,500	147	274,700	143	322,800	136	12.81%
Providence—Fall River—Warwick, RI—MA MSA	1,188,600	39	1,230,900	42	1,313,700	44	3.56%
Provo—Orem, UT MSA	368,500	111	437,900	103	509,200	99	18.83%
Pueblo, CO MSA	141,500	211	150,600	210	160,700	209	6.43%
Punta Gorda, FL MSA	141,600	210	164,400	195	199,500	188	16.10%
Raleigh—Durham—Chapel Hill, NC MSA	1,187,900	40	1,371,100	38	1,568,600	38	15.42%
Rapid City, SD MSA	88,600	266	94,300	261	99,200	263	6.43%
Reading, PA MSA	373,600	109	388,900	114	418,600	117	4.10%
Redding, CA MSA	163,300	187	185,400	182	232,100	169	13.53%
Reno, NV MSA	339,500	119	368,300	120	389,600	124	8.48%
Richland—Kennewick—Pasco, WA MSA	191,800	169	224,600	166	271,600	153	17.10%
Richmond—Petersburg, VA MSA	996,500	50	1,089,400	50	1,214,800	47	9.32%
Roanoke, VA MSA	235,500	150	244,100	156	255,000	161	3.48%
Rochester, MN MSA	124,300	230	134,700	222	146,900	223	8.37%
Rochester, NY MSA	1,098,200	46	1,114,800	49	1,162,000	51	1.51%
Rockford, IL MSA	371,200	110	392,300	112	431,400	113	5.68%
Rocky Mount, NC MSA	143,000	208	148,400	213	154,200	214	3.78%
Sacramento—Yolo, CA CMSA	1,796,900	24	2,227,700	23	3,137,700	18	23.97%
Saginaw—Bay City—Midland, MI MSA	403,100	101	404,000	107	405,500	122	0.22%
Salinas, CA MSA	401,800	102	464,700	95	597,500	87	15.65%
Salt Lake City—Ogden, UT MSA	1,333,900	35	1,507,000	35	1,684,500	35	12.98%
San Angelo, TX MSA	104,000	252	108,100	254	114,500	251	3.94%
San Antonio, TX MSA	1,592,400	29	1,790,800	28	2,099,300	28	12.46%
San Diego, CA MSA	2,813,800	17	3,244,700	15	4,155,000	15	15.31%
San Francisco—Oakland—San Jose, CA CMSA	7,039,400	5	8,111,800	5	10,377,400	3	15.23%
San Luis Obispo—Atascadero—Paso Robles, CA MSA	246,700	145	287,000	138	372,000	128	16.34%
Santa Barbara—Santa Maria—Lompoc, CA MSA	399,300	103	439,900	102	525,600	96	10.17%
Santa Fe, NM MSA	147,600	205	177,000	189	221,600	176	19.92%
Sarasota—Bradenton, FL MSA	590,000	72	664,600	68	779,600	67	12.64%

(Continued)

71

TABLE 4.1 (Continued)

Metropolitan Area	2000	Rank	2010	Rank	2025	Rank	% Change 2000–2010
Savannah, GA MSA	293,000	133	312,800	132	335,400	135	6.76%
Scranton—Wilkes-Barre—Hazleton, PA MSA	624,800	67	619,200	73	608,200	84	-0.90%
Seattle—Tacoma—Bremerton, WA CMSA	3,554,800	13	4,012,600	13	4,670,800	13	12.88%
Sharon, PA MSA	120,300	236	120,000	241	119,400	248	-0.25%
Sheboygan, WI MSA	112,600	244	117,500	248	122,800	245	4.35%
Sherman—Denison, TX MSA	110,600	248	122,100	238	140,100	226	10.40%
Shreveport—Bossier City, LA MSA	392,300	104	409,300	106	438,200	110	4.33%
Sioux City, IA—NE MSA	124,100	232	129,600	230	136,000	232	4.43%
Sioux Falls, SD MSA	172,400	180	198,700	174	221,200	177	15.26%
South Bend, IN MSA	265,600	137	274,700	143	282,900	149	3.43%
Spokane, WA MSA	417,900	98	462,300	98	526,000	95	10.62%
Springfield, IL MSA	201,400	165	207,500	169	218,600	180	3.03%
Springfield, MA MSA	591,900	71	595,000	75	600,700	86	0.52%
Springfield, MO MSA	325,700	122	367,400	121	417,800	118	12.80%
State College, PA MSA	135,800	216	140,700	218	150,300	219	3.61%
Steubenville—Weirton, OH—WV MSA	132,000	219	128,000	232	123,300	242	-3.03%
Stockton—Lodi, CA MSA	563,600	75	676,800	67	915,900	61	20.09%
St. Cloud, MN MSA	167,400	184	178,200	187	190,800	192	6.45%
St. Joseph, MO MSA	102,500	254	105,700	257	109,700	256	3.12%
St. Louis, MO—IL MSA	2,603,600	18	2,666,100	19	2,766,300	22	2.40%
Sumter, SC MSA	104,600	251	106,000	256	107,800	257	1.34%
Syracuse, NY MSA	732,100	59	727,500	64	714,100	69	-0.63%
Tallahassee, FL MSA	284,500	134	322,400	129	380,700	126	13.32%
Tampa—St. Petersburg—Clearwater, FL MSA	2,396,000	20	2,639,600	20	3,015,200	21	10.17%
Terre Haute, IN MSA	149,200	202	150,000	212	150,700	218	0.54%
Texarkana, TX—Texarkana, AR MSA	129,700	220	136,800	221	147,600	221	5.47%
Toledo, OH MSA	618,200	68	619,700	72	621,600	81	0.24%
Topeka, KS MSA	169,900	182	177,600	188	188,600	194	4.53%
Tucson, AZ MSA	843,700	57	936,800	56	1,052,100	56	11.03%
Tulsa, OK MSA	803,200	58	887,700	57	1,019,500	57	10.52%

MSA						
Tuscaloosa, AL MSA	164,900	186	177,000	189	192,100	190	7.34%
Tyler, TX MSA	174,700	177	192,000	178	219,000	179	9.90%
Utica—Rome, NY MSA	299,900	130	292,100	137	270,000	154	-2.60%
Victoria, TX MSA	84,100	269	91,300	264	102,500	261	8.56%
Visalia—Tulare—Porterville, CA MSA	368,000	112	444,600	101	606,300	85	20.82%
Waco, TX MSA	213,500	159	231,600	161	259,700	159	8.48%
Washington—Baltimore, DC—MD—VA—WV CMSA	7,608,100	4	8,292,900	4	9,300,000	5	9.00%
Waterloo—Cedar Falls, IA MSA	128,000	223	129,900	229	132,000	235	1.48%
Wausau, WI MSA	125,800	228	131,600	228	137,900	231	4.61%
West Palm Beach—Boca Raton, FL MSA	1,131,200	44	1,330,000	40	1,636,400	36	17.57%
Wheeling, WV—OH MSA	153,200	196	150,800	209	148,100	220	-1.57%
Wichita Falls, TX MSA	140,500	212	148,100	214	159,800	210	5.41%
Wichita, KS MSA	545,200	77	597,400	74	671,300	73	9.57%
Williamsport, PA MSA	120,000	237	120,600	240	121,700	247	0.50%
Wilmington, NC MSA	233,500	151	267,700	145	304,700	142	14.65%
Yakima, WA MSA	222,600	155	249,000	149	287,000	147	11.86%
York, PA MSA	381,600	107	399,100	110	432,900	112	4.53%
Youngstown—Warren, OH MSA	594,700	70	592,400	78	589,600	88	-0.39%
Yuba City, CA MSA	139,100	214	161,700	198	209,200	183	16.25%
Yuma, AZ MSA	160,000	190	188,000	180	222,600	173	17.50%

ASSUMPTIONS
Base: 2000 US Census
Census Bureau 1995–2025 Projection State Assumptions
Metropolitan Areas Derived from 1990–2000 Share of State Growth.

DEMOGRAPHIA and THE PUBLIC PURPOSE
are undertakings of
WENDELL COX CONSULTANCY

TABLE 4.2   *Top 20 Metropolitan Statistical Areas with Highest Rates of House Price Appreciation Percent Change, Period Ended June 30, 2005*

MSA	National Ranking**	1- Year	Quarter	5-Year
Naples–Marco Island, FL	1	35.60	13.50	114.69
Bakersfield, CA	2	33.88	5.79	114.63
Merced, CA	3	32.67	8.63	131.37
Reno–Sparks, NV	4	32.27	7.29	98.45
Palm Bay–Melbourne–Titusville, FL	5	31.45	6.60	110.25
Stockton, CA	6	31.14	7.37	120.73
Phoenix–Mesa–Scottsdale, AZ	7	30.48	10.90	67.31
Visalia–Porterville, CA	8	30.42	5.49	90.93
Cape Coral–Fort Myers, FL	9	29.84	9.82	106.99
Modesto, CA	10	29.56	8.09	132.29
Sarasota–Bradenton–Venice, FL	11	29.50	6.96	100.77
Punta Gorda, FL	12	29.39	7.80	109.63
Yuba City, CA	13	29.09	7.34	131.86
Coeur d'Alene, ID	14	28.98	8.12	59.90
West Palm Beach–Boca Raton–Boynton Beach, FL (MSAD)	15	28.83	6.68	113.92
Prescott, AZ	16	28.63	10.14	70.57
St. George, UT	17	28.34	10.17	47.66
Port St. Lucie–Fort Pierce, FL	18	27.20	7.12	120.98
Fresno, CA	19	27.01	5.94	123.60
Fort Lauderdale–Pompano Beach–Deerfield Beach, FL (MSAD)	20	26.93	6.87	115.85

in the South and West. This report shows that population growth nationally from 2000 to 2010 will be 8.4 percent. Therefore, 8.4 percent population growth is the benchmark for comparison for your region.

Find your Metropolitan Statistical Area in Table 4.1. Look at the percentage of population change from 2000 to 2010. If your area has projected population growth exceeding 8.4 percent, your

TABLE 4.3   *Bottom 20 Metropolitan Statistical Areas with Lowest Rates of House Price Appreciation Percent Change, Period Ended June 30, 2005*

MSA	National Ranking**	1-Year	Quarter	5-Year
Charlotte–Gastonia–Concord, NC-SC	246	3.75	0.35	18.22
Fort Worth–Arlington, TX (MSAD)	247	3.61	1.29	21.31
Tulsa, OK	248	3.44	1.46	22.04
Detroit–Livonia–Dearborn, MI (MSAD)	249	3.41	0.48	24.43
Dallas–Plano–Irving, TX (MSAD)	250	3.40	1.24	21.36
Macon, GA	251	3.29	0.55	21.71
Burlington, NC	252	3.28	0.06	16.48
Greensboro–High Point, NC	253	3.17	-0.52	17.23
Canton–Massillon, OH	254	2.83	0.60	20.52
Saginaw–Saginaw Township North, MI	255	2.82	-1.47	21.73
Anderson, SC	256	2.69	-0.82	20.44
Michigan City–La Porte, IN	257	2.67	-0.84	24.53
Spartanburg, SC	258	2.67	-1.08	16.35
Battle Creek, MI	259	2.53	-1.71	24.46
Wichita, KS	260	2.50	0.96	20.64
Hickory–Lenoir–Morganton, NC	261	2.21	0.32	18.96
Greeley, CO	262	1.88	-0.01	28.75
Kokomo, IN	263	1.08	0.29	14.65
Lafayette, IN	264	0.91	-1.10	10.88
Mansfield, OH	265	0.44	-2.73	21.01

area probably already has sustained and will continue to sustain higher appreciation rates.

Caution: While a large influx of population is a good thing, any rapid changes increase the possibility of temporary imbalances between supply and demand. Just because an area is thriving does not mean it will never become overextended with supply and experience corresponding price fluctuations.

TABLE 4.4 Total Population and Net Change for States: 1995 to 2025 (Thousands. Resident Population)

| Region, Division, and State | Projections for July 1 | | | | | | | July 1, 1995, to July 1, 2025 Components of Change | | | | |
	1995	2000	2005	2010	2015	2020	2025	Net Change	Births	Deaths	Interstate Migration	Immigration
United States	262,755	274,634	285,981	297,716	310,133	322,742	335,050	72,294	126,986	84,633	—	24,666
NORTHEAST	51,466	52,107	52,767	53,692	54,836	56,103	57,392	5,927	21,585	16,537	(7,168)	6,830
New England	13,312	13,581	13,843	14,172	14,546	14,938	15,321	2,009	5,448	4,096	(1,041)	1,338
Maine	1,241	1,259	1,281	1,323	1,362	1,396	1,423	181	437	402	86	20
New Hampshire	1,148	1,224	1,281	1,329	1,372	1,410	1,439	291	481	344	84	31
Vermont	585	617	638	651	662	671	678	94	221	180	26	7
Massachusetts	6,074	6,199	6,310	6,431	6,574	6,734	6,902	828	2,520	1,860	(815)	831
Rhode Island	990	998	1,012	1,038	1,070	1,105	1,141	151	423	318	(94)	113
Connecticut	3,275	3,284	3,317	3,400	3,506	3,621	3,739	464	1,368	992	(329)	337
Middle Atlantic	38,153	38,526	38,923	39,520	40,289	41,164	42,071	3,918	16,136	12,441	(6,127)	5,492
New York	18,136	18,146	18,250	18,530	18,916	19,359	19,830	1,694	8,117	5,598	(5,038)	3,886
New Jersey	7,945	8,178	8,392	8,638	8,924	9,238	9,558	1,613	3,535	2,542	(747)	1,201
Pennsylvania	12,072	12,202	12,281	12,352	12,449	12,567	12,683	611	4,484	4,301	(342)	405
MIDWEST	61,804	63,502	64,825	65,915	67,024	68,114	69,109	7,305	26,334	19,534	(3,541)	2,365
East North Central	43,456	44,419	45,151	45,764	46,410	47,063	47,675	4,219	18,512	13,557	(3,653)	1,839
Ohio	11,151	11,319	11,428	11,505	11,588	11,671	11,744	594	4,417	3,626	(758)	247
Indiana	5,803	6,045	6,215	6,318	6,404	6,481	6,546	742	2,377	1,879	(35)	110
Illinois	11,830	12,051	12,266	12,515	12,808	13,121	13,440	1,610	5,672	3,582	(1,699)	1,037
Michigan	9,549	9,679	9,763	9,836	9,917	10,002	10,078	528	3,965	2,874	(1,122)	310
Wisconsin	5,123	5,326	5,479	5,590	5,693	5,788	5,867	744	2,081	1,596	(39)	134
West North Central	18,348	19,082	19,673	20,151	20,615	21,051	21,434	3,086	7,822	5,978	112	526
Minnesota	4,610	4,830	5,005	5,147	5,283	5,406	5,510	900	1,993	1,349	(89)	190
Iowa	2,842	2,900	2,941	2,968	2,994	3,019	3,040	198	1,073	958	(97)	83
Missouri	5,324	5,540	5,718	5,864	6,005	6,137	6,250	927	2,260	1,858	255	105
North Dakota	641	662	677	690	704	717	729	88	270	214	(6)	13
South Dakota	729	777	810	826	840	853	866	137	341	246	6	6
Nebraska	1,637	1,705	1,761	1,806	1,850	1,892	1,930	293	718	543	35	29
Kansas	2,565	2,668	2,761	2,849	2,939	3,026	3,108	543	1,167	810	7	102

SOUTH	91,890	97,613	102,788	107,597	112,384	117,060	121,448	29,558	43,142	32,054	11,067	5,273
South Atlantic	46,995	50,147	52,921	55,457	57,966	60,411	62,675	15,680	20,682	16,883	6,707	3,790
Delaware	717	768	800	817	832	847	861	144	313	249	35	24
Maryland	5,042	5,275	5,467	5,657	5,862	6,071	6,274	1,232	2,295	1,537	(251)	593
District of Columbia	554	523	529	560	594	625	655	101	334	213	(156)	135
Virginia	6,618	6,997	7,324	7,627	7,921	8,204	8,466	1,848	2,839	2,074	299	605
West Virginia	1,828	1,841	1,849	1,851	1,851	1,850	1,845	17	555	715	105	14
North Carolina	7,195	7,777	8,227	8,552	8,840	9,111	9,349	2,154	3,039	2,612	1,295	199
South Carolina	3,673	3,858	4,033	4,205	4,369	4,517	4,645	972	1,566	1,313	546	58
Georgia	7,201	7,875	8,413	8,824	9,200	9,552	9,869	2,669	3,571	2,340	953	306
Florida	14,166	15,233	16,279	17,363	18,497	19,634	20,710	6,544	6,169	5,829	3,879	1,856
East South Central	16,067	16,918	17,604	18,122	18,586	19,002	19,345	3,279	6,593	5,791	1,737	262
Kentucky	3,860	3,995	4,098	4,170	4,231	4,281	4,314	454	1,439	1,344	175	67
Tennessee	5,256	5,657	5,966	6,180	6,365	6,529	6,665	1,409	2,217	1,909	845	97
Alabama	4,253	4,451	4,631	4,798	4,956	5,100	5,224	971	1,759	1,563	577	71
Mississippi	2,697	2,816	2,908	2,974	3,035	3,093	3,142	445	1,179	975	140	27
West South Central	28,828	30,548	32,263	34,019	35,832	37,647	39,427	10,599	15,867	9,380	2,624	1,222
Arkansas	2,484	2,631	2,750	2,840	2,922	2,997	3,055	572	1,000	979	436	31
Louisiana	4,342	4,425	4,535	4,683	4,840	4,991	5,133	790	2,054	1,501	45	90
Oklahoma	3,278	3,373	3,491	3,639	3,789	3,930	4,057	779	1,411	1,224	412	92
Texas	18,724	20,119	21,487	22,857	24,280	25,729	27,183	8,459	11,403	5,676	1,730	1,008
WEST	57,596	61,413	65,603	70,512	75,889	81,465	87,101	29,505	35,925	16,508	(358)	10,198
Mountain	15,645	17,725	19,249	20,221	21,122	22,049	22,962	7,317	8,794	4,938	2,490	646
Montana	870	950	1,006	1,040	1,069	1,097	1,121	251	374	316	143	13
Idaho	1,163	1,347	1,480	1,557	1,622	1,683	1,739	576	627	379	257	33
Wyoming	480	525	568	607	641	670	694	214	244	160	111	2
Colorado	3,747	4,168	4,468	4,658	4,833	5,012	5,188	1,442	1,855	1,122	504	123
New Mexico	1,685	1,860	2,016	2,155	2,300	2,454	2,612	927	1,030	526	403	12
Arizona	4,218	4,798	5,230	5,522	5,808	6,111	6,412	2,195	2,542	1,434	753	276
Utah	1,951	2,207	2,411	2,551	2,670	2,781	2,883	931	1,310	486	(31)	80
Nevada	1,530	1,871	2,070	2,131	2,179	2,241	2,312	782	813	516	351	106
Pacific	41,951	43,687	46,354	50,291	54,768	59,416	64,139	22,188	27,130	11,570	(2,848)	9,553
Washington	5,431	5,858	6,258	6,658	7,058	7,446	7,808	2,377	2,600	1,708	931	394
Oregon	3,141	3,397	3,613	3,803	3,992	4,177	4,349	1,209	1,364	1,169	712	197
California	31,589	32,521	34,441	37,644	41,373	45,278	49,285	17,696	22,035	8,248	(4,429)	8,725
Alaska	604	653	700	745	791	838	885	281	422	105	(84)	28
Hawaii	1,187	1,257	1,342	1,440	1,553	1,677	1,812	625	709	339	21	209

Source: U.S. Bureau of the Census, Population Division, PPL-47.

77

Existing Home Sales, New Home Sales, and Condominium Sales

Table A.1 in Appendix A includes an NAR report indicating existing home sales by region (Northeast, Midwest, South, and West). Note the historical trends in home sale volume. Steady or increasing sales reflect a healthy market while declining sales reflect deteriorating market conditions. This report also includes data about the months of supply of existing homes for sale.

Looking at Leading Indicators

Days on the market, supply of homes for sale, and mortgage applications are leading indicators of market shifts. Increasing days on the market and increasing months of supply of homes for sale reflect a softening market. Decreasing mortgage applications signal a decline in sales volume.

Since you are trying to assess local conditions, a local real estate broker or your local daily newspaper is your best source of information on the average days on the market (DOM) to sell a home. One problem with this statistic is that real estate agents will cancel and relist a property that is not moving in order to make the property appear to be a new listing. Therefore, regard any DOM statistic as being a potential underestimate of actual selling times.

A good way to find DOM statistics is to search the home page of the web site for your local daily newspaper and type "days on the market" into the "search articles" option on the web site. Be concerned anytime the DOM exceeds 180 days. Historically, the home inventory supply has ranged between 5.5 and 6.5 months of supply in a healthy real estate market.

There is a wealth of information available on the National Association of REALTORS® web page at www.realtor.org. This site includes national inventory data, mortgage applications, new home sales, housing starts, the Housing Affordability Index (HAI), and interest rate forecasts.

The most recently available information is included in Appendix A. For updates, go to the web site at www.realtor.org and click on Research on the left column. Explore the following subcategories below Research: Existing Home Sales, Economic and Housing Data, and Forecasts and Analysis.

The Forecasts and Analysis subcategory includes the NAR Forecast. This forecast predicts GDP, unemployment, interest rates, mortgage rates, housing sales, median home prices, and the Housing Affordability Index (HAI).

Interest Rates

Reporting on interest rates is ongoing in the business sector of the media. The home section of many Sunday editions of local newspapers often graph interest rates. The NAR site just referenced is also excellent. The direction of interest rates should be considered as you study the Housing Affordability Index (HAI).

Housing Affordability Index (HAI)

Table 4.5 summarizes the HAI by region. All regions of the country face a declining HAI. However, all regions save the West have affordability scores over 100, which means that the median income is more than enough to pay for the median home. In the West, the score is a perilously low 83.6 and declining, down from 95.9 one year ago.

For the most up-to-date information, go to the following address at the National Association of REALTORS® web site: http://www.realtor.org/Research.nsf/files/REL0508A.pdf/$FILE/REL 0508A.pdf. If the address has changed or this link otherwise fails, go to the home page at http://www.realtor.org. At the top of the page, type "HAI" in the "Search REALTOR.org" space. You should be able to access a report that includes an affordability index on the

TABLE 4.5 National Association of REALTORS®: Housing Affordability Index

Year		Median Priced Existing Single-Family Home	Mortgage Rate*	Monthly P & I Payment	Payment as a % of Income	Median Family Income	Qualifying Income**	Affordability Indexes		
								Composite	Fixed	ARM
2002		158,100	6.55	804	18.7	51,680	38,592	133.9	131.6	147.1
2003		170,000	5.74	793	18.1	52,682	38,064	138.4	125.7	140.5
2004		184,100	5.72	857	18.9	54,527	41,136	132.6	121.1	135.4
2004	Sept	185,700	5.70	862	18.8	54,920	41,376	132.7	129.1	140.2
	Oct	185,400	5.70	861	18.8	55,079	41,328	133.3	130.1	139.9
	Nov	188,100	5.70	873	19.0	55,239	41,904	131.8	128.7	137.5
	Dec	188,900	5.76	883	19.1	55,399	42,384	130.7	129.0	134.7
2005	Jan	186,100	5.78	872	18.6	56,125	41,856	134.1	132.1	138.2
	Feb	186,800	5.71	868	18.5	56,323	41,664	135.2	132.7	140.7
	Mar	191,900	5.81	902	19.2	56,521	43,296	130.5	128.3	136.1
	Apr	203,100	5.92	966	20.4	56,719	46,368	122.3	119.8	127.5
	May	203,800	5.85	962	20.3	56,917	46,176	123.3	121.0	127.6
	Jun	216,700	5.71	1,007	21.2	57,115	48,336	118.2	116.4	121.9
	July	215,700	5.73	1,005	21.0	57,313	48,240	118.8	117.5	122.2
	Aug r	219,700	5.87	1,039	21.7	57,511	49,872	115.3	113.9	118.6
2005	Sept p	212,200	5.90	1,007	20.9	57,709	48,336	119.4	118.1	123.1
								This Month	Month Ago	Year Ago
Northeast		248,300	5.83	1,169	21.9	63,961	56,112	114.0	113.1	122.3
Midwest		172,000	5.88	814	16.2	60,425	39,072	154.7	152.9	174.2
South		181,900	5.98	871	19.9	52,474	41,808	125.5	121.4	132.5
West		308,400	5.85	1,456	29.9	58,452	69,888	83.6	77.4	95.9

*Effective rate on loans closed on existing homes—Federal Housing Finance Board.
**Based on a 25 percent qualifying ratio for monthly housing expense to gross monthly income with a 20 percent down payment.
r: revised; p: preliminary.
Source: ©2005 National Association of REALTORS®.

far right of the page. Data are reported for only four regions: the Northeast, Midwest, South, and West.

Projecting New Construction

All the measures discussed to date are an attempt to measure demand in the real estate marketplace. The pace of new construction defines the supply. A healthy real estate market has a vibrant construction industry.

The NAR site referenced earlier has the NAR Forecast, which includes a national forecast of housing starts, new single-family home sales, and residential construction. Historical data can be found at the Census Bureau web site at www.census.gov. Census regional historical data are summarized in Table 4.6. To explore the census web site, type "Housing Starts" in the "Questions" blank on the home page. Go to Housing Starts & Permits for metropolitan areas, then click on building permit data at the metropolitan area level.

To get the best local information, call your local municipal planning department and inquire about historical and forecasted data.

Predicting the Future

All the tools discussed in this section are intended to give you better foresight for the future, but don't expect 20/20 future vision. Forecasting the future is difficult. There are variables that have not even been discussed, such as an act of terrorism, which could upset even the most careful prediction of market direction.

The point is to assess the future with whatever reasonable facts are available instead of relying on media opinion, rumor, and chance.

TABLE 4.6 New Privately Owned Housing Units Authorized by Building Permits in Permit-Issuing Places, Seasonally Adjusted Annual Rate (Components may not add to total because of rounding. Number of housing units in thousands.)

| Month | Total | In structures with— | | | Region | | | | | | | |
| | | 1 unit | 2 to 4 units | 5 units or more | Northeast | | Midwest | | South | | West | |
					Total	1 unit	Total	1 unit	Total	1 unit	Total	1 unit
Jan 1994	1,390	1,112	68	210	102	99	298	246	599	472	391	295
Feb 1994	1,269	1,065	56	148	112	98	278	227	545	466	334	274
Mar 1994	1,342	1,078	61	203	121	103	305	243	576	460	340	272
Apr 1994	1,392	1,084	62	246	135	117	306	237	600	462	351	268
May 1994	1,396	1,110	66	220	143	124	315	240	592	471	346	275
Jun 1994	1,357	1,067	58	232	146	126	301	232	565	450	345	259
Jul 1994	1,335	1,041	60	234	161	137	300	228	567	429	307	247
Aug 1994	1,377	1,054	60	263	143	121	303	225	589	452	342	256
Sep 1994	1,412	1,056	60	296	135	118	295	228	608	450	374	260
Oct 1994	1,397	1,042	68	287	131	113	318	226	591	438	357	265
Nov 1994	1,340	1,014	66	260	137	119	298	229	590	426	315	240
Dec 1994	1,396	1,086	62	248	167	129	323	246	603	466	303	245
Jan 1995	1,282	967	66	249	139	121	285	206	567	412	291	228
Feb 1995	1,254	916	52	286	112	96	274	201	536	391	332	228
Mar 1995	1,226	914	64	248	128	106	274	206	558	404	266	198
Apr 1995	1,259	925	60	274	129	106	278	202	539	396	313	221
May 1995	1,271	958	61	252	121	103	278	209	546	410	326	236
Jun 1995	1,305	982	64	259	119	101	295	218	565	424	326	239
Jul 1995	1,354	1,019	61	274	117	101	303	225	598	443	336	250
Aug 1995	1,386	1,045	63	278	121	107	310	233	600	444	355	261
Sep 1995	1,421	1,079	68	274	128	108	315	234	638	487	340	250
Oct 1995	1,400	1,052	65	283	128	106	322	235	634	458	316	253
Nov 1995	1,430	1,060	70	300	126	101	314	241	622	454	368	264
Dec 1995	1,442	1,091	62	289	129	105	300	232	618	460	395	294
Jan 1996	1,387	1,051	63	273	97	87	313	240	610	461	367	263
Feb 1996	1,420	1,085	60	275	116	105	318	246	615	477	371	257
Mar 1996	1,437	1,108	60	269	137	111	335	244	596	484	369	269
Apr 1996	1,463	1,108	74	281	145	108	333	251	636	485	349	264
May 1996	1,457	1,096	66	295	139	109	314	243	663	485	341	259
Jun 1996	1,429	1,089	64	276	132	109	307	239	640	482	350	259
Jul 1996	1,450	1,074	67	309	137	110	338	243	617	461	358	260
Aug 1996	1,413	1,061	63	289	147	113	312	234	627	459	327	255
Sep 1996	1,392	1,037	70	285	143	113	303	229	598	447	348	248
Oct 1996	1,358	1,010	68	280	142	106	305	222	581	443	330	239
Nov 1996	1,412	1,031	68	313	140	111	313	220	636	454	323	246
Dec 1996	1,411	1,015	62	334	142	111	309	212	629	455	331	237

Jan 1997	1,382	1,046	64	272	160	121	295	215	590	458	337	252
Feb 1997	1,445	1,070	65	310	173	116	301	216	609	459	362	279
Mar 1997	1,436	1,031	66	339	153	114	300	218	647	446	336	253
Apr 1997	1,421	1,054	70	297	129	105	312	228	646	466	334	255
May 1997	1,414	1,046	65	303	132	107	289	216	618	456	375	267
Jun 1997	1,402	1,057	67	278	141	111	301	222	624	467	336	257
Jul 1997	1,440	1,050	74	316	136	109	287	214	658	459	359	268
Aug 1997	1,449	1,061	65	323	141	107	309	221	626	462	373	271
Sep 1997	1,494	1,091	67	336	138	112	304	221	654	472	398	286
Oct 1997	1,499	1,098	76	325	134	114	297	218	677	485	391	281
Nov 1997	1,469	1,093	62	314	141	110	297	220	652	487	379	276
Dec 1997	1,456	1,080	77	299	149	117	307	238	621	461	379	264
Jan 1998	1,555	1,158	71	326	173	132	336	261	655	485	391	280
Feb 1998	1,647	1,191	77	379	170	142	373	268	703	498	401	283
Mar 1998	1,605	1,162	71	372	149	126	316	234	747	511	393	291
Apr 1998	1,547	1,157	57	333	140	118	304	239	690	502	413	298
May 1998	1,554	1,165	66	323	142	113	321	244	723	522	368	286
Jun 1998	1,551	1,148	73	330	155	122	314	234	687	505	395	287
Jul 1998	1,610	1,181	76	353	158	118	313	234	735	527	404	299
Aug 1998	1,654	1,196	72	386	157	124	309	237	790	544	398	291
Sep 1998	1,577	1,187	68	322	162	123	319	241	708	529	388	294
Oct 1998	1,719	1,217	70	432	174	123	338	255	789	536	418	303
Nov 1998	1,672	1,248	59	365	174	130	330	267	717	541	451	310
Dec 1998	1,742	1,317	75	350	179	137	408	302	750	573	405	305
Jan 1999	1,732	1,259	81	392	167	129	321	261	804	556	440	313
Feb 1999	1,720	1,291	68	361	176	144	343	272	802	567	399	308
Mar 1999	1,665	1,239	65	361	167	121	350	264	740	549	408	305
Apr 1999	1,600	1,227	65	308	166	130	341	256	700	539	393	302
May 1999	1,640	1,254	58	328	160	129	347	255	712	558	421	312
Jun 1999	1,702	1,276	64	362	175	127	338	259	762	556	427	334
Jul 1999	1,682	1,276	62	344	162	130	337	258	770	566	413	322
Aug 1999	1,671	1,243	66	362	166	130	344	262	767	554	394	297
Sep 1999	1,551	1,198	64	289	154	119	336	262	682	531	379	286
Oct 1999	1,649	1,208	63	378	146	116	343	263	772	537	388	292
Nov 1999	1,672	1,233	69	370	169	124	378	267	737	548	388	294
Dec 1999	1,683	1,257	71	355	174	131	362	270	746	541	401	315
Jan 2000	1,727	1,277	64	386	192	129	377	280	726	560	432	308
Feb 2000	1,692	1,241	70	381	176	128	366	262	735	555	415	296
Mar 2000	1,651	1,253	65	333	174	132	366	278	715	551	396	292
Apr 2000	1,597	1,192	61	344	167	123	347	261	688	512	395	297
May 2000	1,543	1,182	70	291	162	123	317	242	691	524	373	293
Jun 2000	1,572	1,156	61	355	160	117	318	234	694	513	400	292

(Continued)

TABLE 4.6 *(Continued)*

| Month | Total | In structures with— | | | Region | | | | | | | |
| | | 1 unit | 2 to 4 units | 5 units or more | Northeast | | Midwest | | South | | West | |
					Total	1 unit	Total	1 unit	Total	1 unit	Total	1 unit
Jul 2000	1,542	1,152	57	333	159	117	317	236	691	517	375	282
Aug 2000	1,552	1,173	68	311	155	118	305	235	684	520	408	300
Sep 2000	1,570	1,189	67	314	169	122	304	238	708	524	389	305
Oct 2000	1,577	1,224	68	285	160	126	330	245	695	542	392	311
Nov 2000	1,614	1,208	66	340	165	120	290	239	733	532	426	317
Dec 2000	1,543	1,180	60	303	154	120	268	202	678	522	443	336
Jan 2001	1,699	1,251	61	387	150	117	330	249	740	551	479	334
Feb 2001	1,656	1,242	69	345	189	118	330	253	721	545	416	326
Mar 2001	1,659	1,232	69	358	158	113	336	259	728	541	437	319
Apr 2001	1,666	1,259	65	342	158	112	333	249	744	575	431	323
May 2001	1,665	1,240	69	356	153	118	334	256	756	557	422	309
Jun 2001	1,626	1,252	81	293	151	115	350	262	719	570	406	305
Jul 2001	1,598	1,235	62	301	160	117	338	258	709	554	391	306
Aug 2001	1,615	1,241	65	309	161	121	328	257	711	555	415	308
Sep 2001	1,565	1,192	54	319	149	118	321	239	699	539	396	296
Oct 2001	1,566	1,185	60	321	166	121	310	236	707	546	383	282
Nov 2001	1,651	1,229	62	360	161	116	354	256	757	563	379	294
Dec 2001	1,680	1,251	73	356	171	125	341	251	772	579	396	296
Jan 2002	1,665	1,285	69	311	171	133	344	266	768	594	382	292
Feb 2002	1,787	1,401	66	320	211	146	367	283	808	645	401	327
Mar 2002	1,691	1,289	72	330	151	120	341	254	783	592	416	323
Apr 2002	1,669	1,285	68	316	165	125	334	256	755	581	415	323
May 2002	1,716	1,289	71	356	180	120	346	257	767	583	423	329
Jun 2002	1,758	1,314	82	362	176	127	347	257	817	597	418	333
Jul 2002	1,738	1,307	69	362	177	124	352	254	796	598	413	331
Aug 2002	1,695	1,317	72	306	165	120	341	253	768	602	421	342
Sep 2002	1,803	1,366	92	345	184	130	361	269	790	621	468	346
Oct 2002	1,799	1,382	71	346	172	127	359	267	795	615	473	373
Nov 2002	1,771	1,382	70	319	161	122	338	275	782	621	490	364
Dec 2002	1,896	1,409	78	409	177	134	402	286	856	636	461	353
Jan 2003	1,808	1,416	89	303	169	122	367	276	796	626	476	392
Feb 2003	1,854	1,357	80	417	166	106	330	247	808	621	550	383
Mar 2003	1,757	1,359	74	324	164	116	339	267	801	624	453	352
Apr 2003	1,803	1,391	85	327	172	119	354	272	820	645	457	355
May 2003	1,835	1,389	82	364	177	121	358	278	820	638	480	352
Jun 2003	1,875	1,461	79	335	171	122	387	294	859	676	458	369
Jul 2003	1,885	1,478	77	330	184	130	376	297	845	677	480	374

Aug 2003	1,966	1,521	83	362	204	129	388	297	885	708	489	387
Sep 2003	1,961	1,533	92	336	181	130	393	308	892	705	495	390
Oct 2003	2,012	1,566	80	366	200	134	378	311	907	719	527	402
Nov 2003	1,918	1,513	94	311	190	130	393	296	845	694	490	393
Dec 2003	1,987	1,549	76	362	200	126	370	286	926	723	491	414
Jan 2004	1,913	1,488	96	329	184	120	351	277	880	690	498	401
Feb 2004	1,913	1,516	78	319	183	124	343	285	884	701	503	406
Mar 2004	1,975	1,551	93	331	206	140	350	285	916	723	503	403
Apr 2004	2,006	1,544	99	363	198	139	369	282	905	711	534	412
May 2004	2,097	1,610	96	391	196	127	355	283	994	748	552	452
Jun 2004	1,945	1,546	83	316	197	130	339	278	902	730	507	408
Jul 2004	2,066	1,586	113	367	189	119	358	283	964	747	555	437
Aug 2004	1,969	1,556	82	331	175	119	349	288	910	723	535	426
Sep 2004	1,998	1,559	80	359	191	119	376	287	904	732	527	421
Oct 2004	2,018	1,557	93	368	175	115	358	278	960	748	525	416
Nov 2004	2,028	1,549	89	390	204	124	347	279	920	720	557	426
Dec 2004	2,032	1,567	100	365	206	125	357	285	923	745	546	412
Jan 2004	1,963	1,546	94	323	191	131	368	291	899	713	505	411
Feb 2004	1,984	1,574	90	320	184	132	366	298	912	724	522	420
Mar 2004	2,064	1,633	101	330	207	149	377	303	950	756	530	425
Apr 2004	2,069	1,610	92	367	200	145	381	296	949	742	539	427
May 2004	2,129	1,660	88	381	203	135	360	295	1,012	777	554	453
Jun 2004	2,014	1,606	83	325	208	139	342	286	940	761	524	420
Jul 2004	2,114	1,625	105	384	198	127	363	291	984	765	569	442
Aug 2004	2,058	1,606	85	367	179	120	381	303	964	752	534	431
Sep 2004	2,039	1,593	78	368	200	122	378	294	935	752	526	425
Oct 2004	2,093	1,603	87	403	182	121	370	290	1,011	772	530	420
Nov 2004	2,093	1,588	90	415	203	128	353	281	947	742	590	437
Dec 2004	2,081	1,620	90	371	191	123	392	304	948	768	550	425
Jan 2005	2,136	1,635	84	417	195	119	356	280	1,040	807	545	429
Feb 2005	2,093	1,624	83	386	189	116	381	300	974	777	549	431
Mar 2005	2,021	1,552	85	384	184	107	349	269	961	756	527	420
Apr 2005	2,148	1,640	78	430	200	117	379	289	1,011	795	558	439
May 2005	2,062	1,628	85	349	191	120	354	282	968	781	549	445
Jun 2005	2,132	1,653	87	392	213	124	361	286	1,032	810	526	433
Jul 2005	2,171	1,690	99	382	200	130	379	297	1,010	809	582	454
Aug 2005	2,138	1,676	86	376	186	130	353	287	1,064	830	535	429
Sep 2005	2,219	1,767	88	364	208	139	362	296	1,036	843	613	489
Oct 2005	2,071	1,681	84	306	188	126	368	300	997	824	518	431

NA: Not available.

Source: U.S. Bureau of the Census.

85

CASE STUDY: PREDICTING THE FUTURE

By David J. Decker

Cash In on the Coming Real Estate Crash cannot hope to give you a meaningful forecast of the future for your specific neighborhood. Data research firms break the United States down to more than 100 distinct real estate markets. It would be impossible for us to sift through data to present forecasts of more than 100 markets.

The intention is to equip readers to do their own research. However, there are data that break the United States down into four regions. The data indicate that the South, Midwest, and Northeast regions have steady and stable real estate markets. Statistics for the West are more troubling.

One of the most important indicators is the HAI. At 83.6, the index in the West has declined to the lowest score since before the last real estate crash. As interest rates increase, this index will be strained even further.

This index is offset by robust employment and household growth for the West. Over the long term, this region of the country will do well. The question is whether there will be an interim correction, and if so, how severe.

The leading indicators reflect growing days on the market and growing inventory supply. Does this mean that a crash is imminent? Maybe. The more likely event is that appreciation will cool off. It would still take a decline in employment to trigger a crash. Interestingly, the real estate industry itself could be the industry that triggers the decline.

Recently, the strength of the economy has hinged on the strength of the real estate industry. Should this sector falter in the face of rising interest rates, the setback could be enough to erode values in the hottest bubbles, such as in the West.

This analysis is not intended to suggest that all other areas of the country are immune or that a California crash is imminent. Manhattan and Boston real estate also have shown signs of softness.

The conclusion is that some areas of the country are clearly vulnerable. There are other seemingly safe areas that if caught in a local recession will lose value as well. Study the following chapters carefully and be prepared.

CHAPTER 5

SHOULD YOU SELL NOW?

The past few years have been good years for real estate. Almost any real estate that you have owned in just about any area of the country has probably increased in value. Nationally, according to the FDIC, home prices have escalated about 50 percent. The rising real estate tide has lifted all the boats.

Of course, some areas have done better than others. Homes in Chico, California, appreciated 45 percent in value in 2004 alone. Las Vegas, Nevada, and San Diego, California, are two more white-hot markets. Many homeowners and real estate investors in these areas have done well.

These good times beg a question. How long can the party go on? Some readers of this book will study the chapters on how to evaluate their own market, apply the principles, and conclude that in their region, the party is over and the hangover is imminent. The next logical question then is what to do if a crash is looming?

One solid piece of investing advice is you can never go wrong taking a profit. In the worst-case scenario, you wind up walking away from further profits had you stayed in the market. Understandably, many homeowners and real estate investors would like to lock in their profits. There may be temptation to sell. Should you? The answers depend on your situation.

Strategies for the Homeowner

Some may say that a man's home is his castle or that it is his biggest investment, but either way, it's where he lives. Everyone needs a place to live. That is what makes the answer to the question of selling more complicated.

If you are going to sell your home to lock in your profit, where are you going to live? As we consider this situation, the underlying assumption is that you have elected to stay in the same area. Your job is secure.

One strategy for locking in a profit and rendering yourself bust-proof is to sell your home, rent an apartment, and then buy back in when the market plunges. Let's consider this tactic in detail.

Even in a hot market, real estate is illiquid. It takes time and money to sell. Moving is expensive and inconvenient. Finally, for an interim period, you will be trading your home for an apartment that will probably be smaller and not as nice as the home you have now.

Already we can see the decision to sell your home is not a cold, logical business decision. There are lifestyle considerations as well.

It is impossible to assign a dollar value to your inconvenience with having to downgrade to an apartment. Only you can measure that decision. But much of the rest of the equation can be quantified.

Real estate transactions are costly, and this strategy calls for incurring those costs twice, once as a seller then later as a buyer. Both transactions will not have the same expense items. By going through the cycle of selling, renting, and buying, the homeowner will likely incur one real estate commission, one mortgage origination, one title insurance premium, one transfer tax, and two moves.

The largest cost of selling a piece of real estate is usually the real estate commission. These vary with the proliferation of discount real estate brokerages, but the average commission charged by a full-service broker is 6 to 7 percent of the sale price.

Unless you have already paid off your home, you will be retiring your old loan when you sell and taking out a new one when you buy. While there is little cost to retiring a loan, taking out a new one will require an appraisal, credit report, points, and other origination costs. Again, rates vary by region, but 2 percent of the loan amount is a reasonable budget for a loan origination. Some lenders offer supposedly zero closing cost loans, but this is deceptive. The costs are just built into a higher interest rate.

Title insurance is sometimes paid by the seller and sometimes by the buyer. Customs differ by locality. But either way, if you sell and get back in, on one of the two transactions you will be paying for the title insurance. Title insurance rates also vary, and the buyer is advised to shop for a good deal. Expect to pay at least 0.2 percent for title insurance.

Most states have some transfer tax, typically paid by the seller, but the largest expense after any real estate commission is the cost of moving. Depending on distance and circumstances, moving can cost thousands of dollars, not including your own time and trouble.

Finally, remember you will also lose your home mortgage interest deduction for some period of time and you will also lose the benefit of any mortgage amortization while you are renting.

In all, a reasonable estimate of the transactions cost of pursuing this strategy is 10 percent of the cost of the home you sell. However, this 10 percent may not be the full cost of implementing this approach.

To limit your total costs to 10 percent, you would also have to exercise perfect market timing. That means you must sell at the peak and buy back at the lowest dip in the trough. It would be easy to miss on either or both of these transactions, even while employing the market timing techniques illustrated in this book.

The yardstick for measuring the wisdom of employing this tactic is the outcome you would have experienced had you done nothing. Consider some examples.

Assume that the value of your home had increased to $400,000 by the end of 2004 and you decided to sell. Your decision has put you on a course to incur about $40,000 in transactions costs. Your neighbors in the same $400,000 house enjoyed at least 10 percent of additional gains in 2005. Whether your neighbors will be caught in a bust is a matter of speculation, but one thing is certain. Thanks to the transactions cost and poor market timing, you have manufactured your personal bust.

Continuing the same example, say that your do-nothing neighbors finally get caught in a severe bust, wiping out 20 percent of their home's value. The home that was worth $400,000 grew to $440,000 in 2005 but was whacked down to $352,000 by the end of 2006. All through 2007, the media predicted further doom, seeing no end to the misery in sight (more on that in Chapter 10). So convincing were the reports that when prices began to rebound in 2008, at first you missed it. You were expecting further declines. Before you were able to react, the $352,000 home had battled its way back to $380,000 as markets recovered.

Your neighbors who did nothing now live in a home worth $380,000. You are living in an apartment. But you can buy one of those $380,000 homes, assuming you can come up with the additional $20,000 you lost by pursuing a strategy of sell, rent, and buy.

An argument could be made that both homeowners are in the same boat. Both have lost $20,000 from the $400,000 price that existed at the end of 2004. But that argument would be wrong. The homeowners who did nothing have not lost anything. They can lose only if they decide to sell now. Until that time, the loss is only on paper.

However, for the homeowner who sold, the $20,000 loss is real. In fact, the loss may be sufficient to prohibit the selling homeowner from buying back the same quality of home he or she once had.

The strategy of selling, renting, and buying back can be summed up in one word: folly.

There will be some who read this and, bound by determination, will look for remedies to cut the transaction costs to reduce their exposure in pursuing a sell-rent-buy approach. This is just more folly.

Of course, you could decide to sell your home yourself and rent your own moving van to slash the two largest components of the transactions cost. On the other hand, if you are willing to work so hard, why not just get a second job and enjoy the extra income where you are living now?

Yet the greatest detriment to the do-it-yourself route is not the opportunity cost of your labor; it's the mistake you may make in inaccurately pricing your home. A hot real estate market has two characteristics, if not more. One, properties sell quickly and seemingly easily. Two, prices are increasing rapidly.

In a hot real estate market, when homes are selling quickly and easily, there may be a temptation to forgo using a real estate broker. But if you quickly and easily sell your home yourself, how will you know if it sold quickly because of the market conditions or because you priced your home too low?

If selling your home is the remedy for protecting against a bubble-bust, there would have to be other mitigating circumstances to warrant this action. Empty nesters who were thinking of downsizing anyway might take this step now if they determine that their area is headed for a fall.

If you are a snowbird who owns in a northern climate and rents a season rental in a warmer locale, you may want to reverse this arrangement if your northern market is imperiled and the southern location seems more stable.

Finally, perhaps the threat of a bust is an occasion to examine your lifestyle and take advantage of a once-in-a-lifetime opportunity. If you have enjoyed a brisk increase in home equity that you never expected, maybe you can use that as the springboard to launch a new life in a new area. Maybe you retire early. Maybe you move and make that career change that you have always wanted to make if money was not an issue.

It would be impossible to apply an economic yardstick to this decision. If you do decide to make this kind of move, it would be purely a lifestyle choice made sooner versus later. But it may be a wise move indeed.

If you move to the beach early out of fear of a bubble-bust and the bust never comes, how bad is that? Perhaps your old neighbors will continue to log huge profits. Perhaps they will get wiped out in a bust. Meanwhile, you got out at a profit and are enjoying the place of your dreams sooner than you ever imagined.

Strategies for the Real Estate Investor

Prices are high. Investment properties are moving quickly. Interestingly, residential properties are increasingly difficult to manage. Should you sell?

The same low interest rates that have fueled the boom in single-family homes have been a mixed blessing to real estate investors. While property values have increased, vacancies have increased with them as tenants become homeowners. Easy credit is one of the factors pumping more air into the real estate bubble even as it sucks tenants out of investment properties.

Management difficulty alone is often reason enough to drive investors to sell, but today, investors also face profit-taking temptation. The temptation is similar for investors as it is for homeowners. Should you sell now, wait for the bust, and then buy when there is blood in the streets? Again, the answer can be found by studying this strategy in detail.

The investor selling and buying back is exposed to some of the same pitfalls as the sell-rent-buy homeowner. The investor will experience the same transactions costs as the homeowner, incurring a real estate commission, title insurance premium, mortgage origination fees, and transfer taxes.

Fortunately, the investor is spared the expense and inconveniences of moving, but the investor experiences a greater inconvenience. The investor must grapple with the impact of capital gains taxes and depreciation recapture.

Capital gains taxes are easily understood. A capital gain reflects the higher value today versus the price paid yesterday. However, in real estate, computing the gain is more complicated.

Investment real estate enjoys the added benefit of depreciation. While the property may be increasing in value, the government allows the landlord to write down the value of the property each year by taking the appropriate depreciation deduction. This happy arrangement minimally shelters some of the cash flow from the property and is a boon to real estate investors right up to the day they sell. Then the tax man extracts his revenge.

Capital gains on real estate are computed not based on the initial acquisition cost, but on the original cost plus any capital improvements less depreciation taken. The resulting figure is called the "adjusted basis." Capital improvements include such things as a new roof or the replacement of a furnace. The math would look like this:

$$\text{Purchase Price} + \text{Capital Improvements} - \text{Depreciation}$$
$$= \text{Adjusted Basis}$$

Therefore, the equation determining the capital gain is as follows:

$$\text{Net Sale Proceeds} - \text{Adjusted Basis} = \text{Capital Gain}$$

Again, an example will be helpful.

Two investors each bought residential investment real estate five years ago for $600,000. Both properties had land value of $100,000. No capital improvements were made. Yet happily, today both properties are worth $900,000.

Both investors fear a bust. Investor A decides to sell now for $900,000, wait for the bubble to pop, and then buy back in at a lower

price. In doing so, Investor A incurs 6 percent of the sale price in total transaction costs. Investor B decides to ride it out, continuing to
enjoy whatever cash flow the property provides. Who wins?

Let's begin by computing the basis for the investors. The applicable depreciation for these investors is based on a depreciable life of
27.5 years computed on a straight-line basis. Land cannot be depreciated. Therefore, the depreciation would be as follows:

$$(\text{Purchase Price} - \text{Land Value})/27.5 \text{ years} = \text{Annual Depreciation}$$
$$(\$600,000 - \$100,000)/27.5 \text{ years} = \$18,182 \text{ per year}$$

The period of ownership has been five years; thus total depreciation taken for either investor would be $18,182 \times 5 = \$90,910$.
Therefore, both investors have the following adjusted basis:

$$\text{Purchase Price} + \text{Capital Improvements} - \text{Depreciation}$$
$$= \text{Adjusted Basis}$$
$$\$600,000 + \$0 - \$90,910 = \$509,090$$

Investor A incurred 6 percent of the sale price in transaction
costs; therefore the net sale proceeds are $846,000. Now that the net
sale proceeds and adjusted basis are known, the capital gain can now
be computed:

$$\text{Net Sale Proceeds} - \text{Adjusted Basis} = \text{Capital Gain}$$
$$\$846,000 - \$509,090 = \$336,910$$

Assuming no other offsetting gains or losses, Investor A has a
capital gain of $336,910. Both state and federal long-term capital
gains taxes are owed on the sale. State capital gains tax rates vary.
Let's presume the effective tax rate between the two is 25 percent.[1] If
so, Investor A has a tax liability of $84,228. Therefore, Investor A has
after-tax proceeds of $761,772:

$$\text{Net Sale Proceeds} - \text{Capital Gains Taxes} = \text{After-Tax Proceeds}$$
$$\$846,000 - \$84,228 = \$761,772$$

Investor A's $900,000 asset has just become cash of $761,772. Even if Investor A could avoid a real estate commission on the sale and cut the closing costs to zero, he or she would still have only $815,772:

$$\$900,000 - \$84,228 = \$815,772$$

Even considering the best-case scenario, Investor A's outcomes range from $761,772 to $815,772. Investor A has just experienced his or her own personal bubble pop, equaling a decline ranging from 9.4 percent to 15.4 percent.

For Investor A's tactics to pay off, he or she must again exercise perfect market timing, assuming a bubble pop happens at all. Any timing mistakes will result in still lower outcomes. If Investor A's basic assumption about a bubble pop proves wrong, then the disaster is even greater.

If Investor A's strategy of sell, wait for the bust, and buy is going to beat Investor B's strategy of just waiting out the storm, then first there must be a bust, the reversal has to be at least 10 percent or more, and Investor A must have perfect market timing.

Simply put, Investor A is going to lose. The idea that a real estate investor will be able to profit by first accurately predicting a bubble-bust, secondly timing properly when it will pop, selling, then buying back in, again with perfect timing, is just folly.

However, this analysis should not lead to the conclusion that nothing can be done. There are wiser alternatives.

Alternative Investor Strategies

The reason Investor A's strategy of selling and buying back in after a bubble bursts fails is that the capital gains taxes are too high for the plan to work. If the taxes could be avoided, selling and buying back in could work. Fortunately, there are provisions in the tax code allowing for a seller to do just that.

Section 1031 of the Internal Revenue Code allows a real estate investor to defer the capital gains tax liability from the sale of real estate by using the sale proceeds to buy equal or greater real estate. The transaction is a tax-deferred exchange, often called a 1031 exchange. Another name is Starker Exchange, named after one of the litigants in the case law that established the precedent allowing these exchanges.

While this provision affords tremendous advantages for investors, it still has limits. As you shall see, the time allowed for acquiring additional real estate is too short to provide a remedy for the investor who wants to sell in a bubble market and buy back into the same market after the bubble bursts.

However, a 1031 exchange would allow an investor the opportunity to sell in an overheated market and buy where conditions are safer. This is an investment alternative that is much safer.

Chapter 11 details how to balance your portfolio by acquiring real estate in other markets, but before you do that, you need to have a thorough understanding of 1031 exchanges.

Any discussion about tax-deferred exchanges must begin and end by encouraging you to involve your accountant and attorney early in the transaction. It would be foolish to rely on this book or any other book as your only guide to navigating these complex deals. While you will be relying on your accountant and attorney for the final details, you should have a broad understanding of how an exchange is structured.

Tax-deferred exchanges have a language all their own. The party desiring to sell a smaller property and buy a larger one is referred to as the exchangor. The new property obtained is called the replacement property. The smaller property is not sold, it is surrendered.

All 1031 exchanges have three basic requirements. To qualify, (1) the transaction must be a like-kind exchange, (2) all the equity in the property surrendered must be invested in the replacement property, and (3) the value of the replacement property must exceed the value of the property surrendered. Further, the transaction must meet certain time constraints.

Like-kind exchanges are just as they sound. Investment real estate must be exchanged for other investment real estate. Within this concept, the possibilities are broad. The sale of a single-family rental home exchanged for an office building would qualify as an exchange. A warehouse held for investment sold to acquire a piece of raw land held for investment could also be eligible for treatment as an exchange.

Of course, not every imaginable transaction is like-kind. Selling a duplex where you do not live in one of the units and using the proceeds to buy a personal residence would not qualify as an exchange. Neither would the sale of investment real estate to buy shares of stock, even if the stock was a real estate investment trust.

The second requirement for a proper exchange is that the sale proceeds of the surrendered property must be used to acquire more property. There can be more than one replacement property acquired. But the aggregate of both the equity and the fair market value of the property(s) being acquired must be the same or larger for all the tax liability to be deferred. Similarly, the debt on the replacement property must be the same or greater than the debt on the surrendered property. These circumstances can be better understood by example.

Our Investor A friend is still selling his $900,000 property. The loan balance on the property is $400,000. Therefore, Investor A has $500,000 in equity.

If Investor A buys a property for $1,500,000 with a new 80 percent first mortgage, the financial structure of the new acquisition would look like this:

Purchase Price	$1,500,000
New Mortgage	−$1,200,000
Equity	$ 300,000

Investor A has acquired a larger replacement property, but his equity in the new property is smaller. There will still be some immediate tax liability. To defer all tax liability, Investor A should reduce the mortgage to $1,000,000 so the equity position in the new building will be at least the same. Another alternative would be to use the remaining equity of $200,000 from the first transaction to buy another property worth $200,000 or more.

The third requirement is that the exchange occurs within the time constraints provided by law. There are three timing possibilities: simultaneous, delayed, and reverse.

In a *simultaneous* exchange, there is no time delay. The smaller property is surrendered the same day the larger replacement property is acquired. Simultaneous exchanges can be further divided into two types, direct exchanges and third-party exchanges.

In a direct exchange, two owners are swapping properties. For example, the owner of a single-family rental home might exchange the equity in this house plus added cash for a duplex. The owner of the duplex gets the rental house and the cash.

Although a direct, simultaneous exchange is the most simple, it is also the rarest. Most sellers are interested in receiving cash when they sell. As a seller becomes increasingly motivated, he or she may be willing to participate in seller financing. However, most sellers would prefer to carry seller financing than take title to an unknown, smaller piece of real estate.

The solution to the dilemma of the direct exchange is to involve a third-party buyer. With this solution, the simultaneous exchange becomes a third-party simultaneous exchange.

Continuing the same example, now the owner of the single-family rental home finds a third-party buyer for this property. On the same day, the third party buys the rental home, and the exchangor pays cash to buy the duplex.

The weakness to the simultaneous third-party exchange is the demands of timing. Any real estate transaction between just two individuals is fragile enough. Introducing a third party into the equation adds to the complexity. Practically, whether the third-party buyer is found first or the acquisition property is found first, someone is going to have to wait while other real estate deals are found, negotiated, financed, and prepared for closing. Should either of the transactions fail, the entire transaction falls apart.

The remedy for the timing problem is a *delayed* exchange, also called a Starker Exchange as was noted previously. This is by far the most common exchange.

In a Starker Exchange, the exchangor of the single-family rental home would first find a buyer for this property, close the deal, then acquire the larger replacement property later. As long as proper steps are followed within the time period allowed in the law, this approach qualifies as a tax-deferred exchange.

The proper steps to a Starker Exchange include how sale proceeds are handled and requirements for the exchangor to buy and sell as the same entity. The exchangor of a property intending to complete a Section 1031 exchange should never take possession of the proceeds from the sale of the property being surrendered. If the exchangor accepts the sale proceeds, an exchange is no longer possible. Instead, the seller should place the proceeds with what is called a qualified escrow intermediary.

There are several entities that could serve as an escrow intermediary, but the most common and logical choice is a title company. If you were to call any title company and inquire about help in executing a Starker Exchange or a Section 1031 exchange, you would be immediately transferred to an individual who has probably done hundreds of these transactions. Even though you will have your attorney and accountant guiding you, most title companies can give good direction as well.

The exchange requirement that the exchangor buy and sell as the same entity would at first seem not be a stumbling block. However, this requirement can create difficulties for partnerships that are surrendering real estate. If one partner wants to sell, cash out, and pay taxes, and the other partner would like to buy more real estate by completing an exchange, there may be a problem.

One way in which the problem is solved is by having one partner buy out the other before any other real estate transaction occurs. Another alternative is to dissolve the partnership and change the form of ownership to tenants in common. Owners of property holding title as tenants in common are free to pursue separate courses without disqualifying themselves from an exchange opportunity. Consult with your accountant and attorney for more information.

While the technical details of how sales proceeds are handled and how the same entity needs to both buy and sell are important, the most important aspect of the delayed exchanges is the timing.

Returning to our example of the investor with the single-family rental home who desires to trade up for a duplex, once the exchangor surrenders the investment home, he or she has 45 days to name potential properties to buy. The exchangor can name up to three properties.

The naming process is simple. The title company or other escrow intermediary will probably provide you with a form for naming the properties. The form will likely require the street address of the property or properties, and perhaps some additional information such as the name and address of the sellers.

There is no requirement that an accepted offer be in place for any of the named properties. In fact, the properties named need not even be formally for sale. However, an investor would be wise to have at least begun negotiation to acquire one or more of the replacement properties or the exchange may fall apart.

Once up to three replacement properties have been named, the investor has 180 days in which to actually close on one or all of the properties.

The problem with Starker Exchanges is that the timing constraints can sometimes produce motivated *buyers*. An illustration will prove helpful.

Revisiting our single-family home investor, let's assume the home has been surrendered for $200,000. The investor's basis is only $70,000, so the investor has a large potential capital gain tax liability on a $130,000 gain.

Not wanting to pay any tax, the investor places the net sale proceeds with a title company or other escrow intermediary. On the date of closing, the 45-day clock starts ticking. Within the 45-day period, the investor names three target properties to buy.

However, what happens if other buyers snap up two of the named properties? The exchangor is left with just one property that he or she must buy or no exchange will be possible and the taxes will have to be paid. The exchangor is in a vulnerable position. The exchangor may have become a *motivated buyer*.

Within the 45-day window, the exchangor can make unlimited substitutions should properties previously named become unavailable. However, after the 45 days, the roster is fixed and cannot be changed.

As a practical matter, the 45-day window of time is much larger. When the exchangor first contemplates selling, the hunt for a replacement property should begin. Even once a purchase contract has been accepted with a third-party buyer for the surrendered property, the exchangor probably has at least 30 days before the surrendered property closes in which to continue the search for the replacement property. The effective window of time should be at least 75 days or more.

Starker Exchanges are designed to help overcome timing problems, but this solution is still sometimes incomplete. For example, what do you do if you find a terrific replacement property but the surrendered property has not been sold yet? Perhaps you can persuade the seller of the replacement property to wait while you surrender your exchange property. Many times, however, sellers are not willing to wait and gamble on your ability to sell other real estate.

The solution to this problem is a *reverse* exchange. In the reverse exchange, you acquire the replacement property first and surrender the exchange property later.

In this species of exchange, the escrow intermediary takes title to both the replacement property and the exchange property. Once a third-party buyer for the exchange property is found, the escrow closes, and title to the replacement property is delivered to the exchangor.

Again, an example will help eliminate any confusion.

In our illustration involving the exchangor with the $200,000 single-family home, assume the property has an outstanding mortgage of $50,000. The investor has found a duplex for $300,000 that he or she would like to use as the replacement property in an exchange. However, the investor does not have a third-party buyer for the single-family home and the owner of the duplex is not willing to wait for the single-family home to be sold, nor is the duplex owner willing to take the rental home directly in trade. The solution to this problem is the reverse exchange.

The exchangor refinances the rental home with a new mortgage of $150,000. After the old mortgage of $50,000 is paid off, the investor still has $100,000 remaining for the down payment on the $300,000 duplex. Therefore, the investor makes arrangements for an escrow intermediary to take title to the replacement property, in this case the duplex. On closing on the duplex, the investor has 180 days to find a buyer for the single-family rental property.

One advantage of a reverse exchange is that if the exchange falls apart, no tax liability is incurred. The transaction effectively becomes an acquisition that was funded by refinancing another property.

One disadvantage of a reverse exchange is that because the escrow intermediary is taking title to real estate, the fees for this service are higher. Additionally, not every title company offers this service. You may need to contact title companies that specialize in this area. A few such companies are named here:

LandAmerica Financial Group, Inc.
101 Gateway Centre Parkway
Richmond, VA 23235
Toll Free: (800) 446-7086
http://www.landam.com/Home.htm

Chicago Title
601 Riverside Avenue
Jacksonville, FL 32204
Toll Free: (888) 934-3354
http://www.chicagotitle.com/

Reverse exchanges are newer and complicated. Investors interested in doing a reverse exchange simply must retain an attorney and accountant experienced in these transactions.

CHAPTER 6

SHOULD YOU BUY NOW?

R eal estate prices are at all-time highs. Media speculation about a bubble-bust is rampant. Books like this one are being published to warn investors. It seems like the question of whether to buy now would be folly.

Seemingly, to decide to buy now would be akin to ignoring instructions to evacuate for a hurricane. Surely to be buying now would be like driving toward the eye of the storm.

Or is it?

The premise of this book is that important investment decisions should be made based not on media-fueled, knee-jerk reactions, but on careful analysis of the best facts available. A good fact to begin with is that not every region of the country is poised for a bubble-bust. As we have already explained, there will not be a nationwide real estate contraction. There has never been one since the Great Depression, and there will not be one now. But neither should this thinking lead anyone to turn a blind eye to the real possibility of some markets tanking.

The next section addresses whether a home should be purchased under present market conditions. Real estate investors would also benefit from reading this section because the same logic applies to them, also.

Should You Buy a Home Now?

There are several circumstances where an individual or family might be considering a home purchase. There is the first-time buyer. There are growing families that are bursting out of their smaller starter homes. There are the empty nesters desiring to trade down. There are families thinking about acquiring a vacation home or condominium.

Should any of these people be thinking about a home purchase?

The key to answering this question is to determine whether the potential buyer would be buying in a bust prone market. The final chapter of this book identifies 25 of the most overheated real estate markets in the United States. If the market you are considering is not mentioned on this list, that does not necessarily mean that an acquisition would be safe from a bust. You should analyze appropriate data as outlined in Chapter 4.

One way or another, the potential home buyer must decide about the stability of the market being considered. If the verdict is for a bust, then only the empty nester considering downsizing should proceed to buying a smaller home. All others should wait.

However, to be pragmatic, it is difficult to predict accurately a bubble-bust. It is unlikely that all 25 of the overheated markets are going to experience price reversals. In fact, some areas that are hit hardest may not be on any list at all. Because intense declines in local economic activity are usually required to set off a bubble-bust, any predictions can be subject to inaccuracy.

The bottom line is that anyone wanting to acquire any real estate in vast segments of the country will have to do so in the face of at least some evidence of a bubble. The best remedy for the home buyer or the real estate investor is to return to value investing.

Value Investing in Any Market

Earlier, we said that one premise of this book is that investment decisions should not be based on media hype and speculation. A second premise of this book is that any advice should be effective in any market. To suggest strategies that would be prudent only in the face of a huge market collapse is irresponsible. Most of the country will not have this experience.

Our goal is to share strategies that will serve you well no matter what direction the market takes. Value investing is just such a strategy.

Real estate markets have been in boom mode for sufficient time to lull real estate investors and homeowners into getting sloppy. For several years, almost anyone buying almost any real estate has done well. The strategy has been to pay any price to buy anything, wait, sell, and then count the profits. Historically, real estate markets have not been so kind.

Value investing is just what it sounds like. It means getting a good deal on any real estate you buy. It means buying wholesale instead of retail. It means buying below current or potential fair market value.

Obviously, value investing is always a good strategy. However, value investing becomes even more critical as signs of a bubble become more evident.

Value investing dictates that potential home buyers be more disciplined in their purchase decisions. Much has been written about the merits of buying a dilapidated fixer-upper at a steep discount. Such reporting has become a little cottage industry. However, the fact remains that homes in move-in condition move more quickly than homes requiring repair.

The reasons are many. First-time homeowners may be straining to make the down payment and may not be able to afford any post-closing repairs. Most home buyers behave more like consumers than investors when making a home purchase.

Usually, there is nothing wrong with making a consumer driven decision. Clearly, anyone shopping for a house who is concerned with finding one close to their jobs with a particular set of amenities and concerns about room sizes would also like to get a good deal. But the deal is secondary to getting the right house, the right set of consumer driven benefits. In this case, the home is seen as a place to live that also happens to be an important investment.

For the value investor, a home is an important investment that also happens to be a place to live. The value investor who buys 10 percent to 20 percent below current fair market value is well positioned to weather a bubble reversal or to benefit from continued appreciation. Before delving into the techniques for finding these bargains, anyone contemplating any real estate acquisition needs to be grounded in the fundamentals of real estate evaluation.

Appraisal Theory

The process of determining the fair market value for a parcel of real estate is called "appraisal theory." Fair market value is the price that would be achieved between an unrelated buyer and seller if the property were properly exposed to the marketplace for an appropriate time period. Appraisal theory considers three separate approaches to determining fair market value: the market approach, income approach, and cost approach.

Market Approach.   The market approach considers recent sales of comparable real estate. For example, if the subject property is a three-bedroom, one-bath ranch house with a two-car detached garage, the appraisal should include recent sales of other three-bedroom, one-bath ranch houses with two-car detached garages. The sales should be in proximity to the subject and should have closed not more than six months ago.

Adjustments are made to reflect that comparables are not identical with the subject. The value adjustments would reflect differences in age, construction materials, overall condition, lot size, room sizes, and more.

In plain terms, the market approach is a commonsense method for evaluating any particular deal. You can determine whether a property is a bargain, fairly priced, or overpriced by comparing the subject deal to the done deals.

Income Approach. The income approach measures the income producing capacity of real estate to determine value. Any real estate being offered for sale for investment purposes will probably have an operating statement prepared from information provided by the owner that reflects the income and expenses associated with owning the property. Proper analysis of an operating statement would include a determination of market rents, market vacancy rates, and reasonable operating expenses.

Value investing requires the investor to understand the marketplace, and an important aspect of that understanding is knowledge of market rents. Perform a rent survey if needed. When performing a rent survey, do not try to pretend that you are a tenant. By being forthcoming that you are an investor, you can ask more detailed questions beyond anything that a tenant would ask. Share any information you have to gain cooperation.

Your rent survey should include an inquiry about vacancy rates. Be forewarned that not every landlord will be completely honest in providing this information. Network with other real estate professionals such as appraisers and lenders to get additional input.

Finally, analyze the operating expenses. Property taxes and utilities are part of the public record and can be easily verified by contacting the local taxing authority and utility service providers. Insurance, advertising, and other contracted services can be verified by obtaining estimates from vendors. Repair and maintenance budgets can vary depending on the type and condition of property, but sometimes 5 percent of gross income is a good rule of thumb. Sellers have been known to leave out entire expense line items in operating statements, so give careful thought to not only verifying what is there, but also thinking about what should be added that is missing.

The seasoned value investor will eventually learn how to construct quickly his or her own operating statement for any given property. Sophisticated investors will apply gross rent multipliers and capitalization rates when applying the income approach. A more detailed discussion of these terms and techniques appears in Appendix B.

Cost Approach. The cost approach attempts to measure how much it would cost to buy a comparable vacant lot and build the same building again. Unless the subject property is new construction, an adjustment is made to reflect the age of the subject property.

Having developed three separate values by applying the market, income, and cost approaches, these three values are then considered in determining the final fair market value.

For the value investor, the market approach and income approach are the most valuable. The cost approach has several limitations that render it less important. The cost approach is most meaningful when other comparable sales are not available and the property does not produce an income. The sale of a church building would be a good example. Church buildings do not typically produce income, and there may not be many recent sales of comparable buildings.

An additional weakness to the cost approach is the adjustment that must be made reflecting the age of the subject property. The older the subject property, the greater the opportunity for error in this adjustment. Older properties have areas of obsolescence that would never be duplicated today. For instance, vintage buildings may have 60 amp electric service with fuses. Modern systems have 100 amp service and circuit breakers.

For the individual considering a home purchase as his or her residence, the market approach is the most valuable. Real estate investors will rely most heavily on the market approach and the income approach.

Anyone intending to engage in value investing will need to become fluent in appraisal theory. Part of that fluency includes how to find the right data.

Finding the Data. Understanding the nuances of the market approach, income approach, and cost approach is valuable only if the knowledge can be put into action. That means having meaningful data to analyze.

Comparable sales are the heart and soul of the market approach. There are two resources for obtaining recent sale information, your local property tax assessing authority and a real estate agent.

Your local tax assessing authority, most often called the assessor, will have information regarding any sale in its jurisdiction (county, parish, city, town, or village). This is the most complete, comprehensive sales data available. The problem with this information is that it may not be as timely and it may not be readily accessible.

The assessor gets information from the government agency responsible for maintaining real estate records, usually the Register of Deeds. Owing to the time it takes these two government agencies to process the information, when the information becomes available to the public, it may be six months old or more.

Information can sometimes be obtained directly from the Register of Deeds or equivalent government agency. However, like the assessor, this information may not be readily accessible. For instance, either agency may be able to tell you when and for how much a certain parcel of real estate was sold. But if you wanted to get all the sales for a specific property type or geographical region, these agencies may not be well equipped to help.

Real estate agents often have the best access to information, particularly those agents participating in the Multiple Listing Service (MLS). MLS is a real time database of not only properties for sale, but also properties that have sold. The information is as current as any available. While the assessor may have only limited information on any given sale, MLS may include room sizes, recent capital improvements, digital photographs, and maybe even a virtual tour. Further, because the database is computerized, unique property searches can be performed.

For example, if you are considering the purchase of a three-bedroom, two-bath home with a three-car garage, MLS should be able to produce sales closed not more than six months ago in a 10-block radius of the subject property of other three-bedroom, two-bath houses with three-car garages. Should these criteria be too specific to produce any sales, a new search encompassing more city blocks or going back further in time might produce meaningful comparable sales.

The only weakness to MLS is that the data are not comprehensive. Properties sold without a real estate agent would not be included in MLS. Despite this flaw, MLS is still the best source of sale information.

We have already explored how data can be gleaned from the rental surveys, the property taxing authority, utility providers, insurers, service providers, and other contractors to analyze an operating statement for the income approach. Real estate agents and appraisers are additional resources for the income approach.

When approaching real estate agents for sale data or income approach benchmarks, be sure to inquire with an agent that specializes in your area of interest. That specialty might be houses in the neighborhood where you are considering buying a personal residence or an investment specialist focusing on a commercial investment property niche.

Insurance agents and appraisers are excellent sources of the construction cost data that you would need to make a cost approach estimate of value. In fact, in preparing any insurance estimate for a replacement cost policy, the insurance agent would have to consider construction costs.

Value Investing: Finding the Deals

Understanding appraisal theory helps the home shopper or real estate investor know when he or she has found a good deal. However, the deals still need to be found. An adage in the real estate business is that you make money when you buy. This adage is at the root of value investing.

Good deals can be found even in a seller's market. They are harder to find, but they are still there. Value investing is a numbers game. You will need to kiss plenty of frogs before you find a princely deal.

There are two broad strategies to apply in rooting out a good deal. The first strategy involves finding a motivated seller, and the second strategy involves developing what we call "value vision."

Finding that magical motivated seller is the premise of nearly every book ever written about how to invest in real estate. The strategy may be summarized by saying the buyer is to find an individual who for whatever reason has become desperate to sell his or her real estate. In markets that are crushed by a bubble-bust, there will be plenty of these motivated sellers. Chapter 10 goes into more detail about them.

Nevertheless, in much of the country, real estate is in such demand that buyers are lining up to buy junk. Under these conditions, even a motivated seller will be able to sell quickly at fair market value. The strategies of the past may indeed be passé.

To be successful in value investing in the present market conditions, you will need to sharpen your value vision. Having value vision means being able to see potential that others miss. The seller may be motivated, but probably not.

Value vision strategies include fixer-uppers, repositioning, redeveloping, changing the use, getting involved in gentrification, buying an island, and playing Monopoly.

Fixer-Uppers

Finding a fixer-upper in need of only a few cosmetic improvements is a strategy employed by successful investors for decades. The premise is to avoid any structural or mechanical defects and to hone in on properties needing new carpet, fresh paint, or just a good cleaning.

This strategy is well known and well worn. To beat the competition, try taking this idea to the next stage. You do not have to wait until a property has a broker's sign in the front yard to inquire about whether the building is for sale. If you see an intriguing property, note the address and call your local assessor to identify the owner. Many municipalities have this information online on the World Wide Web.

Do not be discouraged if most owners you call are not willing to sell. Keep going until you find someone who is. Even then, they may not be willing to sell at a price that makes sense for you. If so, keep going. Contact more owners. Keep these property owners' names on file and check back with them periodically. Eventually you will find someone willing to sell under circumstances that meet your goals.

Another way to beat the competition is to be willing to take on the properties that have the structural and mechanical defects. Properties with serious shortcomings will have few interested buyers. Eventually, the sellers could become motivated if they are not already.

One good way to make the most of these opportunities is by partnering with the tradesmen who specialize in making the needed repairs. For example, for a property with a basement foundation problem, you might be able to partner with a contractor willing to do the work at cost or when his or her crew is slow, saving money.

Finally, investors who are already in the building trades or who are mechanically inclined are well positioned to attempt this strategy.

Repositioning

Real estate is often divided into classes. Apartments come in low-, middle-, and high-income segments. Office buildings are described as being Class A or Class B.

The rents charged at these properties correspond to their ranking. High-income apartments obviously rent for more than low-income apartments. The same holds true for Class A and Class B office space.

Therefore, anytime an investor can improve a property in such a manner that the property is repositioned, a new tier of rent can be charged and the building becomes more valuable.

This strategy involves more than just repairing a fixer-upper. Restoring a run-down house in a low-income neighborhood might be profitable, but it would not reposition the property. A hypothetical example would be a stately, old, well-located office building rendered obsolete because it does not have sufficient parking. If the parking problem can be solved, the office building can be restored and repositioned.

Repositioning means thinking creatively. In the previous example, one solution would be to buy an adjacent building and knock it down to provide parking. A more creative solution might be to offer valet service. Use your imagination.

CASE STUDY: DOWNTOWN DOG BECOMES UPTOWN GEM

By David J. Decker

A few years ago, I stumbled across a downtown building in a small town that had been for sale for a long time before I discovered it. I wish I could say that my sleuthing skills helped me find this deal, but the truth is the property had a gigantic FOR SALE sign posted on it by one of the largest real estate brokerages in my state. Anyone could have purchased the property.

The building was a combination of office and residential space. The apartments were definitely low-income. The hallways in the residential floors had almost a continual stream of cigarette burns charred into the carpet. The office areas were decorated in an obsolete, dark color scheme. An eager vandal had decorated the elevator. Low-income residential tenants were filtering into the office areas, causing more problems. Both the apartments and the office space were heavily vacant as a result.

In short, the building was a mess. Regardless, there was enormous potential. Some of the offices featured loft space. The apartments on the top floor were all loft units. Windows were plentiful and huge. The walls of this old building are so thick you can sit on the windowsills. Some of the views are excellent.

This property has always been a mystery to me. Thousands of people drive past it every day. Thousands had to have known it was for sale. Its potential seemed obvious.

The property was acquired for about half of its tax-assessed value. Repositioning the property was merely a matter of making cosmetic repairs and redecorating. Rents were increased and vacancies were filled. What was a downtown dog became an uptown gem. The property never moved, but it was certainly repositioned.

Redeveloping

Redeveloping is a close cousin to repositioning, but since major changes to the structure are part of the strategy, it becomes its own technique.

One investor we know employs a redeveloping strategy within his preferred investment niche. The niche is single-family rental homes. The redevelopment strategy is to buy houses that have no garage and then add a two-car detached garage.

The garage is an important enough amenity that the property becomes repositioned. The investor employing this strategy can use the same contractors and tradesmen repeatedly. The first deal may have been difficult, but each successive deal gets easier as the formula is repeated.

Obviously, before embarking on any redevelopment plan, you will need to obtain proper building permits and even possible zoning permissions.

CASE STUDY: DISCO DUMP TO HIGH-LINE HAVEN

By David J. Decker

Back in the 1970s, platform shoes, disco, and dark brown woodwork were all in fashion. Thankfully, the clothes and the music have all gone away, but the woodwork in 1970s vintage apartments still lingers like an eight-track tape player stuck on repeat.

The strategy here is to pull every stick of woodwork out of these units and replace them with a modern medium oak finish. It's not a clever strategy and it's not cheap. "Brute force method" might be a better name. But it works.

I bought a 24-unit apartment with the intention of employing this technique. The price of the building was no bargain. The cost of the improvements has been high. Besides the woodwork and cabinets, I built 24 garages, too.

The result is a better tenant base and a 25 percent increase in rents.

The interesting thing about this case study is that finding a hot bargain was never part of the equation. The repositioning strategy was not sophisticated. Sometimes the simplest ideas are the best ones.

Changing the Use

The definition of fair market value is that the property must be utilized for its highest and best use. This seemingly obvious concept can be easily understood. For example, it would not make sense to build a single-family home in the heart of a downtown dominated by office skyscrapers.

When real estate is built, it nearly always is built to the highest and best use possible at the time. However, sometimes as buildings age, locations change or technology changes and buildings become obsolete.

There are plenty of examples of this phenomenon. The motel located along an old state highway may have been rendered obsolete when the interstate highways were built. The motel was the highest and best use when it was built, but today it has fallen into disarray.

Old inner city vertical factories are another example of a property in need of a change of use. Modern manufacturing assembly lines require a horizontal structure. Vertical industrial buildings are obsolete.

The answer to obsolescence is to change the use. Changing old vertical industrial buildings into lavish modern loft apartments and condominiums has been the rage for years. Sometimes an office building can be converted to residential use to capitalize on strong residential demand if demand for office space is low. The Downtown Dog case study is an example of a former office building that was partially converted to residential use.

Change of use can be subtle. The conversion of apartments to individual condominium ownership does not involve dramatic change. The units were residences before and they are residences after the change. The units may have even been sold to the tenants who were living in them! Condominium conversions are not as prevalent as they once were, but the trend has begun to take root in converting offices to individual condominium ownership.

Readers of this book may not be likely to embark upon converting a warehouse building into loft condominiums, but change of use strategies can be applied to smaller properties as well.

Gas stations typically used to feature two or more service bays for automobile maintenance. Today, the service bays have given way to convenience store space, rendering the old sites obsolete. We have seen former gas stations being used as coffee shops and pizza delivery outlets. You can bet the investor who found the new use for these sites made money in the process.

Getting Involved in Gentrification

Gentrification is the process where an old, deteriorated neighborhood becomes vibrant and valuable again. Sometimes deteriorated former architectural gems that have been forgotten for years are rediscovered by a new generation of homeowners or investors. From time to time a crime ravaged inner city neighborhood undergoes a rebirth from affluent former suburban commuters who grew weary of the ever increasing drive times.

The point is, for whatever reasons, sometimes a neighborhood is reborn and those wise enough to see the possibilities before the trend becomes common knowledge stand to profit. This statement should not dismiss the importance of understanding the reasons a neighborhood might rebound. Understanding what could trigger a rebirth is the key to spotting the trend early enough to benefit.

Gentrification is more likely to take place as more of the following criteria apply:

- **$** Commute times are increasing and the location is near employment centers.
- **$** While the current condition of the housing stock may be poor, the initial construction long ago featured desirable amenities like high ceilings, crown moldings, leaded glass, and cove ceilings.
- **$** The location is near other popular amenities such as a park, zoo, or entertainment district.
- **$** Other positive change has taken place in the area. Maybe the change is a new sports stadium or the redevelopment of a failed shopping mall.

Changes in Infrastructure

Infrastructure is defined as the roads, schools, utility lines, and other publicly funded assets necessary for a modern society. For our purposes, let's assume that even larger private developments like a shopping mall are part of the infrastructure.

An example of infrastructure change that can trigger real estate development is a new interstate highway exit where none existed before. Count on a variety of expensive new construction on what has just become newly valuable land.

A more subtle change in infrastructure can be the extension of municipal water and sewer service into new territory. Land without this service is restricted to less dense development, such as single-family homes, that can function on private well and septic systems.

Often, municipalities plan these infrastructure improvements years in advance. Therefore, one strategy might be to learn about your local municipality's plans for such utility additions and buy land that will be served by them in the future.

The drawback to this strategy is the carrying cost of undeveloped land. The solution may be to find a way to generate income from the land while you are waiting for development to reach you. One solution would be to lease the land to a tenant willing to operate a golf driving range. Another solution might be to erect ministorage facilities. Right now, the ministorage industry is a growth industry.

Go to Quality.   There is no such thing as a sure thing. But some real estate is so well located that it may become the closest thing to bust-proof as anything anyone is ever likely to see in the real estate business. Further, the best locations, despite what seem like stratospheric prices today, may in fact be undervalued.

Waterfront property is probably the best example of this phenomenon. The amount of waterfront property is mostly fixed. Environmental concerns restrict the development of any such undeveloped land that may remain. The population continues to grow, both in numbers and in affluence. The result is extraordinary price pressure on this real estate segment.

Go for the Unique.   Apartment rental housing tends toward being drab and ordinary. If you find a building with unique views or architectural features, this building is likely to enjoy higher rents, stronger occupancy, and faster appreciation.

CASE STUDIES IN UNIQUE PROPERTIES

By David J. Decker

More than a decade ago, I bought an apartment building that featured several loft apartments. Back in those days in that market, there were very few loft apartments available. Therefore, it was difficult to complete a rent survey since there were no units comparable. But my suspicion was the building was dramatically underrented.

After closing on the property, a few minor improvements were made. Rents were increased substantially, out of proportion to the degree of upgrades. I suffered little turnover from the increases. The tenants must have come to the same conclusion that I did—that even after the increase, the units were still a good deal.

I repeated the same experience a few years later with another apartment building in a small town. The units were huge, multilevel townhouse loft apartments. Again, my suspicion was the rents were low, but there was no evidence to support what the rents should be.

After closing, I passed along an enormous one-time increase. Most of the tenants stayed. Vacant units were rented quickly for even higher rent. To this day, the building remains the most expensive housing in this sub-market, despite an influx of new construction apartments.

More recently, a friend called me because he was considering buying an office building where construction had just been completed. But part of the building had still not been built out from the initial construction. The price seemed high, given that some of the space would require additional expense to be finished off. He invited me to come see the building and join him for some brainstorming about whether he should go through with the deal.

I immediately noticed the entire building was oriented toward a wetland that looked like a nature preserve. The view was spectacular. The property includes a deck and patio area overlooking the wetland running the entire length of the building. In short, the property enjoyed unique architecture designed to take advantage of a terrific location.

I told my friend if he didn't want to buy the building, I would!

He has since closed on the building, moved his offices there, and continues to enjoy his view and his success.

CHAPTER 7

Cash Flow Action Plan for Homeowners (So You Aren't Forced to Sell When the Market Is Down)

Smart Moves for Home Owners

The streets are paved with gold.

This has been the battle cry for home owners and real estate investors for five years or more. For some, the only crying in the future will be about the blood in the streets.

When that day comes, some will be washed away in the storm, but others who took prudent precautions shall emerge unscathed. The good news is that in the wake of a crash, there will be a rebound. The key is to have the staying power to weather the hard times.

The best strategy for beating a bubble-bust is to get out of town. Move to a safer area. Sell and lock in your profits. Unfortunately, as we explored in Chapter 5, for most people pulling up and moving out is not a viable option. People are rooted to their communities.

An additional premise of this book is that not only must the strategies outlined work regardless of whether there is a bust, but also the strategies must not require radical, extreme actions. You might be able to preserve your fortune by leaving your family, your friends, and your job, but would you still be happy? If you are ready for a new start in life, go for it. But most will want to stay where they are. For these people, a course must be charted to navigate any coming squall.

If a bubble-bust touches down in your hometown, here is one piece of advice that you must remember: Never sell when the market is soft. Never sell in an environment of panic. If you do, the blood in the streets will be yours.

The key is staying power combined with calm knowledge. If your community is an otherwise desirable place to live, the real estate market will recover.

Before we explore the specific survival strategies, consideration needs to be given to the circumstance where your community is not an otherwise desirable place to live. Home is where the heart is, and it may be harsh to suggest that your neighborhood may not be a desirable place to live. But if the subject is not addressed here, be advised the rest of the United States is going to voice their opinions as they vote with their feet.

If your hometown is a one-horse town, dependent on one industry for its livelihood, you are vulnerable. If the factory closes down, the community can be shattered. When the economic heart of a city dies, there may not be a recovery. There are plenty of Pennsylvania steel towns still rusting away in the shadows of shuttered steel mills. Yes, someday these areas may come back, but you and I may not live that long.

If this condition describes you, then you will be faced with some difficult decisions. Your family may have roots in the community going back generations. Your neighborhood might be all you have ever known. Whether you decide to stay there is up to you. Just know the premise that the real estate market will rebound probably does not apply to you.

Happily, most people do not face such harsh realities. For most, getting back to sunny days is merely a question of waiting, and more importantly, being in a position to be able to wait.

Consider a scenario: You have a job that you love. Things are going well. You have ingratiated yourself with upper management and your future looks bright. To the best of your knowledge, the company is healthy. In the event of a downturn, those bonuses and promotions may go away, but there will always be a place for you.

You also have a home that you love. It may not be a mansion, but it meets your needs. You have a fixed rate mortgage, and if the payments were a little lower you might be better able to save for the future or live a little better now, but you are making ends meet without a struggle.

Then the bubble hits. Some businesses close. Some of your friends fall on hard times. You read in the newspaper or perhaps hear a segment on TV about how real estate has morphed from golden goose to ugly duckling. You haven't been paying close attention, but hasn't that home just down the street from you been for sale forever?

One day, out of the blue, the morning newspaper is flopped onto your front porch and there's no mistaking the headline: *Real Estate Prices Crash 18% From Three Years Ago.*

You had no idea. Yes, you knew the real estate boom was over. It's been a while since you went to a party and heard someone bragging about the killing they made in real estate. But you had no idea it was this bad.

The news is disconcerting. You dig out your property tax bills from the past few years. Your property taxes have gone up a little every year just like they always do. But you missed the ugly details. Your assessed value has actually gone down. Your taxes went up because the tax rate went up, but according to the assessor, your property is worth less today than it was three years ago.

Now you experience your own adrenaline surge. You were counting on your home serving as your primary nest egg. You've paid down some of the mortgage balance over the years, and the house is still worth more than you paid for it, but you've clearly taken a hit.

So you decide to take a closer look at your 401(k). The statements have been piling up in a folder unopened for months. You've really been meaning to get more involved with that, but you know those statements aren't going to hold good news. You were making only the minimum contribution anyway, so the balance was never huge, but on further inspection, you discover that these accounts are down, too.

Now panic is starting to set in. You never would have said that you were rich, and you weren't thinking about retirement soon, but before, you were never worried. You just figured between the house and a little luck with the 401(k), there would be enough. You were planning on boosting your savings soon, and you know you should have taken that step with the last raise, but somehow the increase just disappeared into the family budget. Now it looks like you'll never be able to retire.

The kids will start going off to college in just two more years. When they were little, you set up a college savings account for them and even made a couple of deposits early on. At first, you had the kids contribute some of their birthday money from their grand-parents each year. But on further inspection, there has been no ac-tivity beyond interest posting in these accounts in three years.

In the back of your mind, you always figured that you should have planned better, but you could always pull out a little cash on a home equity line to make a tuition payment if you needed to. Now you're thinking, "What home equity?"

Could this be you?

Our hypothetical home owner is sloppy with his finances in several areas, but who of us aren't? He should have saved more, paid more attention to his investments, and just been more disci-plined, but it's too late now.

You can be smarter and you will be smarter for having read this book. You will be better prepared. But note one important thing. This home owner hasn't lost anything. All the losses are paper losses. As long as he doesn't panic and sell during the downturn, values will return and things will be fine.

The theme of this story is that it never hurts to be lucky. Had this homeowner been forced to accept a transfer to keep his job, or had he lost his job, the story would have a different, sadder ending. But since that didn't happen, let's learn the moral to the story: While it would be better to not get caught in a bust, if you do, don't panic. Ride out the storm. If you were able to make your mortgage payments before and can still make them now, don't worry about a temporary decline in value.

Another moral to the story would be to be better prepared instead of relying on dumb luck. Preparedness is the subject of the rest of this chapter.

Employment Stability Strategy

In the previous example, despite the anxiety this home owner experienced, at no time was he in any financial peril. Staying power is the best defense against a bust, and staying employed is the best way to have staying power.

Now would be a good time to complete a sober assessment of the health of your employer and your reputation and standing with the firm.

Do you work in a cyclical industry or are you employed in a stable field like healthcare? How did your company weather the last recession? Is your company's customer base well diversified or could losing one contract spell disaster?

The reality is that hard-working, talented individuals get laid off often in the face of business reversals. The fact that you do a great job and are respected by your superiors and your peers will not matter if your company fails. Make sure your employer enjoys sound financial health.

Even if your employer appears ready to withstand the test of time, you could still be in trouble if you are required to transfer amid a crash. Explore this possibility now. What has been the protocol in the past? Have you been in the same location perpetually or have you been jumping from city to city every few years? What assurances can your supervisor give you that you will be in the same location for the next 12 months or the next 3 years?

Regardless of the apparent financial health of your employer, reality can change overnight. If your company is merged or bought out by another firm, you could find yourself unemployed because of a consolidation or facing a move to a new headquarters if you want to keep your job. The one thing you can always count on is change.

For those reasons, start networking now. Call any colleagues that have left recently to stay acquainted. Attend trade shows and industry symposiums. Talk to a headhunter. Have a backup plan.

Cash Cushion Strategy

The worst-case crash scenario is when you have lost your job, can no longer afford your home, and real estate values have crashed. You may not be able to sell your home for what you owe, or you may not be able to sell your home at all. The only remedy is to avoid having to sell your home by having a cash safety net.

The time to prepare for a stint of unemployment is when you still have a job. Too many workers have a false sense of security and overestimate their value to their employer. If your company is losing money, your years of hard work and loyal service could mean nothing.

Developing a nest egg of cash is key. No matter what industry you may be in, a 90-day nest egg is an absolute minimum safety net. Most will need more. There are many different standards for computing how much of a savings cushion is enough. Some say three months of living expenses, others say six months, a year, or even longer. The best standard for a cushion of savings is 150 percent of the living expenses for the average length of unemployment experienced for professionals in your field who lose their jobs. If such a statistic is hard to determine, figure that your stretch of unemployment could be longer than you think.

There are some prudent strategies to be followed in anticipation of hard times. For some, they will seem like just the opposite of what you should do, but on further investigation, these strategies will prove themselves worthy. Understand that liquidity is the key to survival in hard times. Liquidity means having plenty of cash.

Therefore, while it may seem contradictory, if you have substantial equity in your home and fear unemployment, establish a home equity line for the maximum amount you can. Know that you won't be able to refinance your home or establish a new home equity line if you are unemployed. Further, a substantial portion of your equity could temporarily disappear in a crash. Lock in a line of credit now while you can.

If you have a 15-year or 20-year mortgage, think about refinancing with a 30-year mortgage. Your payments will be less and you can always decide to pay your 30-year mortgage on a 15-year schedule. If money gets tight, you can't reduce your payments on a 15-year mortgage to a 30-year schedule.

However, whatever schedule your mortgage is on, think twice about paying it down faster. Pay down your mortgage only if you already have a cushion of savings to see you through a stint of unemployment. Do not be lulled into thinking your house equity is always readily available to you. You may owe only half of what your home is worth, but no home equity lender is going to make you a loan against that equity if you're unemployed. If you lose your job, you would be better off with the equivalent of 30 percent of your home's value in cash and an 80 percent loan to value (LTV) first mortgage than a scenario where you owe only 50 percent of your home's value but you have no cash.

You should refinance your home if your new monthly payment will be less than your present payment or if the new interest rate will be less than your present rate, even if your payment is the same.

Because you have time, shop around for your refinance. Unlike a purchase, where you must line up financing within a specific period, you have less time pressure. This will give you the time to locate the best deal possible.

Avoid an adjustable rate mortgage. The exception would be a scenario where you intend to sell the property in three years and you get a lower rate for five years. Make sure there are no prepayment penalties associated with the loan.

It may seem contradictory, but the rule for weathering a crash is to postpone long-term debt repayment and have cash available. Pay down your mortgage only in good times.

Obviously, for this strategy to be successful, you must have the discipline to not use your new line of credit for fleeting consumer expenditures. In fact, while postponing long-term debt repayment is advantageous, postponing consumer debt repayment is not.

Cut out every nonessential monthly obligation you can. It's strange the things we take for granted as being essential, like cable television and cell phones. Not many years ago, these amenities did not even exist. If you do not have a sufficient cushion of savings, dump these frivolities until you do.

Eliminate consumer debt. Credit card debt is a disaster. Theoretically, if you are carrying high interest credit card debt that you are not immediately able to eliminate, you would be better off consolidating the debt into a home equity line amortized over a longer period of time at a lower interest rate. But this strategy works only if you have the discipline to not run up new debt once the card balance is paid.

Again theoretically, you should not be cutting up your credit cards. A credit card with a zero balance or a balance that you pay off every month is a good last line of defense in the event of a crisis.

However, know thyself. If the only way to pay off your credit card debt is through debt consolidation on a home equity line, you should probably consider yourself disqualified from having credit cards.

Are You in Financial Trouble?

As you have learned, local real estate appreciation rates rise and fall over time in most markets. Even in hard times, the downswings will change direction. It is just a matter of time until the market improves for the property owner. It does matter if you can survive through financial downswings.

Paper profits (and losses) mean little to the long-term property owner. If your property has increased or decreased over the past three years, that translates to nothing if you have no plans to sell. If your local market busts—let's say 10 percent—and the downturn lasts more than three years, at one point your $200,000 property will be worth only $180,000 before it regains its value back to the $200,000 mark. Of course, if you wanted to sell your property over that three-year period, the low point of the 10 percent lesser value spread means a lot to you because of your loss of the $20,000.

The question is always how well you can survive the down times. If you can survive the low points, you can get though any local real estate bust.

Measuring Your Financial Health by Your Banker's Criteria

After decades of data accumulation and lending experience, lenders established the 28/36 ratio as a sound mortgage lending practice. This rule determines how borrowers qualify for home loans. Here's how it works: With a 28/36 ratio, you are allowed to spend up to 28 percent of your gross monthly income for mortgage payments. If you already pay the full 28 percent for housing, then $36 - 28 = 8$ percent of your income can be budgeted for credit cards and other monthly obligations. (These ratios are sometimes stretched to 29/41.)

The two qualification ratios are housing (28 percent) and debt (36 percent), also called the front ratio and back ratio. These are calculated against your gross income before any taxes or withholdings are taken out. The housing ratio covers your monthly PITI (principal, interest, taxes, and insurance) payment. Private mortgage insurance (PMI) payments and condo or home owners fees are also included in this figure. The debt ratio includes the monthly housing expenses (used to determine the housing ratio) plus all other recurring monthly debt. This shows how much you can owe to other people and still qualify for your home loan.

These qualification ratios are what your bank used to approve your home loan. Once you have settled and moved into your residence, there are no more qualifications to undergo. You might have bought a new car and furniture, or overused your credit cards, piling debt on your plastic. Today, your ratios might be out of whack.

It is relatively easy to self-check your ratios. Add all your monthly housing expenses. (You may be making one monthly payment that covers all the expenses.) Multiply your gross (before taxes) monthly salary by .28 (28%). Your housing payment should be 28 percent or less of your gross monthly income.

To determine your debt ratio, total all of your minimum monthly payments, and add in your housing payment. Multiply your gross monthly salary by .36 (36%). Your total debt payments should be less than 36 percent of your gross monthly income.

If your ratios are out of line, you could be heading for serious financial hardship. It's the first sign that you are in serious financial trouble.

A Home Owners Self-Test of Financial Fitness

There are often signs of financial instability. Some are subtle. Short of a sudden job or income loss, it often takes time to slide into a hole. Getting out of trouble is often difficult.

To help you determine your financial fitness and your ability to weather a downturn in the market, use this self-test.

1. Do you have an adjustable rate mortgage (ARM)? If yes, add 30 points. If no, give yourself zero points.
    Your points: ___.

2. Do you have a balloon mortgage? If yes, add 35 points. If no, give yourself zero points.   Your points: ___.

3. Do you have an interest-only mortgage? If yes, add 50 points. If no, give yourself zero points.   Your points: ___.

4. Do you have a nontraditional (lease purchase, rent with an option to buy, etc.) mortgage? If yes, add 20 points. If no, give yourself zero points.   Your points: ___.

5. Does the total of your monthly principal, interest, taxes, property insurance, and home owners fee (if any) exceed 28 percent of your total monthly gross income? If yes, add 40 points. If no, give yourself zero points.   Your points: ___.

6. Does the total of your monthly principal, interest, taxes, property insurance, home owners fee, and all other minimum monthly debts (car payments, credit card payments, personal loans, student loans, court-ordered child support, etc.) exceed 36 percent of your total monthly gross income? If yes, add 50 points. If no, give yourself zero points.   Your points: ___.

7. Do you have at least three months of your total monthly living expenditures in savings on deposit in your bank? If yes, subtract 40 points. If no, give yourself 40 points.
    Your points: ___.

8. Is/Are your monthly income source(s), such as your job, pensions, and so on highly likely to continue without interruption over the next three years? If yes, add zero points. If no, give yourself 20 points.   Your points: ___.

9. Has your yearly income been increasing by 5 percent or more over the past five years? If yes, add zero points. If no, give yourself 10 points.   Your points: ___.

10. Have you been fully funding your IRAs the past three years? If yes, add zero points. If no, give yourself 20 points.   Your points: ___.

11. Have you been saving at least 10 percent of your gross income over the past five years? If yes, add zero points. If no, give yourself 20 points.   Your points: ___.

12. Have you been more than 30 days late on your mortgage once during the past year? If yes, add 50 points. If no, give yourself zero points.   Your points: ___.

13. Do you often argue with your spouse about money? If yes, add 35 points. If no, give yourself zero points.

          Your points: ___.

14. Over the past year, have your monthly bills always been paid on time? If yes, add zero points. If no, give yourself 40 points.   Your points: ___.

15. Over the past year, have you bounced any checks? If yes, add 10 points. If no, give yourself zero points.

          Your points: ___.

16. Over the past 60 days, have you ever been unable to sleep because you are worrying about your bills, your income, or other financial matters? If yes, add 45 points. If no, give yourself zero points.   Your points: ___.

17. Would you describe your current financial situation as "excellent" or "very good"? If yes, add zero points. If no, give yourself 20 points.   Your points: ___.

18. Has your credit score been improving over the past 24 months? If yes, add zero points. If no, give yourself 25 points.   Your points: ___.

19. Have you refinanced your primary residence for any reason other than to get a lower interest rate? If yes, add 30 points. If no, give yourself zero points.   Your points: ___.

20. Have you refinanced your primary residence, gotten cash out, and then used the money for anything other than to purchase an appreciable asset? If yes, add 40 points. If no, give yourself zero points.   Your points: ___.

21. Do you use your credit cards for cash advances? If yes, add 35 points. If no, give yourself zero points.

    Your points: ___.

22. Do you use your credit cards to purchase consumables, like groceries and food when eating out, and do not pay off the balance each month? If yes, add 30 points. If no, give yourself zero points.   Your points: ___.

23. Are your credit card balances increasing each month? If yes, add 30 points. If no, give yourself zero points.

    Your points: ___.

24. Do you have more than three open bank credit cards? If yes, add 20 points. If no, give yourself zero points.

    Your points: ___.

25. Do you carry a balance of more than $1,000 total on all of your credit cards? If yes, add 35 points. If no, give yourself zero points.   Your points: ___.

26. Have you ever refinanced your home to obtain cash to pay off your credit card balances, only to allow balances to build up again? If yes, add 70 points. If no, give yourself zero points.   Your points: ___.

27. Is your home in good to excellent condition, well maintained, ready to sell, and would need nothing more than a good cleaning to place on the market? If yes, add zero points. If no, give yourself 25 points.   Your points: ___.

28. Is the amount of equity in your home more than 25 percent of the present market value? If yes, add zero points. If no, give yourself 35 points.   Your points: ___.

29. Could you realistically expect to sell your home within the next 30 days, if you placed it on the market? If yes, add zero points. If no, give yourself 25 points.   Your points: ___.

After completing the self-test, total your final score.

If your score is 130 or less, you are in a good position to weather any local real estate crash.

If your score is 135 to 190, you probably need to start making some defensive moves to protect yourself from any crash or market fluctuation.

If your score is 195 or greater, you are in serious trouble should a local bust occur. You need to make immediate changes now to prevent the potential loss of your home or bankruptcy.

As part of your financial self-defense to withstand real estate market downswings, remember these points:

$ Update your budget.

$ Check yourself against the 28/36 rule.

$ Curtail your use of credit cards.

$ Stop using your home as an ATM machine.

Maintain a budget. Most people who feel financial squeezes are not in control of their spending. The only way to know what you owe is to keep track of it. Use either a computer or a simple paper system to watch your monthly obligations.

Keep the 28/36 rule in mind. Before taking on a major obligation, such as a car payment, make sure your 28/36 ratios would remain in line. Don't allow yourself to take on debt that would not allow you to maintain these ratios. Just because a creditor is willing to lend you the money or extend credit, that is not a reason in itself to accept it.

Credit card use is a fast way to get into deep financial trouble. Your balances should be decreasing each month. If you have credit card debt of more than $1,000, develop a plan to get yourself out of debt. Focus on paying off one card at a time. Your goal should be to maintain a zero balance on your credit cards.

Stop using your home as an ATM machine. Just because you have equity in your home, that is not a reason to spend it. This is especially true if you were to use it to purchase a depreciable asset, such as a dream vacation, a car, or a motorcycle. Home equity lines of credit (HELOC) are not a good idea for things like paying off credit card debts or purchases of household consumer items. Refinancing your home to pull cash out to buy the car or toy you always wanted (such as a boat or pair of ATVs) never makes financial sense.

CHAPTER 8

Cash Flow Action Plan for the Investor: Make Sure You Can Hold Your Property through a Down Cycle

How Crashes Change Everything

For homeowners in the midst of a real estate crash the key to survival is to have staying power to weather the storm. For investors, the strategy is the same. You must endeavor to maintain cash flow and take whatever additional steps are necessary to avoid having to sell in a downturn.

For the homeowner, unemployment is the greatest threat to staying power. Real estate investors face the same problem, only in addition to the risk of suffering unemployment yourself, there is the additional risk of your tenants losing their jobs or suffering business reversals, resulting in vacancies. Real estate investors, therefore, have even greater risk exposure than homeowners.

Most real estate crashes are caused by unsustainable losses in employment. When jobs are lost, offices close, warehouses sit empty, stores go dark, and apartments remain vacant. Soft real estate markets are plagued by flat or declining rents, tenant incentives like free rent, and landlord funded tenant improvements. All of these measures impact cash flow.

A soft real estate market can become cutthroat competitive. Competing apartment communities circulate flyers soliciting tenants with free rent deals from adjacent competitors. Leasing agents will be approaching your office, retail, and industrial tenants, wooing them to rent different space.

If you fear a real estate reversal, the time to prepare a strategy is now. There are two strategies from which to choose. We already saw in Chapter 5 that selling investment property to lock in a profit with the intention of getting back in after the crash is a foolish strategy. The demands of market timing are too great and the impact of capital gains taxes is too high. However, it would make sense to sell your property and complete a tax-deferred exchange by buying property in a more stable market. Thus the first strategy is to move your equity to higher ground.

The second strategy is to stay put and weather the storm.

Here are the criteria for choosing between these two strategies:

Staying put and waiting out the storm is an option if:

$ Your property is a cash cow.

$ Your property is unique or elite in some way so that it will remain in demand even in a soft market.

$ Your property is in excellent condition and in need of nothing more than routine ongoing repairs.

Moving your equity to another market is an option if:

$ Your property is having cash flow problems.

$ You are already having vacancy problems.

$ Your property has deferred maintenance or obsolescence that you cannot afford to correct.

Moving your equity to a new market will be a considerable inconvenience and includes additional unique perils. These problems are explored in Chapter 9. For now, understand that your inertia or unwillingness to accept these additional risks may have devastating repercussions if you ignore them and your market crashes.

For the rest of this chapter, we have to assume that wise or otherwise, you have elected to stay in your market and take your chances. There are several steps to take to batten down the hatches before any storm hits.

Renew and Extend Commercial Leases

Leases on office, retail, and industrial space usually are for several years. If you fear a crash and have leases that will be expiring in the short term (12 to 36 months), you may want to consider trying to negotiate an early renewal with these tenants.

A key leasing negotiation strategy in commercial leasing is to require the tenant to supply financial statements annually or on request. If this requirement is part of your lease, you have access to key information to determine the financial health of your tenant.

If your tenant is not required to furnish such information, you can try to incorporate such requirements into a lease renewal. However, tenants are not likely to just voluntarily hand out their financial statements. Count on most to be reluctant or completely uncooperative about sharing such information.

One additional strategy for obtaining the information is to suggest a percentage lease. Percentage leases are usually utilized only for retail tenants. In a percentage lease, all or part of the rent paid is predicated on the sales volume experienced by the tenant. The only way to compute the rent is for the tenant to report gross sales, so you would have access to at least some information.

If you suggest switching a flat rent lease to a percentage lease as part of a lease renewal negotiation, you may gain additional input about your tenant's situation. Tenants with a thriving business may be reluctant to enter into a percentage lease. Conversely, tenants who are struggling may welcome the opportunity to cut their rent if sales go south.

Regardless of the circumstances, you need to make some judgment about the financial strength of your tenant before you enter into lease renewal negotiations. Obviously, the best way to enter into negotiations is with tenant financial statements in hand. But even if such information is not available, try to make an assumption about the tenant's financial strength anyway. Maybe the rent payment history tells the entire story you need to know, particularly if the tenant has struggled to make payments.

The point of this exercise is to avoid making renewal concessions with a weak tenant who is vulnerable to a recession. Additionally, try to further strengthen your position by requiring personal guarantees on the lease. Again, the personal guarantees are only as good as the financial strength of the person making them. You would need to review personal financial statements to know whether the guarantees are worth anything.

Understand that the earlier you try to negotiate a renewal, the weaker your negotiating position may be. For most smaller tenants, it is rare for a commercial lease renewal to be negotiated much more than one year before the expiration date. It may be difficult to gain your tenant's attention to earlier negotiations.

Although early lease negotiations are fraught with stumbling blocks, that does not mean that you should not try. If your tenant has a thriving business, they may not want the disruption of moving and may appreciate an early renewal. The goal is to lock in any good tenants whom you can before desperate leasing agents start knocking on their doors with sweetheart deals from desperate landlords.

Before making any renewal concessions, remember the lease is only as good as the tenant's financial strength. If your tenant goes out of business, it may not matter how many years are left on the lease.

Residential Tenant Retention

Apartment communities can be extraordinarily creative in their leasing programs, but sometimes they miss an opportunity to negate the need for creative leasing solutions by failing to actively engage in tenant retention.

Residential leases are rarely longer than one year. Therefore, negotiating new long-term renewals is not an option. When residential tenants lose their jobs, they usually become former tenants before long. There is nothing that can be done about tenants who can no longer afford to pay. Inevitably, if you are caught in a crash, there are going to be higher vacancies as a result.

Since nothing can be done about vacancies driven by job loss, it becomes essential to address all other causes of tenant turnover. The following is a summary of the reasons that tenants move:

$ Loss of a job.

$ Job or school transfer.

$ Marriage.

$ Divorce.

$ Home purchase.

$ Change in family size.

$ Promotion (increase in income).

$ Death.

$ Rent increase.

$ Dissatisfaction.

$ Loss of roommate.

Begin by tracking how you have lost tenants in the past. This will identify where you need to focus your attention. You may find that you do not even know why some of your tenants left. Ignorance in this critical area may indicate hidden potential for making a difference in tenant retention by studying the problem.

Realize that not every vacating tenant will tell you the real reason for moving. However, you will usually have a forwarding address for your tenant. If your former tenant has not left the area and they are still renting their housing, this is cause for further investigation.

Develop your own list of reasons your tenants gave when they left. Your list may look different from the preceding one. Look for areas of opportunity to increase tenant retention. There are some areas where it is difficult to improve on tenant retention, such as the following:

$ Loss of a job.
$ Job or school transfer.
$ Home purchase.
$ Death.

However, even in these more difficult categories, think creatively. Theoretically, if an individual was sufficiently thrilled with the home they were renting, they would never have the desire to own a home of their own. You can spoil your tenant population by being prompt with making repairs and by taking excellent care of groundskeeping and common area maintenance. Take in mail, feed pets, and water plants while your tenants are on vacation if you can. Some communities offer dry cleaning dropoff, daycare, and office services (fax service, etc.).

Other areas affording greater opportunity for reducing tenant turnover include the following:

$ Marriage.
$ Divorce.
$ Change in family size.
$ Promotion (increase in income).
$ Rent increase.

$ Dissatisfaction.

$ Loss of roommate.

Many of these reasons for vacating reflect a need for a different size apartment, including marriage, divorce, change in family size, and loss of a roommate. Make sure that your residents are aware of the different size floor plans you have available. Be certain that your tenants are aware of other buildings you have for rent in the area.

Start a roommate matchmaking service. If your apartment portfolio is seemingly too small for this effort, try combining with neighboring rental communities.

Obviously, pay close attention to any turnover initiated because of resident dissatisfaction. If there is a consistent pattern of complaints about defects within your power to remedy, do so.

Work from the assumption that any resident who moves to another rental apartment in your area represents a potential tenant retention failure.

Residential Leasing Strategies

There are two ways to solve a vacancy problem. Tenant retention is the first way. Aggressively leasing is the second. Aggressive leasing includes having a model apartment available, implementing appropriate concessions, tracking call patterns, and tracking leasing patterns.

Often, large apartment complexes will set aside one unit to use as a model. Smaller apartment complexes cannot afford this luxury. However, even if your apartment community is a single-family rental home, there are steps you can take to adapt the concept of having a model.

Never show an empty, vacant apartment or home that has no decorations at all. Instead, strive to create a mini model. A mini model has new towels hanging in the bathroom and kitchen, an attractive silk plant on the kitchen counter, and other minor touches. Remember, kitchens and baths are what sell housing. Focus your attention on these areas.

A better alternative to the mini model is the ambassador apartment. The ambassador apartment is the existing resident who is a terrific housekeeper and decorator. See if you can gain permission from this individual to use their apartment as a model during certain hours in exchange for a rent discount.

The point of having a mini model or ambassador apartment is to improve your closing ratio on showings. However, it would be impossible to improve this ratio if you do not know what your present ratio is. You should be tracking call patterns and leasing patterns.

Your property is probably experiencing a call pattern, even if you do not know it. You can discern what this pattern might be only if you have been tracking calls. Make sure any telephone voice mail system you use has a time and date stamp. The purpose for gathering this information is to direct how you staff your phone coverage and plan showing times.

Hopefully, tracking your telephone calls will point out a distinct pattern of when you receive most of your calls. Most of your calls may be on evenings or weekends. Your calls may peak around the publication of the mediums in which you advertise. In our office, we experience a spike in call activity on Friday afternoons through the weekend and during the day on Monday. But do not make any assumptions about your call patterns. Track the data.

Once you have identified your call pattern, make sure you have trained, motivated staff available to answer the phones during these peak times. With cellular phones and call forwarding, there is no excuse for not having appropriate phone coverage.

You should also be tracking the source that generated the call, particularly if you are advertising in more than one medium. Adjust your advertising and other efforts according to these patterns.

You should also be tracking the outcome of these phone calls.

That outcome should be a pattern of showing appointments. You want to be able to anticipate the showing pattern so that you can prepare in advance for these appointments. Being prepared means scheduling cleaning and landscaping routines around these patterns so the property will look the best during the showings.

Being prepared means notifying the tenants that have given notice to vacate that you will potentially need to show their apartment during a set time each week. Your vacating tenants will appreciate this courtesy and this will save you from running around trying to notify them on each occasion there is a showing.

If your experience is similar to mine, you will find that most telephone inquiries are from prospects who would like to view the rental unit immediately or later the same day. Being able to accommodate this choice requires you to have either vacant apartments or previous notification of any tenant intending to vacate.

Your properties may also have a leasing pattern. The leasing pattern reflects where your tenants came from, where they are working, and how they found out about you.

To track your leasing patterns, mount a large map on a piece of styrofoam and place colored pins in the map to reflect where your tenants were living before they moved to your facility and where your tenants are working now. If you can discern any patterns from this exercise, you will know where to focus your leasing efforts.

Cash Flow Strategies

Marginal properties are always the last to be leased and the first to sit vacant. Even assuming your properties are not marginal, the time to reposition your properties and prepare to meet the competition is now. You do not want to be caught at the depths of a crash with deferred maintenance, obsolescence, and a vacancy problem.

Making the needed upgrades, improvements, or repairs presents a quandary. Should you borrow money to improve your properties while interest rates are still low knowing the added debt will negatively impact cash flow? Even if you do not need to borrow to upgrade your buildings, that cash could have been retained as a cushion against hard times.

The best answer is to do both: Upgrade the asset while maintaining a cash reserve. However, if both goals are seemingly unachievable, err in favor of upgrading the property. Take the steps most likely to help you keep tenants and stay occupied.

Establish emergency lines of credit now. These credit lines are likely to be based on the value of your properties. You must obtain these credit lines while the values of your properties are still high. If you wait until you need the money, any erosion of value will impair your ability to borrow.

Attack every opportunity to increase revenue and slash expenses. One revenue opportunity often missed is to reconfigure existing space to change non-revenue-producing common area space into leased space. Consolidate any first floor or higher management storage closets and shop areas to make room for rentable tenant storage space.

Use the same idea to convert underperforming space. For example, a den in an apartment is more valuable if it can be made into a bedroom.

Tackle operating expenses the same way. Wring waste from every expense line item. Start with the most expensive costs and work your way down. For most landlords, the greatest expense of ownership is the interest on the mortgage. Can you refinance for better terms and lower payments? Put a good mortgage broker on the case and see if he or she can find you a better deal. If they fail, it costs you nothing.

Water and sewer utilities are expensive enough in most areas of the country to justify replacement of any toilets that are not the newer lower capacity models. Many utility companies will perform energy audits for free. Take prudent action to save energy when the savings justify the move.

Challenge your assessment to reduce your property taxes. Rebid insurance policies. Reconsider any contracts on leased equipment such as leased water heaters, laundry equipment, or water softeners. These line items can be eliminated entirely by buying the equipment. At least contact the vendor and tell them you are considering a purchase. The vendor may respond by reducing the rent or by cutting you a greater share of the revenue in a coin laundry lease.

Revisit any contracted services such as waste hauling or snow removal to make sure that your current vendor is still cost competitive. Track responses to advertisements for space for lease to discern which advertising media are most effective for you.

CHAPTER 9

Don't Put All Your Real Estate Eggs in One Basket: Hedging and Balancing Your Portfolio

You've had a good ride. You never anticipated it, but your real estate has skyrocketed to prices you would never have imagined. But even good tidings can present a problem. Now that you've made your money, how do you keep it from being washed away in a crash?

You have some decisions to make. You have to decide whether to take your chances staying in the market you are in now or moving your equity to safer, higher ground. Either choice carries both opportunity and risk.

This decision needs to be made based on rational thinking and good research, not on media hype about bursting real estate bubbles. Therefore, if you have not already done so, go back to Chapter 4, learn the techniques for assessing a real estate market, and apply the methodology to your neighborhood.

Having taken a sober look at the data, you can make an educated decision about whether to stay in your present market or go elsewhere.

Deciding to Stay Put

Consider the following example.

> Perhaps your area has done well over the past five years. Comparing your MSA to the benchmark five-year appreciation of 50 percent (see Chapter 4), you have done far better than the national average.
>
> A close look at the data explains why. Your region has experienced a boom in job creation that shows no sign of letting up. Not surprisingly, people are flocking to where the jobs are, and both population and the number of households have grown. While there has been robust construction activity, there does not appear to be a glut of new housing. The average days on the market to sell a home remains stable and relatively short. The supply of existing homes for sale is less than five months.
>
> However, home prices have escalated and creative financing packages like interest-only loans are gaining market share because housing would not be affordable for too many otherwise. As interest rates increase, affordability becomes even more of an issue. The Housing Affordability Index (HAI) is well below 100 and falling. The region has experienced boom and bust cycles before.
>
> Despite some foreboding indicators, you decide to stay put. You are counting on continued employment growth and an expanding number of households to cancel the impact of rising interest rates.

This property owner has reached a reasonable conclusion based on careful study of correct data. However, the owner could still be wrong and have his or her equity wiped out in a crash. That is the risk in making a decision to stay put.

This mixed message is what most individuals will experience as they use the techniques in this book to analyze the health of their real estate market. Part of the decision making process will be your aversion to risk. For some, just knowing that their region appears to be at a peak and is one that has experienced boom and bust cycles in the past is reason enough to get out.

Hedging Your Position While Staying Put

Other homeowners or investors may assess their neighborhoods and feel more uneasy. Realistically, many homeowners will not be able to move easily without unwanted disruption. Is there a remedy to staying put without risking your equity disappearing?

Recently, Merrill Lynch & Company and several other investment banks have begun offering investment products designed to move contrary to the housing market. By the second quarter of 2006, the Chicago Mercantile Exchange will have futures contracts based on home prices in each of 10 different cities, plus a composite contract on all 10 cities.

The idea is that by making the correct investment hedge, gains in these indices would offset any loss in equity of your real estate.

These investment products go by a scary name: derivatives. They are complicated, risky, and hardly foolproof, and cannot offer a perfect hedge against a crash. Most homeowners are probably not equipped to sort out the complications of these financial vehicles. Giving you direction on how to navigate this minefield is beyond the scope of this book. However, if you have experience or sophistication in these areas, you might explore this hedge alternative.

Deciding to Move Your Equity Elsewhere

Other investors looking at the same data may conclude that it is time to bail out while their profit is still intact. This property owner needs to visit Chapter 4 a second time, this time to find a place to move his or her equity.

This is an exciting challenge. The goal is to identify the next area of opportunity. Some investors may want to follow a contrarian strategy by starting with the MSAs that experienced the least appreciation in the past five years. After all, every dog has its day. Maybe some of these MSAs are poised for a rebound. Chapter 17 includes a list of the most undervalued cities. Just make sure that your predictions are based on serious analysis of good data and not wishful thinking.

The risk to this strategy is that you could be wrong, miss the continued boom in your old market, and step right into a crash in the new market you choose. Remember, even a real estate market that has not experienced a price bubble is still vulnerable to widespread unemployment.

However, the more likely and unavoidable risk is the competitive disadvantage you will have pitting your wits in a new market against investors who have been active in these markets their entire careers.

CASE STUDY: KNOW YOUR MARKET

By David J. Decker

I have always been an advocate of knowing your market thoroughly. Although I have been investing in the same markets in southeastern Wisconsin for 20 years, I do not claim to have mastered every local marketplace. For example, I have never invested in student housing or management intensive inner-city core type properties.

I know other investors who have been successful in these market segments, and one of them taught me an important lesson. Several years ago, I was involved as a broker helping an investor sell some inner-city apartment buildings. The investor was doing a tax-deferred exchange, trading his equity into more apartments in an area that was easier to manage.

As I got to know this investor, I learned that he continued to enjoy the successful operation of several other inner-city apartment buildings that were within a short walk of the buildings he was selling. While he was anxious to get out of these buildings, he was content to keep the other apartments that were only a few blocks away.

I was curious to know why the ownership experience could be so different for similar apartment buildings seemingly in the same location. The investor explained to me that pedestrian traffic patterns made the difference between failure and success in these buildings.

All of his buildings were on a major east-west street within blocks of one another. The successful buildings were oriented toward this major street, with the main entrance to the building exiting on the main east-west thoroughfare. The failing buildings were on a corner of the main street facing a smaller north-south street running perpendicular to the main street. The entrances to these buildings were on the smaller north-south street.

The smaller street was not as well lit or as well traveled. Few of the tenants owned cars. Most people felt more secure on the main east-west street than on the arterial north-south side street. As a result, the buildings facing the main street fared well and stayed full while the neighboring buildings fronting on the smaller street just a few blocks away were not as successful.

This example highlights the subtleties of the marketplace. Only those working and investing in these markets are likely to know or appreciate this detail. Yet these subtle details can be the deciding factors between failure and success.

It is difficult to beat the local competition in making a value investing play in a distant, unfamiliar market. However, by employing the techniques you learned in Chapter 6, you should be able to at least hold your own.

Sometimes the logistical barriers to distance investing help impose proper analysis. Too often, buyers are overanxious to go out and kick the tires on a real estate investment opportunity. Whether the property is down the street or a thousand miles away, proper investment analysis begins by studying the operating numbers on a property.

While the operating numbers tell an important story, you will need to make an assessment of the local economy in a city unfamiliar to you. The most detailed economic data typically available are broken down only to the level of the Metropolitan Statistical Area (MSA). In other words, the most detailed data you will be able to find apply to *entire cities*. Most cities are large enough such that there can be individual mini booms and busts going on within different neighborhoods within the same city or MSA.

One way to get an indication of local conditions is to follow the home centers. Home centers like Menards, Home Depot, and Lowe's expand only into areas experiencing robust real estate activity. You can piggyback on their research by visiting the company web sites and exploring employment opportunities at new store openings.

However you do it, you must be certain that you are not choosing the wrong location in the right city. Eventually, that means spending some time in your target location.

Maybe you can focus on an area that you have visited frequently on vacation. Perhaps you can return to an area where you grew up. Try to take advantage of any existing knowledge you may have.

If you elect to embark on investing in a new area, consider spending your next vacation there. Gain as much familiarity as you can. Get acquainted with a real estate agent specializing in your desired area of investment.

Regardless of your strategy, there are web sites that can help you search anywhere in the country. Two of them are www.realtor.com and www.loopnet.com. Realtor.com focuses on single-family houses with some multifamily housing. Loopnet.com features commercial properties only. A third site, Realtor.org, referenced earlier, has commercial property listings as well at http://www.realtor.org/cominfex.nsf?OpenDatabase.

Long Distance Property Management

If your efforts to move your equity are successful, then you will be faced with an additional dilemma. How do you manage these distant properties?

One way to overcome the problem is to invest in properties that are less management intensive. The best example is a single-tenant triple net lease investment.

Triple Net Lease (NNN) Investments. A single-tenant NNN investment requires the least management involvement of just about any real estate investment. Examples of single-tenant NNN investments include drugstores, fast-food restaurants, oil change centers, gas stations, and any other office, retail, or industrial real estate that is occupied by a single tenant on a NNN (pronounced "triple net" or "net-net-net") lease.

A NNN lease transfers almost all property management responsibility to the tenant. Under a NNN lease, the tenant is responsible for all costs of operating the property, including property taxes, insurance, maintenance, and utilities.

Not only does the property owner not have any management responsibilities, the tenant has a vested interest in carrying out his or her contractual duties. After all, the leased space is a place of business. The tenant will want to keep the space in good repair, such that deferred maintenance does not become a deterrent to customers.

Often, these leases are for long periods of time, up to 20 years, or even longer. If your lease is backed by a solid corporate guaranty, you will be able to continue to collect rent on your site even if the corporate parent decides to close your location. A long-term NNN lease with an investment grade tenant makes for a trouble free real estate investment.

The financing available for quality NNN lease investments is among the best available in commercial real estate. Most mortgages on commercial real estate are recourse loans, which mean the borrower is personally responsible for the entire debt. In the event of default, the lender could tap the borrower's entire net worth to satisfy a deficiency. However, NNN leased properties are often available with nonrecourse debt.

Not only does the investor not have to place his or her entire net worth in jeopardy, the interest rates and other terms are also favorable. NNN leased properties can be financed for the lowest interest rates for the longest periods of time compared to just about any other commercial property.

One drawback of a NNN lease is that in the final years of the lease term, the property may become illiquid until it is known whether the tenant will renew the lease or exercise a lease extension option. Of course, if the tenant does not renew or the business fails, then you would experience 100 percent vacancy.

Commercial property can suffer months or even years of vacancy before a new tenant is found. You may have to incur the expense of a leasing agent to find a tenant. Even once the new tenant is identified, there may be expensive tenant improvements.

For these reasons, commercial property is inherently more risky than residential properties. While the loan terms can be favorable, loan to value ratios are usually lower, forcing investors to inject more cash into these deals.

NNN leased properties are not a beginner's investment, but for an investor with substantial equity, the NNN lease option is a viable way to move your equity to a safer location without having to be concerned with day-to-day management responsibilities.

Other Long Distance Property Management Solutions

The most obvious solution is to hire a local professional property management company. Look for a company that specializes in properties similar to the one you are buying. Visit properties the company is currently managing on a random basis to be certain the management company is doing a good job with their current portfolio. Talk to some of their management clients to see if they have any complaints.

For anyone determined to own and manage themselves from a distance, there are several strategies. The first strategy is to acquire less management intensive real estate such as the NNN leased properties discussed earlier. While NNN properties offer the least management responsibility, multi-tenant industrial buildings and retail strip centers can also be less management intensive alternatives.

If you are intent on owning office or residential real estate that you intend to manage yourself from a distance, then try to split up the management duties between at least two people. Such a strategy will prove helpful if one person quits, and the two managers can keep on eye on one another. If one individual quits, the remaining person can interview replacements.

PART THREE

HOW TO PROFIT WHEN THE CRASH HAPPENS

LIFE AFTER THE BUST: HOW HOMEOWNERS, INVESTORS, LANDLORDS, LENDERS, AND THE NATIONAL ECONOMY WILL REACT— AND HOW TO PROFIT

O ne of the most interesting phenomena of the present real estate boom is the degree of optimism shared by some homeowners and investors. Today, the print and broadcast media have an
ongoing commentary about the existence of a real estate bubble
and the probability of a bust. It would be nearly impossible to be
unaware of the attention being given to real estate, and most of the
attention lately has been about how the sky may fall.

If you don't hear about real estate on your television set or in
your newspaper, then you are probably hearing about it from your
neighbors. Yet as we read in Chapter 1, a sizable chunk of the population believes that double-digit appreciation will continue not
just next year but also for the foreseeable future.

It is important to understand the psychology behind this optimism because if a bust does occur, the same psychology will be experienced again in reverse. After the bust, a measurable portion of
the populace will believe that real estate should always be avoided
and will never get better.

Entire books have been devoted to the concept of adopting new products, technologies, or ideas. *The Tipping Point* is one such title that comes to mind. The basic idea is that early adopters will discover a new idea first before the idea trickles down to the larger population and finally to the last holdouts in the late adopters. One important concept to keep in mind is that not every idea explored by early adopters becomes successful in the larger marketplace.

In the 1970s, quadraphonic sound was supposed to be the next great thing, making the existing stereophonic sound standards obsolete. It never happened. Today, the concept of a real estate bust is in the early adopter stage.

Some early adopters have already sold their homes and have moved into rental housing. Whether this decision will prove prudent or foolish remains to be seen. Our belief is that few will benefit by following this strategy. This tactic will not become widespread.

What may become widespread is pessimism about real estate. The pessimism will be based upon actual and imagined real estate calamities.

The Impact of a Bust on the National Economy

The present real estate boom has been so pervasive and so strong that it has become the juggernaut driving the economy. Real estate typically suffers with the rest of the economy when the business cycle reaches a contraction stage, but this time a contraction in real estate might be enough to cause broader economic stagnation. "About 43.0% of the increase in private sector payrolls since the economic recovery began in November 2001"[1] has been attributed to real estate activity.

One phenomenon from the present boom is the influence of the wealth effect from ballooning real estate equity. People spend more because they feel they have more. Our economy has always been consumer driven. A decline in real estate values could eliminate or diminish the wealth effect and depress consumer spending.

Today, real estate is struggling to shoulder the burden of higher interest rates. Tomorrow, higher unemployment could be added to that weight. If the combination of higher interest rates and greater unemployment further cools the demand for real estate, a vicious circle can begin to develop.

Business cycle contractions and real estate contractions have several elements in common, like increases in bankruptcies and foreclosures. Any increase in foreclosures could place added pressure on the already troubled mortgage secondary market. To understand this problem, the workings of the secondary market must first be understood.

Few financial institutions making mortgages retain those mortgages for their own portfolios. Instead, the loans are sold on the secondary market. The secondary market injects liquidity into mortgage lending and helps diversify risk. Freddie Mac is one of the quasipublic secondary market companies that engage in the sale of mortgage backed financial securities.

Formerly, stringent criteria were required for mortgages to be sold on the secondary market. Presently, the marketplace has become saturated with easy money interest-only loans and ARMs and hypersegmented with mortgage products aimed at sub-par credit borrowers. Logically, if the mortgage market becomes vulnerable to foreclosures, the riskiest products will be the ones that suffer the greatest default rates.

Depending on how widespread the problems become, the ramifications will range from an elimination of the riskier mortgage products to failure of institutions like Freddie Mac. Although wholesale failure seems unlikely, the outcome is almost certain to be a mortgage market with more stringent lending criteria and a reduction in the number of more risky, creative mortgage products like interest-only loans.

Already, legislators have taken action to rein in the practices of Freddie Mac and Fannie Mae. A new agency has been proposed, the Federal Housing Finance Agency, with the intention that this regulatory body would set capital requirements, potentially reject new business products, and limit portfolio holdings.

This new agency and the legislation to create it are still far from becoming a reality. But what is clear is that lawmakers recognize that this industry is out of control. Whenever or whatever laws are passed, count on them to constrict the easy money financing that has been driving the present real estate boom.

The Impact of a Bust on the Lending Industry

Real estate may be a local business, but interest rates are mostly the same nationally. Tighter money policies will be the same nationwide. In a downturn, transaction volume will fall off. Today, lenders are flush with cash and money is chasing deals. Competitive mortgage quotes can be found for even questionable deals. In a reversal, even sound deals may be hard to finance.

The result will be a resurgence of the creative financing techniques that have been lying dormant recently. Motivated sellers will once again participate in financing their properties that might not sell otherwise. Land contracts and seller-funded second mortgages will become more commonplace.

The Impact of the Bust on Seller Behavior

Again, understanding current conditions will help predict the future in the aftermath of a bust. Currently, real estate is the only game in town. No other investment opportunity can keep pace with real estate. The marketplace is flush with newcomers buying in at new price plateaus. Nationally, home ownership has gained three percentage points, growing to 70 percent. The investment community is similarly crowded with new, less experienced participants.

In a downturn, circumstances will reverse. The rate of home ownership may contract temporarily. The more recent arrivals in real estate investing will be the first to exit. The property flipping schemes involving assigning contracts on new construction condominiums and other new real estate will come to an end.

Perhaps most importantly, the blind optimism of the present may metamorphose into unjustified pessimism tomorrow. Of course, some of the pessimism will be justified, owing to real losses. But just as the marketplace has overreacted to good conditions, the same overreaction may be experienced from adverse conditions. In other words, popular opinion may skew inaccurately negative.

Some real estate owners will go through the following phases during a crash.

The first phase is *surprise*. After all, today large segments of owners are still expecting rapid appreciation. For values to go flat would be a surprise. Values going backward will be a shock.

The second phase is *concern*. A recession is when your neighbors lose their jobs. A depression is when you lose your job. As long as real estate owners are able to continue meeting their mortgage obligations, they will think of the local market being only in a "recession."

The third phase is *panic*. This is when the downturn in the market actually begins to affect them personally. Maybe a pay cut renders their home less affordable. Maybe more vacancies linger longer.

The final phase is *desperation*. At this stage, the status quo is no longer being maintained. The homeowner believes he will not be able to keep his house. The real estate investor thinks the days of positive cash flow are over forever.

Anytime popular perception is inaccurate, opportunities arise for those with better vision.

Post-Bust Profit Opportunities

The most important theme to remember is to make real estate investing decisions based on your own research into the criteria and indicators that drive real estate markets described in this book. Do not rely on media speculation or advice from just one or two supposed real estate experts, not even this one. If there is opportunity in the marketplace, the data will bear it out.

Depending on the nature of any reversal or the kind of investment strategy you follow, you may likely find yourself making a contrarian play. If you decide to invest again in a market that has experienced a bust, you may find yourself all alone.

As much as investors may dislike competition when buying property, the competition verifies the legitimacy and wisdom of the contemplated purchase. In the future, depending on the severity of the downturn, there may be little competition. A lack of competitors will make for more buying opportunities, but it takes greater courage to follow a contrarian strategy.

However, not everyone making a contrarian move will be doing so in the wake of a bust. Some will be making this move now by engaging in tax-deferred exchanges by selling in vulnerable locations and buying in safer areas as described in Chapter 9.

As we have already explored, not every region of the United States has participated equally in the real estate boom. There probably are regions poised for strong growth that may surpass some of the present appreciation leaders. This displacement will occur more from declines in appreciation in leading regions than from growth in appreciation in lagging regions, but the disparity should still be sufficient to warrant exploration of this strategy.

Finding and investing in these regions is a contrarian tactic some real estate exchangers may want to explore now. Because there are few regions that are presently distressed, moving equity to a new location will not give you the opportunity to employ creative financing techniques and other tactics characteristic of a buyer's market. Even in lagging regions, presently it's still a seller's market, although that could change.

The Role of Motivated Sellers

It seems like every book ever written on investing in real estate has the obligatory advice on how to find and exploit motivated sellers. Forgetting any ethical considerations, how would you go about finding such people?

Under current conditions, even a property owner desperate to unload quickly an unwanted piece of property can reasonably expect to be able to sell their real estate rapidly without discounting or offering terms other than all cash. Of course, this situation will change in the face of a bust. Still, expending great effort to find these motivated sellers is a waste of time.

The truth is that you are better served by making aggressive (low) offers based on the value investing strategies outlined in Chapter 6. Don't worry about who your seller may be or his reason for selling. Sellers always have two reasons for selling: the reason they tell you and the real one.

The rule here is not that you should operate under some kind of unspoken rule of chivalry or charity. Take full advantage of the opportunities you discover in the marketplace. For example, if a vacant property has been languishing on the market for months and you are the only one bidding, how much more information do you need to have about the seller to know that you have the upper hand? You can learn the seller's motivation by the best test of all: their response to your low-ball offer.

The Role of Liquidity

Another theme repeated throughout this book is the importance of liquidity in surviving and profiting from a bust. Call it deep pockets, staying power, or a strong cash position, but liquidity means having access to sufficient cash to first survive any reversal and then be able to take advantage of any post-bust buying opportunities.

Chapters 7 and 8 went into the details of how to bolster your cash position to survive a downturn. This section suggests what to do with your cash to profit from a reversal.

Remember, not everyone who prepares for a bust will experience one. In fact, past real estate busts have been localized. Although many regions of the country are vulnerable, there may be only a few areas that actually have a reversal. This does not mean that those who prepared for a bust wasted their time. Those who set aside cash to prepare for a bust that never came to their neighborhood will be well positioned to capitalize on opportunities in any area that did experience a downturn.

Creating a Vulture Fund

In a healthy real estate market, the best real estate is often not available for sale at any price. There are certain trophy properties that, owing to either their unique locations or their exceptional architecture, are simply irreplaceable. Because of their quality attributes, these properties are consistently in demand, resulting in higher cash flow and easier management than typically experienced. These elite properties may be available for sale only under circumstances of distress.

Choice properties can range from the office tower with the elite address to the ornate home in your neighborhood that never comes available for sale that you've always admired. The point is that in a downturn, not only may bargains be available on many properties, but some unique buying opportunities may present themselves that may not have existed alternatively.

The lesson then is to be prepared. Astute real estate investors such as Chicagoan Sam Zell have formed real estate vulture funds to take advantage of such opportunities in the past. You may not have the financial capacity of a Sam Zell, but you can still form a vulture fund of your own.

The best way to proceed is on your own with your own cash reserves. You can act more quickly alone and you have no one to answer to. But if your cash is inadequate, consider pooling your funds with other partners.

Chapter 12 explores some partnership pitfalls. For now, just understand that each partner's role should be clearly understood. The best partnerships are those where the other partners are dependent upon and confident in your real estate investing expertise.

One logical question is where to find these partners. The answer is to network. Real estate always carries a certain mystique. In good times, investors want to join the party. In hard times, people would like to get in on the bargains, but they may be afraid to act alone. That's where you come in.

Real estate should be your topic of conversation everywhere you go. Be sure to mention your desire to form partnerships with your CPA, with your attorney, and with fellow members of your local apartment association or investment club. Your CPA or attorney may want to become your partner or they may know of a client who would.

Regardless of whether you act alone or with partners, an important consideration to keep in mind is that you will need cash reserves not only for making the acquisition, but also for surviving some lean times prior to recovery.

Any real estate you buy under distressed circumstances is at best likely to be suffering from deferred maintenance. More likely, the property may need an entire facelift to successfully reposition the asset to be competitive in a leaner market. Finally, any acquisition made to exploit a market timing strategy must be made with the knowledge that perfect market timing is rare. You must have the staying power to wait for recovery that may be more distant than you had thought.

CHAPTER 11

Signs of Spring: When to Start Buying After a Crash

To know when to buy again after a crash, you first need to have a thorough understanding of how real estate markets react to market corrections and contractions. Real estate markets tend to be "sticky." That is to say that prices do not fall overnight. It takes time for real estate markets to find a new equilibrium once supply and demand factors have changed.

Real estate is not like the stock market. Investors buy stocks with the clear understanding that they could lose money. Most property owners have a clear, fixed expectation that their real estate will at least maintain its value, if not increase. Therefore, in the face of a downturn, property owners can just wait.

Liquidity in the stock market facilitates panic selling. Real estate owners may feel equal panic, but the opportunity to act impulsively on that emotion just isn't there.

Probably the most fundamental characteristic that separates real estate from other investments is that real estate is not entirely an investment. Real estate is also a consumer good. There is no immediate status to be gained by owning 1,000 shares of a particular stock, but owning the right home in the right location says that you have arrived. Even if real estate is not a status symbol, people still need a place to live and work. As we saw in Chapter 7, some homeowners who can will try to ride out the bust, even continuing to make mortgage payments on homes that are no longer worth what is owed against them.

The long-term nature of commercial leases can help blunt an immediate response to negative price pressure. Stores may close, but if a corporate parent backs the lease and the corporation remains in business, the corporation will still have to pay rent on the vacant store. Similarly, a large office tenant may lay off scores of workers, but as long as the company remains in business, it will have to honor its lease, even if the result is that the company has more space than it needs.

The result of these circumstances is real estate prices will not react quickly to changes in demand. At various stages of a real estate crash, prices may have declined substantially without having bottomed out. The question then becomes how to know when the market is showing signs of recovery.

The Role of Employment in a Recovery

Since a decline in employment is the factor most likely to trigger a crash, sustained recovery in real estate markets will almost always be marked by recovery in employment. Review the Projecting Employment and Income section in Chapter 4 to complete an assessment of future local conditions.

The direction of employment is more important than any particular degree of unemployment. For example, a sustained unemployment rate of 10 percent could be good news if previously unemployment was hovering around 12 percent.

The Role of Population in a Recovery

In the southern California real estate crash of the early 1990s, there was a significant loss of population as individuals fled the area for better opportunities. This trend has since reversed itself and a new boom has been the result.

Population gains are not a prerequisite for recovery, but sustained population and household growth will result in restoration to a damaged real estate economy. Review the techniques in Chapter 4 to determine the prospects for population and household growth.

The Role of Interest Rates in a Recovery

Often, a decline in interest rates alone can be enough to lift a depressed real estate market out of recession. However, we are unlikely to experience this phenomenon in the next real estate cycle. Most long-term forecasts for interest rates predict stable and historically moderate interest rates, but rates that are higher than they are today.

These rates will be sufficiently low to sustain a vibrant real estate market over the long term. However, interest rates themselves are not likely to rescue a failing real estate market in this real estate cycle. In fact just the opposite may be true. The pressure of even gently increasing interest rates may aggravate markets where affordability is already an issue.

The Interaction of Interest Rates, Employment, and Income in a Recovery

One of the most important indices in a recovery is the Housing Affordability Index (HAI) discussed in Chapter 4. This index measures the ability of the median income to afford a median priced home. A score of 100 means that median incomes can exactly afford the median home. Scores below 100 reflect increasing difficulty in affording the median home.

In a crash, at least some affordability is restored. Therefore, in a recovery, the HAI may again start to decline. Use the HAI to chart whether the bottom has been reached or the market has established only a temporary plateau before further losses.

For example, the present HAI score for the West is 83.6, a remarkably low figure. A real estate crash would drive the index back toward 100. The index may never reach 100 before a recovery begins, but if the index is still below 100, wait until the index actually declines before investing.

The Role of Leasing Incentives in Commercial Real Estate

In a soft market, effective rents will decline even if nominal rents remain the same. The reason is that landlords will begin to include free rent, tenant improvements, and other incentives as an inducement for new tenants. These kinds of incentives are typically a matter of negotiation for most commercial real estate, and therefore harder to discern for the casual observer. A good commercial leasing agent will be aware of the nature of the additional accommodations landlords are making to attract tenants.

The role of incentives is most clearly witnessed in the residential sector of commercial real estate. For this discussion, residential commercial real estate includes apartment buildings five units or larger.

When apartment rents soften, landlords start giving away free rent, color TVs, MP3 players, even trips to Jamaica and similar locales, in addition to other promotional items, as an inducement to new tenants. These incentives are more easily discerned because apartment communities will boldly declare them in advertisements, signs, and banners. The result is that while nominal street rents may remain the same, effective rents go down.

One of the first signs of recovery is when these incentives start to go away. The incentives will disappear before rents begin to increase.

Signs of Recovery in Commercial
Real Estate Markets

We have already discussed how some companies may remain in business, stuck with unneeded excess space. These businesses will not just absorb these losses without taking action. The result is an increase in sublet space in the marketplace.

There is always a supply of space available for sublease in any market. Even in a healthy market, circumstances change. A business may outgrow its space prior to the expiration of a lease. Growth may dictate a change of address even if it means continuing to pay rent on the old space. Similarly, some businesses fail even in good times. If a corporate parent or similarly strong personal guaranty backs the lease, rent will still be paid on vacant space.

Therefore, in a downturn, there will be more space available for sublease. However, not all space lends itself well to being sublet. The industrial tenant may lay off entire shifts of workers, going from 24-hour operation to just one or two shifts. This tenant may still occupy 100 percent of the space, but be at as little as one-third of capacity.

Similarly, while a large office tenant occupying several floors of an office building may be able to consolidate and vacate entire floors of a building, other businesses will not be able to reorganize to make available sufficient quantities of contiguous space for a sublease. Consequently, there is always excess capacity in commercial real estate markets once a recovery begins. The local economy will be able to sustain some expansion without absorbing vacant space.

Therefore, a decline in available sublease space is not just a sign of recovery in a commercial real estate market, it is a *leading* indicator. When vacancy rates start to decline, recovery has already been under way for some time.

Obviously, declining vacancy rates also indicate a commercial market in recovery stages. As commercial markets recover, sublet and vacant space will be absorbed, rents will increase, and new construction will begin, loosely in that order.

To understand the pulse in the marketplace, keep in touch with a strong commercial leasing agent. These agents will be the first to sense a turn in the marketplace as inquiries for space begin to increase.

The next section deals with signs of recovery in residential real estate, but many of the indicators are also relevant to commercial property as well.

Signs of Recovery in Residential Real Estate Markets

The first signs of recovery in residential single-family homes will occur in the leading indicators, days on the market, months of supply, and mortgage applications. These indicators were discussed in Chapter 4. Before prices begin to recover, homes will be selling more quickly, the months of supply will begin to decline, and mortgage applications will increase.

You may be able to access data for these indicators by using the techniques and sources described in Chapter 4, but if not, a real estate agent should be able to discern decreasing days on the market and declining inventories of homes for sale. A mortgage broker or bank lending officer should be able to give you an idea of the direction of mortgage applications. Title insurance reps will also be among the first to experience an uptick in sales volume.

In Chapter 4, we noted that an inventory of between 5.5 and 6.5 months of supply reflected a sound, vibrant real estate market. Understand that you do not need to wait until inventories have declined to these levels before starting to invest. In fact, those getting in at the beginning of the recovery will do the best. Just know which direction the indicators are headed and invest before they return to normal levels.

Signs of Recovery in Residential Construction

Some residential new construction is sold much like a new car is sold. There are two kinds of residential new construction, spec housing and custom housing. Spec housing is built on speculation of finding a buyer. The builder decides on what home to build on the lot, and further decides which upgrades or improvements to include in the home.

In custom homes, the buyer may order a home from an assortment of model floor plans the builder has available. The buyer may make modification to the floor plan of the "base" home, adding extra rooms or garage space. The buyer may additionally make upgrades to the finishes of the base home. For example, the base home often does not include a paved driveway. A home buyer may elect to upgrade the carpet included in the base price to a better grade of carpet or to a different flooring entirely, such as a hardwood floor.

Builders love the upgrades that a home buyer may choose for a custom home because these upgrades are usually subject to higher profit margins. In a soft real estate market, builders will start to throw in upgrades to attract buyers.

Some builders include certain upgrades as standard in their homes as a way of differentiating themselves from other builders, and other builders toy with upgrade inclusion as a way of gaining additional market share, so some upgrades are always going to be thrown in by some builders even in a seller's market. For changes in this phenomenon to be meaningful to you, you or someone you know such as a real estate agent would have to be close enough to the new construction marketplace to be able to discern these changes.

Strategies for Capitalizing on the Recovery

The key to profiting from a crash is to buy just before the recovery becomes widely obvious. Remember that real estate markets can remain in the doldrums for decades. The real estate market in Japan is just such an example.

In a crash, vacancy will be widespread and effective rental rates will be falling. It is important to consider the mindset of a seller to know when to buy. First, keep in mind that a crash will not occur all at once. Real estate markets move more slowly. The market will cool, and then turn.

At first, real estate owners may not discern their vulnerability. Long-term leases will at first blunt the impact of a crash. However, as leases expire or as businesses fail entirely, rent payments will cease and space will remain vacant. In short, some time will be required for the market to reach bottom.

Some real estate owners will be able to sustain periods of negative cash flow or unemployment by relying on their reserves. Therefore, it takes more time before sellers become truly desperate.

While all of this is occurring, you may be tempted to buy. After all, you may be seeing prices not experienced in a decade. However, lower prices alone should not be the sole impetus in a buying decision. Look at the data and indicators outlined in this book. Make an educated guess at whether the market has hit bottom.

It is important not to buy in too soon. Whenever you buy, buy under the assumption that you will have to weather a period of difficulty. Perfect market timing plays are rare. Deep pockets are a must or you may become a motivated seller yourself.

By waiting, you may be able to take advantage of increasingly desperate sellers. Even if you wait too long to catch the exact bottom, there will still be plenty of profits available in the early and obvious stages of a recovery. For the investor with limited staying power, having the patience to wait until recovery is certain is a must or you may pay a high price for any mistakes you make in timing the recovery.

CREATIVE FINANCING WHEN NO ONE WANTS TO LEND: DESCRIBING THE CONDITIONS THAT ARE LIKELY TO PREVAIL UNDER ILLIQUID LENDING POLICIES

One of the problems with real estate busts is that lenders stop lending. Without financing, buying property becomes difficult, if not impossible. Despite the lack of regular financing, there are still ways to make deals.

The good news about lenders is that they will start lending again sometime in the future. They have to do that to stay in business. Nonperforming loans are pushed into foreclosure. Good loans are paid off, and their book of business begins to dwindle. To uphold profits, they have to lend again. In the early stages of recovery, they will be more choosy, but as markets begin to improve, they lend more and are willing to take more chances. Until that happens, you can always use creative financing to acquire properties that make sense to buy.

What Is Creative Financing?

Traditional financing is what we know. You want to buy a $200,000 home. You ask the bank for a loan of $160,000. The other $40,000 is your down payment, from your funds, on deposit in the bank or in equity in a property you are selling. You have enough money to pay for the closing costs. Your income and employment situation allow you to qualify for the loan, and you have few other monthly obligations. You have excellent credit. The property appraised for $210,000. It's an easy loan for a bank to make. At closing, you give the seller $200,000. You own the property, and you make your monthly payments to the lender. It is a typical real estate purchase and loan scenario. This is traditional financing, a mortgage that any lender should willingly make.

Creative financing is when you use other than traditional financing to buy and control real estate. There is nothing wrong with creative financing. It is just different from traditional financing.

Creative financing is used to buy and trade real estate every day, regardless of whether the real estate market is up or down. There is nothing illegal or dishonest about creative financing. However, in down times, creative financing is used more often.

Everything from owner financing to borrowing money from the real estate agent falls under the broad umbrella of creative financing. Keep in mind that regular or traditional financing is not the only way to buy real estate. Many of these techniques follow.

No Money Down Financing

Author Robert Allen published a book called *Nothing Down* in 1979. Because of the media-fueled popularity of the book, there was a flurry of people seeking to purchase real estate with nothing down.

As with anything else successful, others have followed in the footprints of *Nothing Down*. Following its publication and success, many others hawked the idea of buying real estate with no money down. Today, there is a new generation of gurus selling books, CDs, and seminars. To maintain the sale of their training materials and seminar seats, the real estate gurus promote creative ideas to buy real estate with no money down.

Some of the ideas are old and stale. In the real world, it is doubtful if they work. For example, one of the gurus promotes the idea of acquiring properties with assumable mortgages. It's a great idea, but impractical in today's world.

Assumable mortgages are now nearly gone from the marketplace. Years ago, it was the norm to allow a mortgage to be assumable by anyone else. Things have changed. For the past decade or more, most loan notes included a *due-on-sale* clause. This clause inserted in loan contracts limits or eliminates the ability for anyone to assume mortgages.

The due-on-sale clause typically states, "The Lender may, at its option, declare immediately due and payable all sums secured by the Mortgage upon the sale or transfer, without the Lender's prior written consent, of all or any part of the Real Property, or any interest in the Real Property." As you can see, even the term "due-on-sale" is misleading. The contract language says the mortgage may be declared due if there is any transfer of any interest in the property, and not just the sale of the real estate.

If you can find an assumable mortgage, it is likely to be older, and have only a small principal balance. Following the advice of present day gurus, you could offer the seller a second mortgage for the balance of the purchase price greater than the first mortgage assumed. That would make this technically a "nothing down" deal, where you purchased the property without any down payment. The problem is finding assumable mortgages, and then finding a seller willing to carry a large second mortgage. Of course, it is possible. So is buying the winning ticket of next week's PowerBall lottery. It is possible, but not probable.

Keep in mind that many creative financing ideas or concepts touted are possible, but are unlikely to work in the real world.

Seller Financing

As traditional lenders adopt increasingly stringent financing criteria, owners motivated to sell become more willing to consider purchase offers that propose seller financing.

Seller financing is uncomplicated when the property is free and clear. When seller financing is involved, the seller may or may not require a down payment. The seller may or may not require a credit check. The terms of the loan (interest rate, amortization, time to pay off the loan, etc.) are negotiated between you and the seller. When you finally agree to terms, you can move quickly to closing.

Remember to make sure to obtain title insurance. You do not want to be buying any property without assurance of having clear title. Have your attorney prepare the paperwork and close the transaction.

Seller financing becomes complicated when the seller does not own the property outright. Even though the seller might agree to seller financing, you could be stepping on quicksand.

Wrap Around Mortgages

When the seller does not own the property free and clear, one solution is to create a wrap around mortgage. The idea is that a new mortgage "wraps" around the current mortgage.

To understand this concept better, consider this example:

Property value: $100,000.

Financing in place: $85,000.

Seller willing to finance $15,000 equity.

The seller accepts a mortgage from you for $100,000 (a "nothing down" deal). Each month you make your payment to the seller. The seller then makes the payment to the mortgage company that holds the original mortgage of $85,000.

Why would a seller agree to do this? Sometimes, it is because of a spread. For example, you agreed to pay 8 percent interest on the $100,000 loan, but the $85,000 loan is at an interest rate of only 6 percent. The seller keeps the difference of the 2 percent spread each month.

Sounds like a workable plan. Sounded good to Patricia and Patrick, too.

REAL CASE SCENARIO

Pat and Pat is what their friends called them. Patricia, a forever smiling waitress who often worked 16-hour days for the extra cash, and her husband Patrick, an auto mechanic, bought their first home using a wrap around mortgage.

It was a modest house, the couple's first, but still their dream house. It was a decent home where they planned to raise their three children.

They had put down $7,000 to make their wrap around mortgage financing work. It had taken them years to get that amount of money saved.

After buying their home, it took 14 months before Pat and Pat realized they were in deep trouble. There was the notice tacked on the front door. It was an order to vacate the property.

Each month, they had made their payment, on time, and as agreed to the seller. Pat and Pat even had cancelled checks to prove they had made their payments.

The seller had indeed cashed the checks. He kept every cent, never paying the original mortgage. By this time, he had received Pat and Pat's $7,000 down payment, and 14 months of their mortgage payments. The total was nearly $20,000.

Pat and Pat lost everything. Sure, they sued the seller, who filed bankruptcy (seems he had a gambling problem). After being court-ordered to vacate the property, Pat and Pat moved to a small apartment.

Pat and Pat made several mistakes. They trusted the seller to be honest and fair. They should have paid a loan servicing company, directing their payment to be sent in two portions. The underlying mortgage would have been paid by the servicing company, with the remaining balance being sent to the seller. They could have even paid the underlying mortgage directly. They did not have the transaction recorded. Their biggest mistake of all was not using an attorney to oversee the closing.

An unrecorded wrap around mortgage is often used as a way to beat or get around a due-on-sale clause. The underlying premise is there would be no way for the lender to know about the un-recorded sale, so there would be no opportunity for the lender to exercise the due-on-sale clause.

Some real estate gurus advocate unrecorded wrap around mort-gages as an effective buying strategy. A recent real estate book about property flipping published by a major publishing company cheerfully proclaims that it is not a criminal act to transfer a prop-erty while ignoring the due-on-sale clause.

That is true. Ignoring the due-on-sale clause is not a crime. It is a contract violation for the seller. You (the buyer) are not violating the contract between the original lender and the seller. You won't go to jail, but you could—just like Pat and Pat—become the victim of the lender's foreclosure on the seller.

Anyone advising you to enter into an unrecorded land contract or wrap around mortgage in an effort to avoid a due-on-sale clause is dispensing horrible advice. Unrecorded land contracts make lit-tle sense for a buyer or seller. There is no logical reason not to record the contract, except to avoid detection. That in itself should set off alarm bells in your mind.

A due-on-sale clause does not have to negate the opportunity to structure a deal with seller financing. You just need to approach the existing lender with your plans to gain permission from them to allow the deal to move forward. Your plan may meet with success, particularly if the seller is not released from liability on the original indebtedness.

When the seller is not released from liability on the underlying financing on the property with a due-on-sale clause, the seller may have a problem qualifying for another home loan. The current mortgage on the property could curtail the buying power of the seller in acquiring another mortgage.

Properly Using Land Contracts

If there is no underlying debt or if the lender is willing to release the seller from the due-on-sale clause, land contracts may be creatively employed to acquire real estate. A land contract purchase works like this:

1. You agree to buy the property for a specific price.

2. You negotiate all of the financing terms with the seller, including the amount of down payment, rate of interest, schedule of payments (amortization), and any balloon payments.

3. If there is an underlying debt, provisions should be made to be certain that payments are continued on this existing debt.

4. Monthly payments may include provisions for establishing an escrow to insure payment of property taxes and insurance.

It is not unusual for sellers to be interested in getting cashed out of the land contract before the loan is entirely paid or fully amortized. Such a desire necessitates a balloon payment. Balloon payments can be dangerous.

One of the reasons for entering into a land contract is because conventional financing is not available. The underlying assumption is that by the time the balloon payment comes due, conventional financing will be available or the borrower will be unable to perform. Therefore, an imperative is to defer any obligation to make large balloon payments to a time in the future when you can be certain that conventional financing will be available.

You may want to build some kind of extension option into your land contract in case you are not able to obtain conventional financing as originally planned. Sometimes an increase in the interest rate or a smaller reduction in the principal balance is enough to induce a seller to agree to a land contract extension. Just make sure you negotiate these extensions when you purchase the property, long before you ever need them.

The following is an outline of a sample land contract purchase:

Buyer and seller agree to a land contract purchase of a $100,000 property.

The buyer makes a $10,000 down payment to the seller.

The $90,000 balance is amortized for 30 years, at 7 percent interest. The monthly payment is $598.77.

The buyer must pay off the land contract within 3 years. Therefore, assuming the buyer makes all payments as agreed, the buyer faces a balloon payment of the entire remaining loan balance of $87,054 no later than the thirty-sixth month following closing.

When a land contract agreement is used, it should be recorded.

An attorney should close the transaction.

The land contract should allow you to take control of a property quickly and easily.

Renting with Option to Buy

A fast and simple way to control real estate is to rent it with an option to buy it. You simply rent the property, but with a slight difference: You have an option to buy the property as well. A portion of your rent may or may not be applied to the agreed purchase price.

For example, you might agree to rent a property for $900 a month, and $100 of your rent applies to the purchase price. You and the owner agree to a purchase of $97,000. If you rent the property for 10 months, you will need $96,000 to purchase the property (10 payments with $100 credit = $1,000. Purchase price of $97,000 − $1,000 credit = $96,000 balance).

The property owner cannot sell the property to anyone other than you for the agreed-to price during the rent option period. You can sell the property to someone else—at a profit—during the option period. If it took you the 10 months to sell the property, and you sold it for $110,000 after some cleaning and fixing, you would turn a profit. Consider these computations:

$110,000 sales price from your buyer.

$97,000 paid by you to property owner.

$13,000 gross profit.

$8,000 rent paid (10 payments of $900 − $100 credit = $800).

$5,000 net profit.

Of course, the sooner you sell the property, the higher your profit. If you cannot sell it, you lost only your rent.

During tougher times, like when a real estate bubble has broken, a property owner is more likely to accept a rent-to-own deal when they need the monthly income to make their mortgage payments.

Your rent check can cover their mortgage payment, insurance, taxes, and so on. Your rent-to-own offer takes over the responsibility of the maintenance of the property. The rent-to-own strategy may work with a harried investor sinking deeper into debt each month.

You do not need more than a month's rent to make this deal work. It will often work best with property that needs a cosmetic update and cleaning. Absentee out of town property owners may be more likely to agree to a rent-to-own proposal.

Creative Borrowing

Sometimes the deal can be made by using creative borrowing techniques. You may need to ask the seller to hold a note for a second mortgage.

CASE STUDY: (ALMOST) NO MONEY DOWN

By David J. Decker

Years ago, I bought a 32-unit apartment building with a very low down payment. There was little wrong with the property, but for some reason, it had languished on the market for more than a year. I was sure that the rents on the unique loft floor plans could be increased substantially while I made only minor cosmetic improvements.

I was short of cash and in no position to make a large down payment. The deal I proposed was more straightforward than creative. I merely suggested the seller hold about a 16 percent second mortgage, while I obtained a new first mortgage of 80 percent of the purchase price. The transfer of security deposits and other closing credits reduced my 4 percent down payment even further.

The first mortgage was difficult to find. Finally the financing was obtained and the deal closed. Rents were increased substantially, and the property provided strong cash flow.

The only sad part of the story is that I had to sell the property a few years later to be sure that I could meet the balloon payment obligation on the remaining balance of the second mortgage. Even so, I was able to sell the building at a profit.

It is also possible to borrow money from the real estate agent. An agent may be willing to leave part (or all) of the commission on the table for a later payment. There are also nontraditional loan sources throughout your community. They are sometimes called "hard money loans." Another name is "private lender." These people are private individuals in your community who have the cash and are willing to lend it for loans secured by real estate.

They probably do not advertise. You have to find them by networking. Local insurance agents, certified public accountants, real estate attorneys, and title companies may know of people in your local area who make these loans.

Private lenders will want a reasonable return on their money. They are not going to lend their money for less than they can get with it safely tucked away in a bank. You may need to offer points. They are less likely to make a long-term financing commitment. Private lenders work best for properties that you are buying and selling quickly. The less time you need their money, the more likely they will be agreeable to lending it.

Forming Partnerships

Another way to find financing is to form partnerships to acquire investment properties. Partnerships can be set up any way that the partners agree. It does not need to be a 50–50 relationship.

REAL CASE SCENARIO

One real estate partnership is set up this way: There are two partners. The first partner receives the first $435,000 of income. The next $200,000 goes to the second partner. After $635,000, the first partner receives 42.5 percent while the second partner receives 57.5 percent.

Who came up with this agreement? The two partners. Just remember the formal agreement of profit split is whatever the partners agree.

A partner or partners can legally form a partnership or corporation for conducting business. That business can acquire one or many properties.

Partnerships can be a great thing or a source of heartache. To make certain that your venture is successful, be sure that each partner adds a vital ingredient to the partnership. One partner may have the money, while the other partner may have the real estate expertise and handle the day-to-day management. Each partner's role and responsibilities should be clearly defined.

It's great to do business with your family or friends, but apply the same rules that you would with a stranger. Each partner has to have something essential to add. Even then, have a partnership exit strategy. Craft a dispute resolution mechanism before you ever think you will need it. Agree to binding arbitration or a similar remedy in the event that the partnership breaks down and the members can no longer agree.

This partnership does not need to be on paper. But it should be. Any deal worthy of two or more honorable people going together to do business should be reduced to writing.

When you start thinking about partnerships, keep in mind that things can go wrong. You need to discuss with your partners how to undo a partnership, when one of the partners wants out. That happens too often.

Formal partnerships should be put together with an attorney. A good legal mind can guide you through the process and can help the partners decide how they want to structure the partnership, so everything being done is in all parties' best interests. You want to discuss the correct way to form and dissolve a partnership, and consider tax ramifications as well as expenses of the partnership. You always want to understand fully your duties, obligations, and responsibilities of being a partner in the partnership.

Partnerships can help you acquire funds needed to purchase real estate, especially multiple partners. Once you have completed deals and made money for your partners, finding additional partners will be easier.

CASE STUDY: PARTNERSHIP SUCCESS AND FAILURES

By David J. Decker

Early in my career, I seemed to make a living brokering real estate deals for dissolving partnerships. Some dissolutions were friendly, others not so friendly. I remember one 25-year partnership ending in a bout of fisticuff. I have seen families destroyed over ventures gone wrong.

I have known other partnerships that have never had more than a handshake agreement, yet the union has endured for decades and scores of transactions. From these experiences, I would give any partnership odds of about 50–50 for enduring success.

In tough times, conventional money is harder to find from traditional lenders. This often occurs at a time when great opportunities in the real estate market are available. Be prepared to acquire property with alternative methods and sources of funds to buy property offered for sale at fire sale prices.

CHAPTER 13

The Best Way to Time the Market Rebound: Use Options

W hat if you could buy real estate without much money? And let's make it even more enticing: without credit checks, qualifying for loans, or paying costs, either. The answer is simple: Use real estate options to acquire properties. You can control vast amounts of real estate quickly and easily.

Real estate gurus sometimes tout using options, but they often do not get the facts straight about the effective use of options, or how they work. Because of the misinformation, many do not understand when to use a real estate option. When you fully understand options, you can use them to create leverage, reduce risk, and conserve capital while holding the controlling interest in undervalued properties.

With a properly prepared option, you take control of undervalued properties with immediate resale profit potential. You can then sell either the property or the option, quickly receiving your profit.

A real estate option grants control of the property without your buying it. By holding the option on the real estate, you have the exclusive right either to buy the property or not to buy it. The final choice is yours. The option also permits you to sell or assign the option to someone else.

A real estate option creates an *exclusive* right. That right means that no one else can buy or sell the property during the entire term that your option remains in effect. No one can buy or sell the property without first satisfying the option.

Many investors do not understand the mechanics of using real estate options, or if they do, they do not use them. Options are one of the most powerful tools in real estate investing. Many supersuccessful investors routinely use real estate options for maximum leverage in acquiring real estate.

Before you can successfully use real estate options to acquire properties, you need to understand their use in your state. Because a real estate option is a legally binding contract between you and the seller, you need to verify its legal status in the state where you are investing. This means a consultation with a competent real estate attorney.

Your attorney will be able to explain to you how options work in your state. You will need to understand the differences between a real estate option and a lease option. In a lease option, you are renting the property with the option to buy. Technically, you have a leasehold estate. With a real estate option, you have the option to buy without the leasehold estate.

Your attorney will also provide you with the essential elements of a valid real estate option for your state.

On the following pages, a representative real estate option agreement is shown. It is placed here only for educational purposes, and is not intended for use in any or all states. You should not use this option agreement. Rather, obtain a valid agreement from your attorney.

OPTION TO PURCHASE

THIS OPTION AGREEMENT entered into this ___ day of _____, 20___, between the SELLER, _____, and the BUYER, _____, hereby grants to the Buyer an option to purchase (OPTION) for the property known as [Street Address]

_____

in the _____ of _____, County of _____, State of _____, more particularly described as (insert legal description): _____

_____

_____

_____

_____

_____

Option Terms

Within ____ days of acceptance of this Option, a nonrefundable option fee of $_____ will be paid by the Buyer. If the Option is exercised, $_____ of the option fee shall be applied to the purchase price at closing. The Option may only be exercised by delivering written notice to the Seller by no later than midnight of _____.

The Option may be extended until _____, by an additional nonrefundable extension fee payment of $_____ to Seller by no later than _____. If the Option is exercised, $_____ of the option extension fee shall be applied to the purchase price at closing.

This Option may be recorded.

This Option is void unless a copy signed by both Buyer and Seller is delivered to the Buyer before _____.

Purchase Terms

If this Option is exercised as described under the Option Terms, the terms of the purchase shall be as follows:

Purchase Price $_____

Additional Items included in the purchase price: _____

_____

Items not included in the purchase price: _____

_____

Title shall be conveyed with merchantable title by warranty deed (or as otherwise agreed in writing) free and clear of all liens and encumbrances, except: recorded municipal and utility easements, recorded building and use restrictions and covenants, municipal and zoning ordinances, general taxes levied in the year of closing and _____.

Seller shall deliver title evidence in an owner's policy of title insurance in an amount equal to the purchase price issued by a licensed insurer authorized to write title insurance in the state where the subject property is located. Seller shall bear the cost of providing the title insurance. A commitment for title insurance shall be delivered to Buyer at least two business days prior to closing, showing merchantable title subject only to appropriate customary title insurance requirements and exceptions and liens to be paid out of closing proceeds. Buyer may notify Seller in writing of objections to title up until the date of closing. If such notification is received, Seller shall have up to 14 days to cure any objection and the closing date shall be changed as needed for this purpose. If the Seller fails to cure the objections, the Seller shall so notify the Buyer in writing. Upon receipt of such notice, the Buyer shall have 5 days to provide a written waiver of the objections, and if so provided, the time for closing shall be extended accordingly. If the Buyer does not so waive the objections as described, this Option shall become null and void. Providing title evidence acceptable for closing does not terminate the Seller's obligation to deliver merchantable title to the Buyer.

Seller shall assign seller's rights under any leases and transfer all security deposits and prepaid rents to Buyer at closing.

The following shall be prorated at closing: fuel, real estate taxes, rents, private and municipal charges, property owner's association assessments, and _____.

Occupancy of the premises shall be given to the Buyer at closing subject to tenant's rights.

Representations and Warranties: Seller warrants and represents to Buyer that as of the date of this Option, Seller has no notice or knowledge of any conditions adversely affecting the property, except as follows: _____. Conditions adversely affecting the property shall be understood to include:

1. Completed or pending reassessment of the subject property for property tax purposes.
2. Repair orders issued by government agencies or court order.
3. Any land divisions of the subject property for which required approvals had not been obtained.
4. Violation of any laws regarding or regulating the use of the subject property.
5. Violation of any environmental laws regarding the subject property.
6. Any portion of the subject property being in a shoreland zoning area, wetland, or 100 year floodplain, according to any government laws.
7. Any adverse condition constituting a health or safety hazard at the subject property.
8. Septic tanks, cisterns, 100 KV or higher high voltage electric, steel natural gas lines, or similar systems on the subject property that do not service the subject property.

9. Public improvements, planned or commenced, which may result in special assessments or otherwise materially and adversely affect the subject property or its use.

10. Conditions which would adversely affect the cost of building on the subject property including, but not limited to, unstable fill, subsurface foundations, disposal or dumping on the subject property of toxic or hazardous materials, high water table, or materially adverse soil conditions such as low load bearing capacity or excessive rock conditions.

11. Underground storage tanks (USTs) or aboveground storage tanks (ASTs) on the subject property for storage of flammable or combustible liquids or materials including but not limited to gasoline, heating oil or similar substances which are currently or which were previously located on the subject property.

12. Other conditions or circumstances which would materially and adversely impact the value of the subject property to a reasonable person with knowledge of the kind and type of the condition or circumstance.

Seller shall notify Buyer of any adverse conditions inconsistent with the above 12 representations which arise after this Option is granted but prior to it being exercised.

If the property was built before 1978, Buyer and Seller should enter into a separate Lead Base Paint disclosure agreement and Seller should provide Buyer with a copy of the government pamphlet *Protecting Your Family From Lead In Your Home*.

Seller shall maintain the subject property until closing in materially the same condition as of the date the Option is exercised, excepting ordinary wear and tear.

If the subject property is damaged prior to closing in an amount determined to be not more than 5% of the purchase price, Seller shall restore the subject property and return it to materially the same condition that it was on the Option exercise date. If the damage is determined to have exceeded 5% of the purchase price, Seller shall notify Buyer in writing of the damage and this Option may be withdrawn by the Buyer. If withdrawn as provided herein, all Option fees and Option Extension fees paid by the Buyer shall be refunded to the Buyer. Should Buyer elect to exercise this Option despite damage exceeding 5% of the purchase price, either: (1) the Seller shall return the subject property to the same material condition existing prior to exercising this Option, excepting ordinary wear and tear, OR (2) the Buyer shall be the beneficiary of any insurance proceeds awarded relating to the property damage, in addition to a credit at closing in the amount of the deductible on the Seller's insurance policy.

Any special assessments for work levied or commenced prior to the date this Option is exercised shall be paid by the Seller by closing. The Buyer shall pay any other special assessments.

Time is of the essence as to deadlines and dates excepting: _____.

Default Remedies

1. Default by Buyer. If the Buyer exercises the Option but fails to proceed with the closing of the purchase of the subject property pursuant to the terms and provisions as contained herein, Seller shall be entitled to retain the Option Fee as liquidated damages and shall have no further recourse against the Buyer.
2. Default by Seller. If the Seller fails to close the sale of the subject property pursuant to the terms and provisions of this Option, the Buyer shall be entitled to either sue for specific performance of the real estate purchase or terminate this Option and sue for money damages.

Notices

All notices, waivers, demands and/or consents provided for in this Option shall be in writing and shall be delivered to the parties by facsimile, by hand or by United States Mail with postage pre-paid or by any other recognized commercial carrier. Such notices shall be deemed to have been served on the date faxed or mailed, delivery charges or postage pre-paid. All such notices shall be addressed as follows:

To the Seller:

Name: _____

Address:_____

_____

Phone: (___)___-_____

Fax: (___)___-_____

To the Buyer:

Name: _____

Address:_____

_____

Phone: (___)___-_____

Fax: (___)___-_____

Signatures

This Option is an enforceable contract.

BUYER:

Name: _____

Print Name: _____

Date:_____

SELLER:

Name: _____

Print Name: _____

Date:_____

BUYER:

Name: _____

Print Name: _____

Date:_____

SELLER:

Name: _____

Print Name: _____

Date:_____

Understanding the Option

To understand the technical workings of a real estate option, you must first understand the terms or words used throughout the agreement. The key terminology is:

- $ *Exercise of option* occurs when the *buyer* notifies the *seller* in writing that the *buyer* decided to exercise their *real estate option* and purchase the property under terms of the option.

- $ *Expiration of option* occurs when a *buyer* fails to exercise the option within the *option period* stated in the *real estate option* agreement.

- $ *Option consideration* is the amount of money paid by a *buyer* to purchase a real estate option from a *seller*.

- $ *Option period* is the specific time stated in the agreement while the *real estate option* remains in effect.

- $ *Real estate option* is bought by a *buyer* from the *seller*: What has been bought is the option, which consists of the exclusive, unrestricted, and irrevocable right to purchase a property at a specific purchase price within a specified period.

- $ *Real estate option agreement* is the document signed by both parties intending to be legally bound to the terms and conditions.

Now with an understanding of the general terminology used in a real estate option agreement, it's time to look closer at an actual agreement. A real estate option agreement is unilateral. The one-sided agreement binds only the seller. The property owner is bound and promised the exclusive, unrestricted, and irrevocable right and option to purchase the property to the buyer. The real estate option agreement does not impose any obligation on the buyer to exercise the option, and there is no requirement to purchase the property. The buyer buys this exclusive right from the seller, paying for it with a nonrefundable payment.

Once the buyer exercises the option to buy the property, the real estate option agreement becomes a bilateral contract. It now binds both parties to complete the transaction.

Each state has established laws as to when and how an equitable interest is created and passes from the seller to the buyer. This is why you must consult with a competent real estate lawyer practicing in the state where you want to acquire property.

The real estate option agreement is structured in most cases so the property owner continues paying all the costs of owning the property. This includes taxes, insurance, and maintenance. Since you do not own the property, you are not obligated to make any monthly loan payments. You also don't have to deal with tenants.

While your option is valid and binding, should the property owner sell the property to anyone else, you are entitled to damages. Your attorney can explain what you might be entitled to claim and receive within your jurisdiction.

The option allows you to lock in the price of the property, and you can then sell the option to another investor or someone interested in buying and using the property. As an investor, if you use options to control real estate, you are not spending money on closing costs. When you transfer the option to another, there are no fees or costs associated with the transfer. In other words, it costs nothing to transfer an option, whereas it costs thousands of dollars to transfer real estate.

How to Use Options

Getting started with real estate options is easy. The following section deals with how to employ options in any real estate market. The final section details how to employ options in a real estate crash.

There are three ways to profit from an option. One is to exercise your option because you believe the property has increased in value to warrant a purchase at what has now become a below market sale. The second profit opportunity is to just sell the option to another investor. Believe it or not, the third way to profit is by selling the option back to the seller. If the seller would like to be rid of the property and another buyer comes along during the term the option is in effect, the seller would not be able to take advantage of this alternative sale without first clearing your option rights. You may be able to sell your option rights back to the seller at a profit.

Once you have consulted your lawyer and understand how options work in your state, you can start making offers. It does not require a lot of cash. While you could offer thousands of dollars as an option fee, many investors offer only a token payment. One investor offers only $20, and has been successful in controlling properties that sold for $100,000. Another investor staples a $50 bill to the lease option agreement when presenting the offer to the property owner.

Options are a fast way to generate income. As soon as you have obtained the option, you start to market the property. As soon as you locate a buyer, you can generate quick cash. One investor structures his deals to make a minimum of $5,000 on each transaction. Another investor obtains options on properties that rehab investors buy. After getting the option in place, she e-mails her property to the investors. Based in New Jersey, she has been able to close deals in less than two weeks. She prices the properties with a $3,000 to $4,000 profit. While she does not want to be identified, she said her best month was 19 properties acquired and sold. And she is doing this part time while raising two children.

Real estate options are flexible. They can be used with all types of properties. This includes everything from land to single residential homes, multi-family units, apartment buildings, and commercial properties.

Remember that you specify the option period, which offers additional flexibility in controlling the property. In many cases, you may be able to extend the option period. Sometimes this can be done with no additional fee paid to the property owner.

In summary, using a real estate option is an ideal investment technique for anyone to use. Because options do not require much cash, you can begin investing quickly and easily. As a beginner to options, you need to locate properties, execute an option, and then start selling the property for more than your optioned price. It is that simple.

Employing Options in a Crash

As you learned in Chapter 1, today many real estate owners have expectations of continued robust growth in appreciation for the coming years. Remember, as you read in Chapter 10, these owners hold these beliefs even in the face of nearly constant questioning about the status of a real estate bubble and whether it will burst. It only takes a few years for a trend to become fixed in people's minds as the norm.

The same way that today's good times have become an assumed expectation, if bad times come, some owners will have a similar overreaction. Some will believe things will never get better.

Anytime investors have unrealistic expectations of the future, an opportunity is created for better informed players. That player in the know could be you.

The strategy is to use options in making a timing play in a recovering real estate market. The danger in any market timing move is that if your forecast is wrong, you could be stuck holding a property mired in a price plateau, or worse, still subject to further declines. Options remove the risk. With an option, you can lock in the upside potential without having to risk more than the option fee.

During the darkest hours of a real estate crash, some investors and real estate owners will view your option fee as found money. To exercise a cliche, it is always darkest before the dawn. Chapter 10 explored the mental reactions property owners may experience in a bust. To paraphrase, sellers will experience growing desperation if there is no relief from a real estate contraction.

Interestingly, the most desperate of sellers will not be candidates for an option. Their problems are too immediate to gamble on whether you will ever exercise your option. However, there will be those sellers who will not have your perspective for a brighter future. These individuals are option candidates.

There are several strategies for employing options under these circumstances:

1. *Option One:* You believe the market is poised for recovery. In this circumstance, you simply offer the owner an option for the property at a value more than the property is worth today. The key to this strategy is negotiating for as long an option period as possible. You make this gamble only if you have studied Chapter 4 in detail and have concluded that statistical evidence suggests a rebound.

2. *Option Two:* You have inside information. If you have inside information, you don't have to wait for a real estate crash to occur before profiting from your exclusive wisdom. Inside information might be the knowledge that water and sewer laterals will be extended to a specific location. Such infrastructure improvements will allow more dense development, making the land in this area more valuable. The strategy is to gain control of real estate in these areas before this knowledge becomes widespread.

   Another example is by engaging in assemblage. Assemblage is combining smaller parcels of real estate together to make a new, larger parcel that is more valuable than the individual pieces. The problem is that one holdout can spoil the entire effort. The remedy is to employ options.

3. *Option Three:* You control a tenant. Even in good times, commercial real estate can sit vacant for years. In a crash, owners can lose all hope of ever finding a tenant. If you have control of a tenant, you might be able to view that vacant commercial property in a new perspective—one that includes your new occupant.

In some cases, the tenant you control could be you, if you are a business owner looking for space. Even if you do not control a tenant, if you think you would be able to act as your own commercial leasing agent and find a tenant for the space within the option period, take a gamble on an option.

You can combine these strategies within and without a real estate crash to maximize your opportunities with options.

CHAPTER 14

PROFITING FROM SHORT SALES AND BUYING PREFORECLOSURE

W hen the bubbles burst, some owners of real estate will find themselves in deep financial trouble. Whether from their own fault because of overextension of credit, or from no fault of their own because of job cuts, these homeowners are losing their homes. Foreclosure is never pleasant. No one signs the loan papers expecting to lose their home because of nonpayment.

Real estate investors are always looking for opportunities to buy properties at reasonable prices and terms. Most investors look at foreclosure properties as potential deals, seeking them because they might be priced less than their fair market value.

Understanding the Foreclosure Process

Foreclosure is a legal process by which the mortgagor's (borrower's) rights to their property are terminated. It takes time to complete a foreclosure. The legal process moves slowly, and it is not uncommon for months to pass before the foreclosure is complete.

There are various stages of a foreclosure. From the first late notice mailed to the borrower to the actual sale of the property at the county courthouse, each step could be called "foreclosure." Most people pay their mortgage off or bring the payments current before legal action is finalized. There are some who cannot or refuse to do so. That is when an attorney is hired, and the legal process begins.

Often, the property owner has no equity in the property. More is owed than the value of the property. This phenomenon can occur anytime, but it occurs more often during a bust, when property values reverse, or remain flat. This situation presents the possibility of a short sale.

There are opportunities for profits in short sales for investors willing to do the work. A short sale is also sometimes called a "short pay." Before you can delve into the mechanics of a short sale, you must first understand the foreclosure process.

Before the lender formally starts foreclosure proceedings, the borrower receives many communications. It all starts with the first missed payment. There are phone calls and attempts to contact the borrower. If the lender and borrower cannot work out a payment schedule, the lender moves to foreclosure.

If the decision was made to commence the foreclosure, the lender files a lawsuit in the county court where the property is located. By this time, the property owner is usually three or four months behind in the monthly payments. When the lawsuit is filed, it has become a public record in the courthouse. The case is reported in some local newspapers, and in the local legal newspaper.

For the investor, finding properties in foreclosure—after the legal action has started and a lawsuit has been filed—is easy. It's just a matter of finding the list. It is public information, available at the county courthouse.

Finding people in preforeclosure is not as easy. There is no public list or anyplace you can go to find people who are three or four months behind in their monthly mortgage payments.

However, people in preforeclosure status offer great opportunities for the enterprising investor. They are in trouble, and they know it. Most likely, they are scared, and do not know what to do or which way to turn. They may be considering bankruptcy. They are going to lose their home, and they don't know where to go for help. They know that within weeks a deputy sheriff will be at their door serving legal papers on them.

If you can find them, you help them out of the jam by completing a short sale. To find the people in trouble, you must implement a marketing plan that allows them to call you. This is usually done with advertisements in the real estate sections of newspapers, or with bandit signs erected at busy intersections. The verbiage goes something like this: FACING FORECLOSURE? SELL YOUR PROPERTY TO US. FAST CLOSINGS.

Sometimes, property owners facing foreclosure advertise their homes for sale. You may learn about their foreclosure property when inquiring about their property.

A short sale is where the lender agrees to take less than is owed to pay off the loan. Consider this scenario:

Loan on property: $125,000.

Fair market value: $120,000.

The borrower cannot sell the property and walk away with any cash. In fact, the borrower cannot sell the property without paying cash at settlement. Of course, this may be impossible. If the borrower had the money, the loan would not be in default. Most likely, the lender has tacked on late fees and other charges, making the amount owed greater than the amortized balance.

The owner of the property could surrender the deed in lieu of foreclosure. If the lender agrees, the owner could turn the property over to the lender, and leave. The lender is then stuck with the property, and it becomes part of their inventory. When the lender acquires properties from its borrowers, that property is called Real Estate Owned (REO). The lender has a department that manages its REO properties. It is usually called the "loss mitigation department."

When the lender receives property with a deed-in-lieu transaction, it eliminates legal expenses. But the lender has a property that needs selling. There are expenses associated with the sale, including sales commission and transfer costs. The property needs to be maintained until it is sold. Owning real estate is not what lenders do. So many times, but not always, they will accept a short sale. In the preceding example, you could offer $105,000. If it is accepted, you have a property that you purchased $15,000 below fair market value.

How much discount a lender might accept is never known. You can offer anything. Your first offer might be 60 cents on the dollar. They can say yes, no, or make a counteroffer. It's just business. Don't be surprised if your first offer is turned down. The person you are dealing with in the loss mitigation department at the lender's office is not emotionally involved in the property. Their job is to mitigate losses, not give property away to investors.

Getting Involved Early

At other stages in the foreclosure process, you may not be able to view the inside of a property. But at this stage, your odds will be better. Before you consider making an offer for a short sale, you should inspect the property for defects and other problems. Your first meeting with the property owner facing foreclosure is likely to be difficult. They will possibly be emotional. They may not yet have accepted that they are going to lose their home.

There are several reasons for getting involved in troubled properties early in the process. You have a better chance to view and inspect the property. You can avoid the competitive environment of an auction, and the short sale puts you in control; no one else sees the entire transaction. While there is nothing wrong with buying property via a real estate auction, getting in before others gives you more control, and the ability to wiggle. For example, you might find that mechanic's liens are easier to resolve. Mechanic's liens can result when a homeowner fails to pay a contractor for work performed on his or her home.

One mechanic's lien might be settled for 10 percent of its value, another at 50 percent. Later, when everything turns public, the mechanic who was willing to accept just 10 cents on the dollar is likely to say no, especially when learning another is getting 50 cents for each dollar owed.

If you can find the property before legal foreclosure commences, you can control not only the property, but also the owner. This gives you tremendous leverage and ability. Usually, by this point in the progress, the owner just wants out. They are more interested in making a deal work than anything else. They just want to sign their names, and make everything bad go away. The faster and easier you can make this happen for them, the more likely they will cooperate and agree to your proposals and solutions.

The homeowner is lost, with debt mounting and no foreseeable way out. Often, with some counseling and assistance, the property owner might have been able to solve the financial crisis. But as things got worse, the property owner opted to ignore rather than attempt to solve the problem.

As you inspect the property, look for severe maintenance problems or necessary repairs. Remember that if the property owners were unable to pay their monthly loan payment, they may also have been unable to afford to maintain the property. Look for building code violations and inspect all mechanical systems. Make sure the plumbing, heating, and electrical systems are functional. Remember the seller is in a difficult financial position and may attempt to hide problems with the property.

You need to have an honest discussion with the homeowner. Keep in mind that property owners facing foreclosure probably had a sudden change in their lives, which caused their financial distress. At one point, they were able to qualify for the mortgage. Something happened that prevented them from making their payments. If you are successful, they will be out from under the foreclosure, which will give them a chance to start over.

You will need to get the property owner's written authorization for their lender to disclose information about the loan to you. Ask the lender for an appropriate form that the owner can simply sign.

Your first contact with the lender is to gather information. Fax the authorization to release form to the lender, and then ask for loan balance information and a breakdown of all fees. While speaking to the lender's representative, your message should go something like this:

> When I heard about Fred and Ethel's problem, I told them I would try to help. Fred's job loss and Ethel's illness set them back. They want to sell their property and just move on with their lives. I own several rentals near them, and I am willing to buy their property. But there is a huge problem. Based on what I know about the area and the comps, Fred and Ethel owe far more than their property is worth. I'm willing to help get them out of foreclosure and help you get a defaulted loan off your books, but there is no way I can even consider paying the loan balance. Would you consider a short payoff?

You will soon know from the response how likely it is for you to proceed with trying to acquire the property. If the lender's representative gives you an indication that a short sale is possible, you can then continue your work. If they flatly refuse, it is time to move on to another property.

Your next step is to check the courthouse for liens. If the property owners were unable to pay their monthly mortgage payment, it is likely that many other things have gone unpaid, too. You need to look for outstanding liens. Your search should include looking for municipal liens. The landowner may not have completed required maintenance, so the local municipality did the work, and billed the owner for it. When they did not pay, the municipality filed a lien against the property. There could also be unpaid water or sewerage use fees. Municipal liens are not wiped out by foreclosure.

Look also for property tax liens. If the property taxes have not have been paid, there may be a lien against the property.

There could be outstanding mechanic's liens for repairs made to the property as discussed previously.

The Internal Revenue Service, seeking payment of unpaid taxes, may also have filed a lien against the property.

When you find lien holders, you will have to contact them and see if they will accept a payoff. Some will accept pennies on the dollar, as it is better to get something, rather than nothing.

Once you have gathered all the information, you can proceed with your offer to the owner and lender. The owner of the property is in control, because it is their property. You need to sign a purchase agreement with the property owners.

In that purchase agreement, to protect the property owners, you want to include the following stipulation: "This offer is predicated upon the seller's lender accepting payment in full of the current loan without pursuit of any deficiency judgment."

The reason for this contingency is to protect the homeowners. With a short sale, they would still owe their lender the difference between the mortgage balance and the discounted amount, creating a "deficiency judgment." If granted, the judgment would follow the homeowners for as long as it existed. It would appear on their credit report just as any other judgment is reported.

To be fair to the homeowners, you should explain that the discounted amount (the difference between the mortgage balance and the short sale) may be declared as income on their income tax return with a 1099 reporting this to the IRS. You should advise them that they need to speak with their tax adviser for advice. Because of their financial distress, which most likely was caused by loss of income, the 1099 may have little effect on their tax situation.

Your next step is to prepare your justification as to why the property is not worth what is owed on it. Your report should list all the problems you have found. Include what needs to be fixed, repaired, or replaced. Your list should include retail pricing for the lists of materials and labor to get the work completed. Include your comparable properties (comps) justifying a lower price. Include newspaper clippings that report crime in the area, or neighborhood decline. Include photographs, too. Build a convincing case about why the property is worth less.

You are now ready to submit your purchase offer to the lender. Fax works best. Send the following to the lender:

- $ A cover letter.
- $ The sales contract between you and the borrower.
- $ Your justification document.
- $ A HUD1 settlement statement.

Your package can include other items. One effective item is often a hardship letter from the borrower. The more desperate they sound, explaining their situation (job loss, illness, etc.) and saying that unless the lender accepts this offer, they will have to consider bankruptcy, the more effective it will be. In other words, the better the sob story, the more likely the offer will be accepted by the lender. Estimates for repair are also good.

The HUD1 settlement sheet should show that the sellers will be receiving no money from the transaction. You may have to pay the closing costs. The amount of money the borrowers would receive would be the amount you are proposing to pay off the loan. A financial statement from the sellers is also helpful, especially if it shows that the borrower has no other source of income or assets to repay their loan.

One of the things the lender will focus on is what the property is worth today. The lender usually hires a local real estate broker or appraiser to evaluate the property. The report produced is called a broker's price opinion or "BPO." Remember that you can also submit your own appraisal or comparable sales information to the lender for consideration. You will want to submit as much negative information about the property as possible, to justify your offer. If your offer is too far off the BPO value, it is likely to be rejected. The lender is not interested in giving you a good deal.

Lenders accept short sale purchases regularly. They do not want to be carrying properties on their books. They are under constant pressure to get rid of the REO properties they are carrying. The lenders know that a short sale saves the costs associated with the foreclosure process. They know about the expenses of attorney fees, the eviction process, delays from borrower bankruptcy, damage to the property, costs associated with resale, and so on. Additionally, the seller is likely to be uncollectible. With a short sale, the lender gets rid of the property faster, so it can cut its losses. Your goal is to convince the lender that it is better to accept less money now.

One of the problems in dealing with a loss mitigation department is locating the person with the authority to accept the proposal. Most representatives will not have the authority to approve a short sale. When it comes time to negotiate, it can save you much time and aggravation to get to the decision maker, the one who can accept the proposal.

As you can see, working out a short sale can take much time. But the rewards are worth it. Often, you can pick up a property that with some work can be sold quickly for a profit. Buying a property with a short sale is one way to get those discounted priced properties. When the real estate market is down, lenders are more likely to agree to a short sale. They want to get properties they own off their books as soon as they possibly can.

CASE STUDY: PREFORECLOSURE PROFITS

By David J. Decker

One way to profit from preforeclosures is to buy the mortgage. When you buy the mortgage, you step into the bank's shoes. Obviously, you should take this step only if there is equity or *potential equity* left in the property.

I helped a friend with exactly such a transaction a few years ago. I had been involved in several foreclosure situations and had built a solid rapport with a local bank. Through that connection, I discovered a nine-unit apartment property that was in the process of foreclosure.

The bank was willing to sell their mortgage for about $100,000, a slight discount. There was a second mortgage on the property for about $38,000. I helped my friend get in contact with an attorney that specialized in foreclosures. After consultations with the attorney, my friend bought the mortgage from the bank.

As we began to discuss a bidding strategy for the auction, my friend decided to look into buying the second mortgage as well. We were concerned that if other parties bid at the auction, any price bid over the value of the first mortgage would go to pay other creditors, such as the second mortgage holder.

I was able to persuade the second mortgage holder to accept a short sale of $1,500 for the second mortgage—a discount of 96 percent! Owning both mortgages, my friend was ready to bid at the auction.

Not surprisingly, bidding at the auction was intense. For most properties, there is only one bidder—the bank. But when investors sniff equity, the sharks start to circle, and this property had clear potential equity.

Interestingly, the bidding went all the way to $138,000, the combined values of the first and second mortgages. My friend could have let another bidder win and have walked out the door with a profit of $36,500.

Instead, he kept bidding and won the final bid at $138,000. Remember, he could bid up to $138,000 without it costing him anything additional since he already owned the first and second mortgages.

My friend went on to rehab the property, investing another $80,000 in improvements. On completion, he refinanced the building a few months later, obtaining a new 75 percent first mortgage on an appraisal based on its new value of $360,000! The new loan was for $270,000.

His costs in the deal were about $181,500 ($100,000 for the first mortgage, $1,500 for the second mortgage and $80,000 in improvements). After the refinance, he recovered his costs and had about $88,500 to spare, plus he owned a property with solid cash flow.

This was hardly a no money down deal. This investor put up $181,500 in real cash before getting any return. But after the deal was done, he owned a cash flow property with an equity position of $90,000 and he recovered all of his cash invested plus an additional $88,500, all in less than a year.

CHAPTER 15

Buying at the Auction

When people think of a real estate auction, they usually assume the real estate being sold has been foreclosed. That is not always the case. According to the National Association of REALTORS®, "the value of residential and commercial properties at auctions climbed from $49.5 billion to $58.5 billion between 1998 and 2002." Investors are often attracted to auctions as a method of acquiring properties quickly at a bargain price.

As real estate bubbles break and owners are anxious for a quick sale, one option to get rid of property is to sell it by auction. In today's electronic world, the auction can be online, and not just the traditional sale with an auctioneer standing in front of a group of interested bidders.

The government is well known for using auctions as a way of disposing of property. Real estate is just one of many items the various governments (federal, state, local) use to dispose of property. The government uses both live and online auctions. Banks and lenders sometimes use auctions as a way to dispose of property. The courts authorize auctions to sell real estate.

Finally, auctions are used as part of the legal process of foreclosure. While the process varies from state to state, the general steps remain the same.

While the auction is one of the final steps in the foreclosure process, most foreclosures never make it this far. Once the lender starts the legal action, the property owner resolves the outstanding debt. Usually the property is sold or refinanced, the debt is satisfied, and the foreclosure suit is ended. However, sometimes owners are not able to solve the problems and the property is sold at a public auction at the courthouse.

Occasionally when a property is scheduled for sale, a property owner may file a bankruptcy action and seek protection from the federal courts. This delays the public sale of the property.

At a public sale resulting from a foreclosure action, there is always at least one bidder there, the party who brought the foreclosure action. In most cases, that bidder is the lender or the lender's representative. Depending on the customs of the court, local tradition, and law, sometimes the bidder might be the auctioneer, or an attorney representing the lender. Sometimes the official auctioneer is the county sheriff. Often the only bid received at the public sale is the one from the lender's representative in the outstanding amount of the loan. Again, based on tradition, sometimes these sales are held on the steps of the courthouse. In other locales, they are conducted in the main courtroom.

The auctioneer invites an opening bid, and any subsequent bids, until a final bid amount has been offered and accepted. What typically happens is the lender's representative begins the bidding at the amount of the outstanding loan. There may be others there to continue bidding on the property. When the bidding stops, the auction for the sale of the property is completed.

If you are interested in bidding at the auction, the terms of the auction are what you need to be most concerned with. There are three types of auctions:

1. *Absolute Auction* (or sometimes called an "auction without reserve"). The property is sold at the time of the auction to the highest bidder, regardless of the price. A sale is guaranteed, which often feeds buyer excitement, and greater participation by more buyers is often the result. Many property

sellers, including financial institutions and government agencies, use this auction type frequently.

2. *Reserve Auction* (or sometimes called an "auction subject to confirmation"). In this type of auction, the seller reserves the right to accept or reject the highest bid within a specified time. Often the period is from immediately following the auction up to 72 hours after the auction closes. When you think about it, the highest bid is nothing more than an offer to buy. With a reserve auction, the property owners predetermine the price they want and are not obligated to sell other than at a price that is entirely acceptable to them.

3. *Minimum Bid Auction*. When the auction begins, the auctioneer accepts bids only at or above a published minimum price. This minimum price is always stated in the brochure and advertisements and is announced at the auction. While this type of auction offers a reduced risk for the seller (since the sales price must be above a minimum acceptable level), it does not insure a sale on the day of the auction. There may simply be no bidders.

Although auctions can be a lot of fun, and a good way to buy anything, including real estate, an auction can be a dangerous way for the uninitiated to purchase. Auctions are a buyer-beware world, where real estate is sold as is and all sales are final. Partly because of the historic nature of auctions in the United States, what the auctioneer says is final and unquestioned. (This goes back to the days of the Civil War, where a colonel sold off captured military items or surplus. That is why some auctioneers are still called colonels.)

The terms of a real estate auction can vary from sale to sale, and with jurisdiction. Most require cash or certified funds of 10 percent of the final bid. If your bid is $150,000, you need $15,000 at the conclusion of the auction. Normally, you have 30 days to come up with the balance of $135,000, and the property is yours.

Remember, it is sold as is. If you find a leaky roof later, that's too bad. "As is" means you bought a property with a leaky roof. If you change your mind and do not want to buy it, you lost your 10 percent deposit.

The terms of sales of a real estate auction often require that you pay all closing costs associated with the transfer of the property. That means you need to pay all transfer taxes, recording fees, deed preparation, and title insurance.

Also be aware that the title you receive may not be free and clear of all liens that have been placed against the property. You may have bought not only the property, but also the liens, which need to be settled to obtain a free and clear title on the property.

When a property is sold at auction because of a foreclosure, the first bid received usually covers the outstanding loan. If no one else bids, the property is transferred to the lender. Title and ownership of the property leave the defaulted borrower and go to the lender. The property becomes a Real Estate Owned (REO) asset. The lender will eventually sell the property to recover the money from the loan. If there are additional bidders, the winning bidder's payment pays off the loan, with the excess distributed first to other secured lien holders, then to the property owner.

As an investor, you should realize this simple fact: The more equity in the property, the more likely there will be competitive bids from other investors. Many will try to capture that equity.

What often seems like an easy way to make a fast profit in real estate has some pitfalls. For example, you must pay that 10 percent minimum of your bid in certified funds to the auctioneer at the time your bid is accepted. Concluding the sale within the specified time is also a problem, unless you have the cash. Lenders can close loans in less than 30 days, but depending on a financial institution to do so with your 10 percent payment at risk could cause some sleepless nights. Further, you may find that lenders are not always anxious to make loans on properties that just suffered a foreclosure.

This is not a game for beginners. Before trying to acquire a property in a real estate auction, make sure you have a clear understanding of the terms of the auction. Some auctions require the buyer to pay a "bidder's premium." Unlike property sold by a real estate agent, where the seller pays the agent's commission, the buyer pays the auctioneer's commission. This is done by adding on the bidder's premium.

Discuss your plan with your real estate attorney. Don't bid without the assistance of an attorney. You have to be ready to walk away from a real estate auction. Don't get carried away in the bidding process and overpay for a property.

A title search on any property you are buying through foreclosure is a must. You can obtain the necessary information from any title insurance company. Always be cautious of liens placed against the property. Make sure that you understand which liens will not be removed by the foreclosure action, and if there could be any problems with the title to the property. Tax liens, in particular, remain fully enforceable against the real estate, even when a foreclosure occurs.

Another lien that can cause real problems for you are those placed by the Internal Revenue Service. The IRS enjoys special powers to collect income tax, including placing liens on real estate properties. If the title report shows an IRS tax lien, determine if the IRS has been duly notified of the pending foreclosure. If the IRS has been notified at least 25 days prior to the auction, the current law allows the agency to seize the property to cure the lien for up to 120 days following the sale. If this were to happen to you, you would be entitled to a refund of all of your money with interest. Should the IRS not proceed with a seizure, their right to do so expires after the 120th day following the sale.

Even so, be aware of the special notification requirement. If the IRS was not notified properly of the public auction, their lien remains in place as long as it is on file in the county recorder's office. If you have purchased the real estate and the IRS opted to enforce its lien against the property, you would not be compensated. In effect, you get to pay someone else's income taxes!

One of the other problems with real estate auctions is that they are often cancelled, many times at the last minute. The property owner may have satisfied the debt or a legal procedure may have postponed the sale. It is best to check the day before any scheduled real estate auction to make sure the sale is still scheduled.

Court ordered sales are public information. You can find information about any public auction in the courthouse. They are also often listed in the legal notices section of circulated newspapers.

Auctioneers have moved into the electronic age. Many have web sites, where they list the properties they are offering for sale. While auctioneers have not accepted electronic bids, expect that to change in the future. EBay offers real estate for sale on an ongoing basis. As bubbles burst in specific real estate markets, expect anxious investors and property owners to list their properties for sale, trying to get out from underneath the costs of ownership as quickly as they possibly can.

The IRS, as well as other government entities, are also using the Internet to conduct auctions of real estate. Some sites offer only listings and notifications of sales, while others actively accept bids.

CASE STUDY: BUYING A DRUG HOUSE AT FORECLOSURE

By David J. Decker

Several years ago, a friend brought to my attention a 28-unit apartment complex that was in trouble. I drove past the building to investigate. One of the two buildings was abandoned and boarded up. Both buildings were in a poor state of repair. The location was not an area where you would expect to find boarded up, abandoned buildings. I was immediately curious.

I called my title agent from my cell phone as I sat in my car in front of the building. The agent was quickly able to tell me who the lender was on the property. The lender happened to be a bank that I have an ongoing relationship with spanning 17 years. By the time I got back to my office, I had already had a nice conversation with the appropriate decision makers at the bank.

As it turned out, the local folklore on the property was that the previous owner had gotten involved in dealing drugs with his tenants and trading rent for sex. What is known is that 129 crimes were allegedly committed at this complex and one other apartment building owned by the same gentleman. The crimes included soliciting a child for prostitution, drug dealing, and homicide.

One of the crimes included the robbery of the former owner at gunpoint. He was shot six times in front of the property I eventually purchased. Thankfully, the owner survived, but the property did not fare nearly as well.

The local municipality had seized the property because of the nuisance and crime problems. The building that was boarded up and abandoned sat through the winter with every window broken and the boiler turned off. As a result, once I purchased the property, installed new windows, and turned the boiler back on, I began to discover all of the ruined plumbing. As more pipes thawed, new leaks were discovered. For about two weeks, it was raining in the basement.

The drug people had removed the drywall between the apartments so in the event of a drug bust, they could literally disappear into the walls. There was gang graffiti everywhere. Trash was piled five feet high. The parking lot was full of potholes. Fortunately, the problems were nothing that a little TLC and a few hundred thousand dollars couldn't fix!

Before I bought the property, I had to traverse the foreclosure minefield. I hired an attorney who specialized in foreclosures. We obtained a title search. I had more conversations with the bank trying to learn how they intended to bid.

At most foreclosure auctions, the lender makes the opening bid and drops out immediately if there are other bids. That didn't happen to me. I think the bank wanted to entice other bidders by starting from a lower number. For whatever reason, the bank continued to bid after their opening bid. But I was still the only other bidder.

Since I was the only other bidder, there was no reason to reach to get the property. The bank continued to bid and I dropped out. The bank won the auction. I contacted them after the auction and we cut a deal at a more leisurely pace a week or so later.

As I have already mentioned, I had to stick tons of money into the project. But I was able to obtain financing not only to buy the property, but to fund the improvements, too. I did make a 20 percent cash down payment, but it was based on the dirt cheap price I paid for the building.

I still own this building. It's a real cash cow. I also made some great contacts with the city officials, and they later brought more deals to my attention. There is a sad part to this story, however, and it contains an important example you can learn from.

The previous owner who sold this property to the investor who was eventually foreclosed on made some terrible mistakes. He allowed the investor to assume his existing first mortgage without getting released from liability. Further, he made this investor a second mortgage as well.

The entire second mortgage was wiped out in the foreclosure and the bank went after the previous owner for a small deficiency on the first mortgage. The moral of the story is that when you go to sell, get released from liability on any mortgage that gets assumed. And be careful about any second mortgage that you make. You know what can happen.

CHAPTER 16

How to Buy REOs

When real estate bubbles break, borrowers lose their homes and investments. When those properties are foreclosed by a lender and no other party bids successfully at the auction, the properties become the property of the lender, known as Real Estate Owned (REO) properties. They are an excellent source of bargains.

REO is an ambiguous term. It does not describe a specific property type, such as single-family residences. Rather, it means any property that has been foreclosed on or has been taken back by the lender. The REO label should not dissuade a buyer from the property. In many cases, there is nothing wrong with a property offered for sale by the lender, other than that the previous owner could not afford the repayments. REOs range from farms to multi-family units, from single-family homes to condos. Any real estate that could be financed could become REO and offered for sale by a lender.

Builders and developers can run into financial problems. While they usually look for another builder or developer to take over their unfinished projects, sometimes banks find themselves holding title to building lots or partially built homes. Builders' tracts can offer some interesting investment opportunities for the real estate investor. The value of a partially erected house is always difficult to set. Before buying a property in this condition, make sure you know what it will cost to complete the work. Also, realize that it may be more difficult to arrange financing for a partially built home.

Sometimes, REOs are the result of abandonment. The borrower has just disappeared, and can no longer be found. In other words, the borrower just walked away from the responsibility of owning the property.

In some cases, the borrower simply gives up, and turns the property over to the lender, surrendering the deed in lieu of foreclosure. Deed in lieu of foreclosure, sometimes called a "friendly foreclosure," avoids the public stigma of a foreclosure. This often happens when the property is worth less than the amount owed.

It is safer to buy a REO property than it is to buy a property at any other point in the foreclosure process. REOs are safer because there is an opportunity to inspect the property, there are likely to be fewer title defects, and there is less time pressure. Also note that the bank has the deepest pockets and can therefore afford to lose more—the foreclosed owner may bargain harder for a higher price because he must in order to pay off the debt.

Foreclosure helps to eliminate title defects like second mortgages, mechanic's liens, and other liens junior to the first mortgage, but foreclosure cannot eliminate every lien. For example, property tax liens are not eliminated by foreclosure. You still need to pay close attention to the title report.

At any other point in the foreclosure, a seller may be racing against time to avoid an auction. If the property goes to auction, not only do you have to decide during a few minutes of bidding how much you will pay, but, assuming your bid is successful, you will likely have only 30 days to close. With REO properties, none of these time constraints exist.

For any properties that you just cannot make work on a short sale basis in preforeclosure, don't give up. You may be able to pick up the property at the auction or as a REO.

Another reason a REO is better to purchase than a property in foreclosure is that the lender is now totally in control of the property. When a property is in foreclosure, both the lender and the property owner are in control. The lender obviously wants to be paid off. The property owner is emotionally involved in the property. Those emotions could vary, and often the owner does not want to lose any money. The property owner may be unrealistic about the property's value. With a REO, the lender is not emotionally involved, and simply wants to get rid of the property as quickly as possible.

REO properties are easier to finance, and can often be purchased far below market value. When you are bidding at an auction, you had better have your financing lined up in advance, or you may not be able to meet the typical 30-day closing requirement, sacrificing your 10 percent deposit. When you buy a REO, the bank selling the property may be willing to finance the property for you. At least you won't have to risk 10 percent of the purchase price if you cannot arrange financing.

REO properties are real estate that the lender wants to sell, and as soon as possible. Lenders do not always act like other rational sellers. They are sometimes quick to dump properties, and from the outside, it often makes little sense when they do. Internally, there could be pressure to get the REOs off the books. Last week, an offer of 70 cents on the dollar was turned down, and this week, an offer of 60 cents on the dollar is accepted. It often does not make sense. Management changes, a sudden influx of more REOs, or changes in lender policies could be reasons why property is suddenly sold far below market value. You just never know what is going on inside the REO department of a lender.

Properties on the REO books are probably still accumulating losses. Taxes are accruing, utilities have to be paid, and the lawn has to be cut. Vacant properties are a magnet for vandalism. Lenders are not likely to utilize a handyman for repairs, opting instead for licensed plumbers and electricians. In other words, their operating costs will be higher.

Understandably, a bank does not want a property on its books for long. They are in the real estate business only as lenders, not as owners. Banks want to make money by lending money. They do not want their money tied up in repossessed real estate. Any real estate that the bank owns represents a future, potential financial investment that could be generating a profit, rather than a liability that generates expenses.

In addition to not generating money (and probably generating further losses) for the bank, REOs may suggest mismanagement. The bank will be anxious to dump these properties as a result.

REO properties are not limited to just banks and mortgage companies. The government also has quantities of REOs. Housing and Urban Development (HUD), the Veterans Administration, and the U.S. Department of Agriculture (USDA) always have properties that have been returned because of borrowers' inability to pay the government backed loans. They are listed for sale on each agency's web site:

http://www.va.gov

http://www.hud.gov

http://www.rurdev.usda.gov/

Lenders usually hire a local real estate broker or appraiser to evaluate their REO property. After inspecting the property, the broker produces a report called a broker's price opinion (BPO). This report include comparables (comps) of other nearby properties. It also includes items that need to be repaired or replaced. If your offer is too low compared to the BPO value, it is likely to be rejected.

The weakness to these appraisals or BPOs is that the methodology for developing these reports usually assumes that the property being evaluated is in a marketable condition. Of course, many REO properties are in a poor state of repair, far from being marketable. The result is that the value judgments made may reflect two values, "as is" and "as improved."

Pay close attention to the "as improved" number. This value is an attempt to reflect what the property could be worth if it wasn't trashed. Theoretically, this is the value you are shooting for as you make your improvements. However, this value could be slightly in error.

When you rehab a property, everything may be new. The comparable sales that were the basis for the "as improved" value may not actually be as nice as your freshly remodeled gem. Your property could be worth more. Before you get too excited, beware that underestimating time and expense is rampant in the remodeling business, even for experienced specialists.

The variability of remodeling costs is why an "as is" value can be so difficult to estimate. Additionally, the market dynamics for a dilapidated home are completely different. Despite all that has been written counseling buyers to acquire fixer-uppers, most home buyers are looking for something in move-in condition. A hardy few may be willing to apply a little elbow grease, but the market for real estate that is in need of extensive remodeling can be limited.

That's why you should be skeptical about any of these reports. Find out how long the property has been in the REO inventory. If the reports are accurate, the property will sell within a reasonable length of time. If the property has been on the lender's books for months, these value claims are more suspect.

In the end, you may be best off ignoring these reports and making offers that make sense to you, even if your offer is considerably lower. Build in plenty of cushion and profit margin in your remodeling cost. If the lender rejects your offer, citing the appraisals they have on file, be patient. The lender may grow to doubt the value of any appraisal if the property languishes on the market long enough.

CASE STUDY: REMODELING COST CRAZINESS

By David J. Decker

In the late 1990s, I bought 14 rental apartments in 7 townhouse style duplexes in a prestigious suburb. The buildings were being sold to settle an estate and had been neglected for years. All of the properties had gravel driveways and no paving. The weeds in the middle of these drives were waist high. Inoperable cars were parked in the yards.

The buildings had been built in the 1960s and nothing had been updated since. The kitchens and baths were obsolete and in poor condition. Paint had been slopped onto woodwork, and carpets were worn and dirty.

My plan was to buy the properties for $180,000 per duplex, spend $20,000 per building in improvements, and sell them to individual owners for $240,000.

The day after closing, I had an asphalt contractor at the properties grading and pouring asphalt. The contractor started grading a neighbor's property that I didn't own, a bad omen of things to come. A few weeks later, I got busted by the building inspector for not pulling a permit for the asphalt work. I have contracted plenty of asphalt work both before and after this job and was never required to have a permit. Live and learn.

My intention was to install new kitchen cabinets, remodel the bathrooms, add central air conditioners, and provide new appliances, carpeting, and vinyl flooring. I missed the budget number by only 100 percent! Instead of spending $20,000 per building, it wound up costing about $40,000. The remodel took twice as long, too. Fortunately, I was able to sell the properties for more than expected, about $260,000 or more each. Everything worked out in the end, but I'm still never going to drive down that street ever again!

To make your offer stronger for the REO property, you can also submit your own comparable sales information and repair costs to the lender for consideration. Include a report with as much negative information about the property as possible, to justify your offer. A long list of repairs will get the REO manager's attention. An effective strategy is to include photos of damage and defects.

Don't be intimidated by the asking price. Lenders often set the price for as much as, or more than, other similar properties in the neighborhood. Of course they want to sell it for as much as possible. But that does not mean they will not accept less.

One strategy when buying REOs is to make two offers. One is the bottom line number, with the property purchased as is. The second offer is to pay the bottom line number, plus what it would cost to make the property in pristine condition. With a long list of legitimate repair costs, the lender is likely to accept the first, lower offer.

Another strategy for acceptance of a lower offer it to show your preapproval for financing, and your willingness to close the loan in less than 30 days. Generating a quick sale for the lender is important. With financing already approved, you are a cash buyer. The REO manager will be hard-pressed to turn down the offer. Remember the lender may want to get rid of the property as soon as possible.

Your property inspection should include a careful look at any recent repair work. It is not uncommon for a REO property to have had recent repairs made improperly or in an attempt to hide more serious problems. Sometimes the repairs are more cosmetic than substantive. A professional property inspector should be able to detect such work and alert you to the potential problems.

Of course, you should demand clear title for the property. Most likely, with REO properties, this will be less of a problem. The title had to be clear before they invested in the property with their borrower. The foreclosure process normally eliminates many of the miscellaneous liens on the title. However, foreclosure does not eliminate tax liens, and there can be additional problems. Deed-in-lieu-of-foreclosure REO properties can have second mortgages or other liens in place on the title. When the property owner surrenders the deed and the property to the lender, these junior liens are not eliminated.

There could be tax, municipal, and mechanic's liens placed against the property. If you demand and accept only clear title, it does not matter to you about the unpaid obligations from the previous property owner. They will have to be cleared by the bank. Accepting less than clear title could cause you problems in the future. For example, you could be stuck with having to pay junior liens or back taxes. Have your attorney review the title to make sure that all liens are cleared.

If you are buying the property as your primary residence and not as an investment property, the lender may extend financing to you under different than normal terms. For example, the lender may accept less than a normal down payment. When a lender wants to sell their REO, they may accept only a token down payment from an interested buyer. The reason is simple: They want to get the property off their books and their money back to producing interest income. So they may be willing to make exceptions to sell the home. However, there are restrictions.

If the lender intends to sell the mortgage on the secondary market, then all of the ordinary criteria still apply. Further, federal regulators often frown on sweetheart foreclosure deals and may require the lender to establish higher reserves or impose other sanctions.

Finding REOs is not that difficult. Many are offered for sale through real estate agents, and can be found on your local Multiple Listing Service. Some lenders erect signs, or advertise their properties for sale in the real estate sections of local newspapers. Some list their REOs for sale on their web sites. Most lenders will add your name to their investor list, and send you listings of their REO properties. Depending on the lender, you may receive property information via regular mail, e-mail, or fax. A quick chat with the local branch manager of your bank can put you in touch with the right person in the REO department who can get you on the distribution list of the bank's real estate for sale.

It may take a little work on your part to locate the current REO offerings, but you might find great bargains, making your effort worthwhile and profitable.

CHAPTER 17

THE MOST OVERVALUED AND UNDERVALUED MARKETS IN THE UNITED STATES

Where are the most overvalued real estate markets in the United States? As interest rates rise, markets already straining the limits of affordability will be further tested.

As you know from reading this book, there is no evidence or suggestion of a national real estate bust. What will happen are regional bubble pops, creating localized real estate market crashes, or flat markets. The most likely scenario is that when the bubbles pop air will escape slowly. There will not be an alarm bell, and the next day, all real estate in a region will be reduced by 20 percent or 25 percent. Rather, markets slowly decline.

Jobs and the economy will greatly influence any real estate busts. Local economies will be greatly affected with any downturn in local real estate markets. For example, in Riverside and San Bernardino counties, California, jobs in construction accounted for 33 percent of all jobs created between August 2004 and August 2005. Should construction slow to the point of layoffs, expect ripples through the local economy.

The areas most likely to see the fastest decreases are those oversaturated with investor ownership. The overexuberance of investors to make money quickly is what will make them drop out of a real estate market without rationale. Once they believe the market is falling, they, too, will want to sell, adding more housing inventory on the market. That will add more downward price pressure.

One area particularly vulnerable from investor hyperactivity is Miami. Condos have been overpriced, oversold, and overbought. This market is vulnerable.

Most Overvalued Areas

The most overvalued areas in the United States are located in California, Florida, the Washington, D.C. area, and the Northeast, particularly Boston and New York City. Based on the employment forecasts, population forecasts, current income level, the Housing Affordability Index (HAI), and growth compared with housing prices, key market areas were identified.

By alphabetical order, here are the 25 most likely locations for real estate busts to occur:

Bakersfield, CA

Baltimore, Towson, MD

Bethesda, Frederick, Gaithersburg, MD

Boston, Quincy, MA

Edison, NJ

Fort Lauderdale, Pompano Beach, Deerfield Beach, FL

Fresno, CA

Las Vegas, Paradise, NV

Los Angeles, including Glendale and Long Beach, CA

Miami, Miami Beach, Kendall, FL

Naples, Cape Coral, Fort Myers, FL

New York City

Phoenix, Mesa, Scottsdale, AZ

Providence, RI, New Bedford, Fall River, MA

Riverside, San Bernardino, Ontario, CA

Sacramento, Arden, Arcade, Roseville, CA

Salinas, CA

San Diego, Carlsbad, San Marcos, CA

San Francisco, San Mateo, Redwood City, CA

San Jose, Sunnyvale, Santa Clara, CA

Santa Barbara, Santa Maria, Goleta, CA

Santa Rosa, Petaluma, CA

Sarasota, Bradenton, Venice, FL

Washington, DC, Arlington, Alexandria, VA,
and the greater MD & WV areas

West Palm Beach, Boca Raton, Boynton Beach, FL

The fact that your hometown is not found on this list does not mean that a bust cannot occur in your region. All local economies are always vulnerable to local recessions. The cities on this list are more vulnerable because they are already straining the limits of affordability.

Similarly, just because your neighborhood is included on this list is not grounds for panic. A bust is not likely to occur in every one of these regions. Some of these regions may continue to enjoy robust growth.

Whether this list is good news or bad, it is still not a substitute for you doing your own research and paying attention to changing market conditions in your region.

Most Undervalued Markets

On the other end of the spectrum are areas with undervalued real estate markets, and those less likely to experience any real estate bust. These areas are:

Atlanta, GA

Augusta, Aiken, GA

Charlotte, Gastonia, NC

Cleveland, Elyria, Mentor, OH

Columbus, OH

Dallas, TX

Davenport, Moline, Rock Island, IL

Dayton, Springfield, OH

Denver, Aurora, CO

Detroit, Livonia, Dearborn, MI

El Paso, TX

Fargo, Moorhead, ND

Fort Wayne, IN

Fort Worth, Arlington, TX

Greenville, Spartanburg, SC

Harrisburg, Lebanon, PA

Houston, TX

Indianapolis, IN

Jackson, MS

Kansas City, MO

Little Rock, N. Little Rock, AR

Memphis, TN

Montgomery, AL

Nashville, Davidson, Murfreesboro, TN

Peoria, Pekin, IL

Raleigh, Durham, NC

Rochester, NY

Rockford, IL

San Antonio, TX

Sioux Falls, SD

Syracuse, NY

Tulsa, OK

Warren, Farmington Hills, Troy, MI
Wichita, KS

Again, just because a city appears on this list does not mean that properties in these markets are a bargain poised for a growth spurt. Values may remain stagnant for years.

Some Other Things to Consider about the Lists

These lists presented here were compiled in late 2005. Factors change, such as employment, the general economy, and local market factors. As new data emerge, cities on these lists would likely be added or dropped. By looking at these factors, as well as analyzing a local real estate market, you can do your own computations. You can determine the strengths or weaknesses of your own market.

Supply and demand in any metro area is always vulnerable to local economic conditions. As these words were composed, both Ford and General Motors were reporting record losses. If they close a plant in an area, that will have an effect on that local real estate market.

While shore and other vacation locations are always going to be desirable, overinvestment by investors will weaken or soften markets. There are just not enough investors to keep repurchasing properties at even higher prices.

The areas listed are just that: areas. Within those markets, there will be strong pricing, but generally, overall the areas will likely show weakness in prices. Those weaknesses will become evident when prices flatten or decrease.

Areas where there is little additional land available for development—such as New York City, Washington, D.C., and most shore locations—will enjoy strong markets, even if there are drops or hiccups in the real estate market. Overall, the value will return after falling or leveling off. In time, prices will even rise, but most probably, at a slower rate. Areas with limited or no area to grow—such as Manhattan—will see price increases after any bust. Areas where there are still places to build and expand, such as Dallas, will see slower price gains. Rather than pay high prices for land, developers and builders can just go down the road and buy. That's possible in Dallas, but not Manhattan.

Some areas have already experienced slowdowns, such as Las Vegas. From 2004 to 2005, Las Vegas' growth dropped from 48 percent to 11 percent. San Diego slowed from 29 percent to 8 percent during the same period.

Suburban areas on the fringes of metropolitan areas may lose some steam, because of gas prices. This is even more likely in areas without mass transit. If energy prices and gas costs increase, fewer people will likely be willing to drive an hour or so to work each day. They just won't be able to afford it. Housing in those areas could lose value.

Closing Thoughts about Bubbles and Busts

When bubbles pop, and real estate busts develop, there is one sure-fire way to make money. Although you can no longer rely on a spiraling upward market, you can make profitable investments.

There's a saying in real estate: *You make your money on the buy, not the sale.* Buying property at the right price is both critical and essential. As interest rates rise, resale values fall. Your best investments are value investments, properties that are undervalued, properties that are ugly, in need of work or updates, or a combination of these. Finding underused properties or properties in an up and coming neighborhood makes sense, too.

Relying on local market momentum to make money is always chancy. Any fast moving real estate market may slow, flatten, or even decline. Busts can follow booms. The current boom in housing in the United States is uneven. Because of weaker local economies, cities like Detroit have not seen a real estate boom. Atlanta has seen a boom in new home building, but home prices have not increased. While the sprawl continues in the greater Atlanta area, only time will determine how higher energy costs for commuters will affect housing prices. With rebuilding required from 2005's hurricanes, building materials and skilled workers will be in shorter supply. New home prices should increase.

When markets slow, invest for the long term. Allow your tenants to pay the mortgage. Return to old-fashioned fundamentals for safe investments in real estate. Forget the fast flip. The only flips that make sense are those properties bought low, rehabbed, and resold.

Buying undervalued property is always a wise investment. Common sense value investing, while never risk free, makes more sense than blindly jumping on a real estate bandwagon.

Two questions for you to consider:

- **$** When you pay $120,000 for a $150,000 property, who would buy it from you?
- **$** When you pay $180,000 for a $150,000 property, who would buy it from you?

Buy wisely, and you don't ever have to worry about a real estate bubble.

APPENDIX A

The advice in this book is timeless. Unfortunately, the data presented are not. Thanks to the Internet, terrific information is available at the touch of a button. The most recently available information is included here and throughout *Cash In on the Coming Real Estate Crash*. However, in our fast-paced world, these data will quickly change. Therefore, we have included the Internet links and instructions on how to access these data yourself.

There are limitations to these data. The most precise information is broken down only by city. Some of the data are presented only by region. This information is intended to provide direction about general trends in the market. How things will pan out in your neighborhood is still something you will need to continually evaluate.

Existing Home Sales

These data (see Table A.1) supply a snapshot of the volume of sales regionally, as well as changes in median home prices. By examining the history, a trend can be forecasted for the future. Note also the months of supply and remember that healthy markets have an inventory of less than 6.5 months.

Updated data are available at http://www.realtor.org/Research .nsf/files/REL0509EHS.pdf/$FILE/REL0509EHS.pdf.

TABLE A.1 Existing Home Sales

Year		U.S.	Northeast	Midwest	South	West	U.S.	Northeast	Midwest	South	West	Inventory	Mos. Supply
2002		5,631,000	950,000	1,346,000	2,065,000	1,269,000	*	*	*	*	*	2,108,000	4.7
2003		6,183,000	1,022,000	1,468,000	2,282,000	1,404,000	*	*	*	*	*	2,250,000	4.6
2004		6,784,000	1,114,000	1,549,000	2,542,000	1,577,000	*	*	*	*	*	2,214,000	4.3
		Seasonally Adjusted Annual Rate					Not Seasonally Adjusted						
2004	Sept	6,790,000	1,130,000	1,540,000	2,520,000	1,600,000	572,000	95,000	137,000	211,000	127,000	2,382,000	4.2
	Oct	6,840,000	1,120,000	1,560,000	2,580,000	1,580,000	555,000	94,000	121,000	210,000	132,000	2,465,000	4.3
	Nov	6,980,000	1,140,000	1,570,000	2,640,000	1,640,000	531,000	87,000	116,000	202,000	127,000	2,539,000	4.4
	Dec	6,810,000	1,130,000	1,550,000	2,550,000	1,580,000	547,000	90,000	120,000	212,000	124,000	2,214,000	3.9
2005	Jan	6,820,000	1,090,000	1,470,000	2,650,000	1,590,000	382,000	64,000	77,000	146,000	95,000	2,147,000	3.8
	Feb	6,820,000	1,140,000	1,520,000	2,560,000	1,600,000	402,000	68,000	89,000	156,000	89,000	2,330,000	4.1
	Mar	6,870,000	1,150,000	1,550,000	2,560,000	1,610,000	558,000	84,000	126,000	212,000	134,000	2,297,000	4.0
	Apr	7,180,000	1,200,000	1,640,000	2,740,000	1,600,000	626,000	98,000	142,000	234,000	151,000	2,474,000	4.1
	May	7,140,000	1,190,000	1,600,000	2,710,000	1,640,000	668,000	104,000	156,000	253,000	156,000	2,556,000	4.3
	Jun	7,350,000	1,230,000	1,640,000	2,740,000	1,740,000	753,000	129,000	171,000	280,000	174,000	2,678,000	4.4
	Jul	7,150,000	1,190,000	1,610,000	2,750,000	1,600,000	690,000	128,000	158,000	254,000	150,000	2,756,000	4.6
	Aug r	7,280,000	1,200,000	1,660,000	2,730,000	1,690,000	743,000	128,000	169,000	280,000	167,000	2,841,000	4.7
	Sept p	7,280,000	1,210,000	1,610,000	2,830,000	1,620,000	627,000	103,000	147,000	243,000	134,000	2,849,000	4.7
vs. last month:		0.0%	0.8%	-3.0%	3.7%	-4.1%	-15.6%	-19.5%	-13.0%	-13.2%	-19.8%	0.3%	0.0%
vs. last year:		7.2%	7.1%	4.5%	12.3%	1.3%	9.6%	8.4%	7.3%	15.2%	5.5%	19.6%	11.9%
year-to-date:							5.449	0.906	1.235	2.058	1.250		

Sales Price of Existing Homes

Median

Year	U.S.	Northeast	Midwest	South	West
2002	$156,200	$160,300	$137,200	$144,200	$211,500
2003	169,500	188,500	143,400	154,800	231,500
2004	185,200	219,800	152,300	168,500	263,300
Not Seasonally Adjusted					
Sept	187,000	221,000	153,000	170,000	263,000
Oct	187,000	228,000	154,000	166,000	272,000
Nov	190,000	229,000	154,000	170,000	275,000
Dec	191,000	220,000	156,000	174,000	279,000
Jan	189,000	231,000	149,000	169,000	278,000
Feb	189,000	250,000	154,000	163,000	273,000
Mar	193,000	242,000	156,000	165,000	293,000
Apr	205,000	243,000	166,000	175,000	307,000
May	206,000	245,000	167,000	179,000	303,000
Jun	217,000	250,000	174,000	189,000	319,000
Jul	216,000	251,000	175,000	187,000	324,000
Aug r	220,000	254,000	176,000	189,000	327,000
Sept p	212,000	245,000	175,000	184,000	302,000
vs. last year:	13.4%	10.9%	14.4%	8.2%	14.8%

Average (Mean)

Year	U.S.	Northeast	Midwest	South	West
2002	$199,200	$205,200	$165,400	$181,200	$259,500
2003	215,000	231,500	175,600	195,000	277,000
2004	236,600	259,200	184,800	214,700	309,800
Not Seasonally Adjusted					
Sept	237,000	259,000	186,000	216,000	308,000
Oct	239,000	267,000	186,000	212,000	317,000
Nov	242,000	267,000	188,000	218,000	319,000
Dec	244,000	263,000	189,000	223,000	324,000
Jan	241,000	268,000	180,000	219,000	322,000
Feb	241,000	281,000	187,000	211,000	319,000
Mar	247,000	275,000	192,000	214,000	336,000
Apr	254,000	280,000	195,000	224,000	346,000
May	257,000	280,000	195,000	232,000	344,000
Jun	266,000	286,000	204,000	242,000	355,000
Jul	267,000	286,000	205,000	240,000	359,000
Aug r	269,000	289,000	207,000	241,000	361,000
Sept p	260,000	279,000	207,000	234,000	345,000
vs. last year:	9.7%	7.7%	11.3%	8.3%	12.0%

r: revised; p: preliminary.
Source: ©2005 National Association of REALTORS®.

Pending Home Sales Index

Pending home sales are a great forecast tool. (See Table A.2.)

The most recent data can be found at http://www.realtor.org/ Research.nsf/files/PHS0508.pdf/$FILE/PHS0508.pdf.

TABLE A.2 Pending Home Sales Index (PHSI)

Year		United States	Northeast	Midwest	South	West	United States	Northeast	Midwest	South	West
2002		102.2	103.3	103.0	99.7	104.7	*	*	*	*	*
2003		107.4	101.0	109.8	107.4	110.0	*	*	*	*	*
2004		120.9	109.7	118.6	126.8	122.9	*	*	*	*	*
		Seasonally Adjusted Annual Rate					Not Seasonally Adjusted				
2004	Aug	123.7	110.9	118.8	132.1	125.8	132.1	116.5	131.2	137.8	136.5
	Sept	124.7	109.5	120.2	130.8	131.9	118.6	105.9	115.5	120.1	129.6
	Oct	128.1	108.7	124.9	133.8	137.5	118.6	104.6	114.1	122.0	128.8
	Nov	123.7	101.4	120.4	130.5	133.8	103.6	87.5	97.3	107.9	115.9
	Dec	123.2	102.1	118.9	130.5	132.7	82.0	66.2	74.1	88.3	92.9
2005	Jan	120.6	105.9	113.5	123.2	135.3	101.4	83.9	89.5	107.8	117.8
	Feb	123.2	108.4	121.1	127.6	129.9	113.3	98.2	109.9	116.8	123.4
	Mar	123.7	116.0	116.7	128.9	128.9	142.8	135.0	136.0	148.0	148.0
	Apr	127.5	120.6	122.0	138.9	120.8	147.4	139.8	144.1	164.1	130.7
	May	125.6	117.0	115.5	137.5	124.5	148.4	141.5	140.6	162.4	140.1
	Jun	126.4	113.2	117.2	137.6	128.9	150.4	136.6	141.7	163.7	149.6
	Jul r	125.5	109.0	116.2	139.0	127.0	136.3	114.9	126.9	153.0	136.8
	Aug p	129.5	108.5	119.4	142.1	136.7	139.8	114.5	132.2	150.5	150.8
	vs. last month:	3.2%	-0.5%	2.8%	2.2%	7.6%	2.6%	-0.3%	4.2%	-1.6%	10.2%
	vs. last year:	4.7%	-2.2%	0.5%	7.6%	8.7%	5.8%	-1.7%	0.8%	9.2%	10.5%

r: revised; p: preliminary.
Source: National Association of REALTORS®.

Median Sales Price of Existing Single-Family Homes for Metropolitan Areas

Table A.3 provides great historical data on median home prices by city. Again, note the trends to predict the future.

Obtain the most recently available data from http://www.realtor.org/Research.nsf/files/REL05Q2T.pdf/$FILE/REL05Q2T.pdf.

TABLE A.3 Median Sales Price of Existing Single-Family Homes for Metropolitan Area

Metropolitan Area	2002	2003	2004	2004:II	2004:III	2004:IV	2005:I r	2005:II p	%Chya
				(Not Seasonally Adjusted, 000s)					
U.S.	158.1	170.0	184.1	183.5	188.2	187.5	188.3	208.5	13.6%
NE	164.3	190.5	220.0	214.9	220.2	222.5	246.2	243.1	13.1%
MW	136.0	141.3	149.0	149.7	153.2	151.0	148.2	167.8	12.1%
SO	147.3	157.1	169.0	169.8	172.1	169.7	165.2	179.4	5.7%
WE	215.4	234.2	265.8	261.6	271.0	278.0	284.1	312.6	19.5%
Akron, OH	115.3	116.7	116.9	116.0	122.9	117.2	111.2	119.8	3.3%
Albany-Schenectady-Troy, NY	125.9	141.6	161.3	157.8	168.9	167.7	170.4	176.1	11.6%
Albuquerque, NM	133.8	138.4	145.4	145.4	144.5	155.8	149.7	171.7	18.1%
Allentown-Bethlehem-Easton, PA-NJ	161.1	184.7	207.3	201.1	222.6	210.5	214.8	249.1	23.9%
Amarillo, TX	91.9	95.7	97.1	96.4	98.1	100.4	102.6	107.4	11.4%
Anaheim-Santa Ana, CA (Orange Co.)	412.7	487.0	627.3	655.3	643.6	627.5	656.9	696.1	6.2%
Appleton, WI	112.7	118.6	122.9	125.6	122.1	123.3	128.0	129.6	3.2%
Atlanta-Sandy Springs-Marietta, GA	146.5	152.4	156.9	156.8	159.7	157.7	159.5	166.5	6.2%
Atlantic City, NJ	143.6	166.5	197.9	194.8	202.4	216.5	217.4	244.9	25.7%
Austin-Round Rock, TX	156.5	156.7	154.7	158.8	158.7	151.3	154.1	166.8	5.0%
Baltimore-Towson, MD	154.8	180.0	217.0	225.2	232.8	220.6	194.2	264.7	17.5%
Barnstable Town, MA	279.6	330.3	377.2	372.6	382.9	395.5	388.8	398.6	7.0%
Baton Rouge, LA	116.9	121.2	127.7	128.2	130.8	128.2	130.5	135.4	5.6%
Beaumont-Port Arthur, TX	84.3	88.4	93.5	95.9	95.3	87.8	90.0	96.5	0.6%
Binghamton, NY	75.3	82.2	85.3	84.7	89.8	85.8	87.1	93.3	10.2%
Birmingham-Hoover, AL	137.4	137.5	146.6	149.5	147.8	149.7	152.1	156.1	4.4%
Bloomington-Normal, IL	N/A	141.0	147.8	149.2	149.3	153.8	141.5	155.8	4.4%
Boise City-Nampa, ID	123.2	130.6	135.9	139.7	140.1	N/A	N/A	161.8	15.8%
Boston-Cambridge-Quincy, MA-NH	335.4	358.5	389.7	392.7	407.2	390.5	396.2	418.5	6.6%
Boulder, CO	317.6	313.0	325.3	331.2	334.9	299.2	337.2	346.2	4.5%
Bridgeport-Stamford-Norwalk, CT	377.0	422.0	441.3	452.9	444.9	434.7	455.5	487.3	7.6%
Buffalo-Niagara Falls, NY	86.6	90.5	95.0	96.0	99.3	94.9	92.9	97.5	1.6%
Canton-Massillon, OH	109.0	114.4	115.2	115.6	119.3	106.1	103.4	N/A	N/A
Cape Coral-Fort Myers, FL	133.3	151.9	187.2	183.8	194.8	198.0	226.0	266.8	45.2%
Cedar Rapids, IA	118.8	122.8	129.5	131.9	129.8	133.4	118.7	131.6	-0.2%
Champaign-Urbana, IL	111.6	122.6	127.2	125.2	133.9	128.5	128.3	137.6	9.9%
Charleston-North Charleston, SC	159.4	168.9	183.5	191.9	184.0	180.4	189.3	193.6	0.9%
Charleston, WV	107.2	110.9	111.3	115.1	119.7	107.2	112.5	121.7	5.7%

(Continued)

TABLE A.3 (Continued)

Metropolitan Area	2002	2003	2004	2004:II	2004:III	2004:IV	2005:I r	2005:II p	%Chya
					(Not Seasonally Adjusted, 000s)				
Charlotte-Gastonia-Concord, NC-SC	149.1	151.5	168.0	172.2	171.0	173.3	169.4	N/A	N/A
Chattanooga, TN-GA	112.3	116.7	125.4	131.8	125.8	126.4	123.8	130.5	-1.0%
Chicago-Naperville-Joliet, IL	205.1	220.3	240.1	244.1	248.0	238.9	237.4	263.6	8.0%
Cincinnati-Middletown, OH-KY-IN	134.1	138.9	142.5	147.5	146.1	143.0	139.6	148.5	0.7%
Cleveland-Elyria-Mentor, OH	N/A	N/A	136.4	139.3	139.6	138.3	135.4	144.7	3.9%
Colorado Springs, CO	176.9	184.5	187.6	189.6	N/A	192.3	192.2	214.2	13.0%
Columbia, SC	119.5	123.6	123.4	120.7	N/A	127.0	129.5	133.7	10.8%
Columbus, OH	140.3	146.3	146.7	150.4	151.1	143.4	140.1	155.9	3.7%
Corpus Christi, TX	94.4	102.1	112.7	111.5	116.9	114.5	116.5	123.0	10.3%
Cumberland, MD-WV	66.5	69.5	72.7	74.7	72.2	71.6	80.6	88.6	18.6%
Dallas-Fort Worth-Arlington, TX	135.2	138.4	138.2	141.0	140.3	137.3	140.0	149.1	5.7%
Danville, IL	N/A	61.5	62.2	62.8	70.2	56.7	59.4	73.4	16.9%
Davenport-Moline-Rock Island, IA-IL	95.0	100.6	107.8	108.0	119.5	104.4	103.0	133.9	24.0%
Dayton, OH	112.6	114.6	115.8	119.7	118.5	113.8	110.0	119.4	-0.3%
Decatur, IL	74.4	74.1	75.5	77.3	78.1	78.7	70.0	86.8	12.3%
Deltona-Daytona Beach-Ormond Beach, FL	108.3	124.9	148.6	147.9	155.6	162.6	169.5	194.0	31.2%
Denver-Aurora, CO	228.1	238.2	239.1	241.8	N/A	237.1	236.0	248.4	2.7%
Des Moines, IA	130.2	133.9	140.8	141.8	144.5	141.6	139.0	145.1	2.3%
Detroit-Warren-Livonia, MI	116.9	N/A	161.0	168.6	168.2	156.8	151.0	169.2	0.4%
Dover, DE	N/A	128.3	150.1	147.6	155.1	157.4	164.4	176.3	19.4%
Durham, NC	N/A	N/A	149.0	151.6	147.0	146.6	152.4	198.5	30.9%
Elmira, NY	68.2	77.9	78.8	81.4	81.5	76.3	74.5	N/A	N/A
El Paso, TX	88.9	92.9	94.7	96.0	95.1	96.1	104.8	108.9	13.4%
Erie, PA	89.4	89.9	98.6	94.1	107.1	102.7	86.9	98.5	4.7%
Eugene-Springfield, OR	143.7	151.7	164.9	163.0	165.9	174.1	178.5	192.4	18.0%
Fargo, ND-MN	107.7	115.1	124.2	124.2	124.6	128.0	125.3	132.6	6.8%
Farmington, NM	118.8	127.2	134.6	134.8	135.1	132.8	148.2	151.8	12.6%
Ft. Wayne, IN	94.9	93.2	96.6	98.6	99.7	94.9	93.4	102.8	4.3%
Gainesville, FL	130.0	145.0	159.0	167.1	166.9	168.0	159.3	178.8	7.0%
Gary-Hammond, IN	114.3	119.2	122.6	124.6	125.6	125.8	120.9	129.6	4.0%
Glens Falls, NY	99.9	113.3	129.3	132.7	127.6	141.2	127.6	142.0	7.0%
Grand Rapids, MI	125.3	129.9	132.9	134.5	133.8	132.1	136.4	139.0	3.3%
Green Bay, WI	130.6	137.3	143.3	141.7	145.1	144.7	152.8	159.2	12.4%

Greensboro-High Point, NC	135.8	137.3	139.8	140.3	143.1	140.3	136.8	148.0	5.5%
Greenville, SC	132.5	136.9	135.8	136.3	139.3	133.5	133.5	143.2	5.1%
Gulfport-Biloxi, MS	100.2	107.6	113.9	113.1	115.8	117.3	121.1	124.0	9.6%
Hagerstown-Martinsburg, MD-WV	N/A	141.8	165.9	160.1	171.7	175.7	185.5	206.0	28.7%
Hartford-West Hartford-East Hartford, CT	179.3	207.9	231.6	226.2	239.8	237.5	244.5	257.7	13.9%
Honolulu, HI	335.0	380.0	460.0	451.1	469.0	490.0	529.1	577.8	28.1%
Houston-Baytown-Sugar Land, TX	132.8	136.4	136.0	139.2	137.5	135.5	138.1	142.5	2.4%
Indianapolis, IN	116.8	121.1	121.7	125.9	128.5	113.4	116.3	124.6	-1.0%
Jackson, MS	N/A	110.7	118.1	118.6	121.1	123.6	123.5	131.7	11.0%
Jacksonville, FL	117.8	131.6	150.7	154.5	157.6	153.7	164.4	166.6	7.8%
Kalamazoo-Portage, MI	117.8	123.4	123.1	127.1	126.8	126.2	117.0	122.6	-3.5%
Kankakee-Bradley, IL	105.8	109.7	120.0	115.4	130.9	119.0	115.4	132.3	14.6%
Kansas City, MO-KS	137.4	144.2	150.0	152.1	152.3	149.3	148.3	157.1	3.3%
Kennewick-Richland-Pasco, WA	140.8	145.3	147.6	147.2	150.8	148.5	144.8	152.7	3.7%
Kingston, NY	156.1	185.1	216.8	220.3	216.4	227.6	227.7	250.7	13.8%
Knoxville, TN	118.4	130.5	132.2	131.4	135.0	135.2	135.2	143.4	9.1%
Lansing-E. Lansing, MI	126.4	133.6	137.9	140.4	139.2	140.7	135.2	143.6	2.3%
Las Vegas-Paradise, NV	159.8	179.2	266.4	269.9	283.2	281.4	291.0	300.1	11.2%
Lexington-Fayette, KY	127.1	133.4	138.7	139.4	139.5	143.5	141.5	144.8	3.9%
Lincoln, NE	122.4	131.5	134.4	135.3	139.6	133.1	133.5	138.3	2.2%
Little Rock-N. Little Rock, AR	95.7	104.8	108.4	110.4	110.9	108.0	108.6	118.9	7.7%
Los Angeles-Long Beach-Santa Ana, CA	290.0	354.7	446.4	438.4	452.4	470.9	474.7	474.8	8.3%
Louisville, KY-IN	125.2	131.7	131.5	133.4	132.5	131.8	130.1	136.8	2.5%
Madison, WI	172.4	183.8	200.8	194.7	209.5	208.1	209.4	220.1	13.0%
Memphis, TN-MS-AR	129.4	133.8	136.2	138.3	140.0	134.8	131.5	150.1	8.5%
Miami-Fort Lauderdale-Miami Beach, FL	192.7	231.6	286.4	282.1	299.9	315.7	339.0	371.6	31.7%
Milwaukee-Waukesha-West Allis, WI	173.8	182.1	197.1	197.3	205.1	199.3	198.9	216.8	9.9%
Minneapolis-St. Paul-Bloomington, MN-WI	185.0	199.6	217.4	218.0	219.8	220.6	218.7	237.7	9.0%
Mobile, AL	104.8	109.1	115.2	116.8	115.6	114.5	117.4	129.1	10.5%
Montgomery, AL	113.6	115.7	116.6	116.9	120.6	119.0	118.3	133.3	14.0%
Nashville-Davidson-Murfreesboro, TN	N/A	N/A	145.4	147.4	149.0	148.7	152.1	159.7	8.3%
New Haven-Milford, CT	191.4	223.9	249.2	246.8	260.5	264.6	244.5	283.8	15.0%
New Orleans-Metairie-Kenner, LA	123.5	130.8	137.4	137.5	143.5	140.3	141.2	152.6	11.0%
New York-Northern New Jersey-Long Island, NY-NJ-PA	296.0	343.5	385.9	382.8	398.2	396.2	412.5	452.7	18.3%
New York-Wayne-White Plains, NY-NJ	348.0	387.3	436.6	422.5	459.1	450.8	456.6	506.8	20.0%
NY: Edison, NJ	245.7	287.6	328.1	320.9	340.6	343.6	343.1	394.1	22.8%

(Continued)

255

TABLE A.3 (Continued)

Metropolitan Area	2002	2003	2004	2004:II	2004:III	2004:IV	2005:I r	2005:II p	%Chya
					[Not Seasonally Adjusted, 000s]				
NY: Nassau-Suffolk, NY	312.9	364.5	413.5	414.8	422.2	431.9	446.7	467.7	12.8%
NY: Newark-Union, NJ-PA	306.8	336.3	375.8	377.2	397.2	372.9	380.4	414.4	9.9%
Norwich-New London, CT	174.8	202.7	231.5	236.7	235.4	235.6	243.0	246.8	4.3%
Ocala, FL	N/A	N/A	110.1	112.3	114.9	114.1	122.2	135.3	20.5%
Oklahoma City, OK	100.1	103.0	112.4	107.0	125.8	109.7	110.3	115.7	8.1%
Omaha, NE-IA	122.4	128.1	131.3	133.2	134.1	N/A	132.4	137.3	3.1%
Orlando, FL	136.6	145.1	169.6	170.1	180.5	184.4	194.4	232.2	36.5%
Palm Bay-Melbourne-Titusville, FL	105.2	123.7	153.4	145.7	159.3	166.3	184.1	204.0	40.0%
Pensacola-Ferry Pass-Brent, FL	112.2	116.4	131.1	132.7	133.8	139.6	143.8	163.6	23.3%
Peoria, IL	88.0	93.1	96.3	98.4	113.0	95.2	91.5	110.5	12.3%
Philadelphia-Camden-Wilmington, PA-NJ-DE-MD	146.9	168.8	185.1	188.0	193.8	189.1	191.2	211.0	12.2%
Phoenix-Mesa-Scottsdale, AZ	143.8	152.5	169.4	165.6	172.7	180.2	193.8	243.4	47.0%
Pittsburgh, PA	102.4	108.2	113.4	117.5	117.4	107.6	106.4	118.5	0.9%
Pittsfield, MA	149.2	163.2	192.8	198.7	196.5	204.0	212.5	211.8	6.6%
Portland-South Portland-Biddeford, ME	172.1	193.1	224.8	227.2	233.5	227.3	236.0	247.2	8.8%
Portland-Vancouver-Beaverton, OR-WA	177.5	188.9	206.5	204.2	211.5	214.5	219.8	238.0	16.6%
Providence-New Bedford-Fall River, RI-MA	203.3	242.9	276.9	274.3	289.4	285.0	278.5	291.6	6.3%
Raleigh-Cary, NC	160.1	162.0	169.9	172.5	172.0	171.6	166.6	185.2	7.4%
Reading, PA	94.7	106.5	121.1	120.5	131.8	122.5	122.2	140.4	16.5%
Reno-Sparks, NV	183.2	204.9	284.3	270.5	299.2	286.2	N/A	357.4	32.1%
Richmond, VA	142.3	155.1	170.7	173.0	174.6	176.2	180.5	198.4	14.7%
Riverside-San Bernardino-Ontario, CA	176.5	221.0	296.4	294.5	311.7	322.4	343.4	367.6	24.8%
Rochester, NY	93.8	99.4	106.5	105.1	114.9	106.2	107.8	110.7	5.3%
Rockford, IL	83.6	99.4	103.6	103.5	105.9	110.9	111.5	122.7	18.6%
Sacramento–Arden-Arcade–Roseville, CA	210.2	247.6	317.6	308.2	329.2	343.9	352.9	377.4	22.5%
Saginaw-Saginaw Township North, MI	N/A	N/A	N/A	N/A	N/A	N/A	N/A	N/A	N/A
Saint Louis, MO-IL	118.7	123.0	128.7	131.5	136.5	128.6	109.4	141.9	7.9%
Salem, OR	N/A	150.6	154.6	151.3	163.7	151.3	156.5	172.0	13.7%
Salt Lake City, UT	148.8	148.0	158.0	161.5	161.3	159.7	157.0	169.9	5.2%

San Antonio, TX	110.4	118.1	122.7	124.7	126.5	122.5	123.6	134.0	7.5%
San Diego-Carlsbad-San Marcos, CA	364.2	424.9	551.6	559.7	578.3	569.9	584.1	605.6	8.2%
San Francisco-Oakland-Fremont, CA	517.1	558.1	641.7	647.3	646.3	656.7	686.2	726.9	12.3%
Sarasota-Bradenton-Venice, FL	168.3	193.3	255.7	273.9	285.9	288.4	341.9	367.8	34.3%
Seattle-Tacoma-Bellevue, WA	229.4	239.1	284.6	258.8	278.2	299.8	290.8	310.3	19.9%
Shreveport-Bossier City, LA	90.3	100.7	110.6	111.4	111.6	115.5	110.6	125.1	12.3%
Sioux Falls, SD	116.7	123.2	129.2	129.7	129.6	127.3	132.9	137.7	6.2%
South Bend-Mishawaka, IN	91.0	91.1	93.6	93.8	98.5	96.4	91.1	102.1	8.8%
Spartanburg, SC	105.2	109.2	110.8	115.2	113.9	111.2	114.5	118.7	3.0%
Spokane, WA	108.7	120.3	128.5	127.3	132.4	138.8	136.3	158.6	24.6%
Springfield, IL	95.5	101.0	103.3	104.5	106.5	109.1	100.1	109.0	4.3%
Springfield, MA	146.9	162.3	180.3	177.6	187.3	187.7	188.5	197.9	11.4%
Springfield, MO	N/A	N/A	114.1	127.4	110.2	109.1	126.4	N/A	N/A
Syracuse, NY	86.4	95.0	98.4	94.7	102.7	98.6	94.4	108.7	14.8%
Tallahassee, FL	136.9	137.1	152.5	148.8	155.6	156.3	156.7	163.3	9.7%
Tampa-St.Petersburg-Clearwater, FL	133.5	138.1	159.7	158.2	167.0	168.5	172.8	195.0	23.3%
Toledo, OH	109.6	111.4	113.5	116.7	114.1	112.4	118.6	118.6	1.6%
Topeka, KS	89.0	97.3	102.1	103.7	109.7	99.1	95.5	103.1	-0.6%
Trenton-Ewing, NJ	179.5	212.4	234.2	235.9	250.4	229.4	225.4	267.7	13.5%
Tucson, AZ	146.4	156.3	177.3	175.8	179.9	185.3	199.0	228.5	30.0%
Tulsa, OK	106.7	110.4	113.1	113.3	115.8	118.1	112.3	117.4	3.6%
Virginia Beach-Norfolk-Newport News, VA-NC	N/A	138.8	163.0	155.1	182.2	167.7	174.0	192.0	23.8%
Washington-Arlington-Alexandria, DC-VA-MD-WV	242.3	277.9	339.8	340.1	349.4	359.0	380.6	429.2	26.2%
Waterloo/Cedar Falls, IA	87.8	91.3	95.2	95.4	96.7	97.9	86.5	100.7	5.6%
Wichita, KS	98.1	100.5	103.9	105.8	106.6	105.5	105.1	106.3	0.5%
Worcester, MA	225.6	252.6	275.9	279.2	284.0	276.5	279.3	292.3	4.7%
Yakima, WA	115.7	123.4	129.9	133.0	136.3	128.1	126.9	134.8	1.4%
Youngstown-Warren-Boardman, OH-PA	N/A	N/A	86.0	85.2	91.1	86.2	82.4	82.9	-2.7%

*All areas are metropolitan statistical areas (MSA) as defined by the U.S. Office of Management and Budget as of 2004. They include the named central city and surrounding areas.　N/A Not Available　p Preliminary　r Revised
©2005 National Association of REALTORS®.

Total Sales: Single-Family, Apartment Condos, and Co-ops

These data (see Table A.4) track regional and state trends in home sales volume.

Updated data can be accessed at http://www.realtor.org/Research .nsf/files/REL05Q2S.pdf/$FILE/REL05Q2S.pdf.

TABLE A.4   *Total Sales: Single-Family, Apartment Condos, and Co-ops*

State	2002	2003	2004	2004.II
United States	5,631	6,183	6,784	6,900
Northeast	950	1,022	1,114	1,123
Midwest	1,346	1,468	1,549	1,597
South	2,065	2,282	2,542	2,567
West	1,269	1,404	1,577	1,627
Alabama	82.2	93.7	112.0	110.2
Alaska	17.2	18.4	23.0	22.7
Arizona	128.2	149.6	186.8	182.5
Arkansas	52.2	53.8	60.9	59.6
California	565.1	577.6	610.1	605.5
Colorado	109.4	112.4	126.0	132.6
Connecticut	64.2	63.5	72.5	72.7
Delaware	14.5	15.8	18.9	18.4
District of Columbia	11.2	12.1	13.4	14.1
Florida	429.3	476.1	526.5	560.3
Georgia	173.9	174.0	215.8	216.2
Hawaii	28.1	34.4	35.5	35.3
Idaho	25.7	27.6	32.0	35.4
Illinois	269.0	275.1	307.5	306.0
Indiana	125.2	120.4	130.5	129.0
Iowa	58.4	62.4	71.1	71.0
Kansas	60.0	65.3	73.4	75.3
Kentucky	73.5	81.1	89.3	88.2
Louisiana	71.7	76.2	79.6	82.9
Maine	28.8	30.7	33.6	33.9
Maryland	117.6	120.8	140.6	138.0
Massachusetts	115.9	118.3	141.7	138.3
Michigan	203.5	207.4	213.4	215.3
Minnesota	122.6	126.7	137.4	146.6
Mississippi	48.0	51.5	58.1	59.7
Missouri	115.2	131.1	141.8	142.2
Montana	22.6	23.2	24.2	23.8
Nebraska	34.3	38.0	39.8	48.0
Nevada	63.5	80.9	99.8	94.1
New Hampshire	23.8	25.4	27.2	27.6
New Jersey	166.0	174.1	188.7	200.1

2004.III	2004.IV	2005.I r	2005.II p	%Chya
		(Seasonally Adjusted Annual Rate, 000s)		
6,797	6,877	6,837	7,217	4.6%
1,123	1,130	1,127	1,207	7.5%
1,550	1,560	1,513	1,623	1.6%
2,560	2,590	2,590	2,730	6.3%
1,573	1,600	1,600	1,657	1.8%
111.7	118.2	123.7	125.6	14.0%
23.0	23.2	28.4	21.5	−5.3%
195.9	199.4	206.2	194.8	6.7%
63.6	61.5	65.7	69.0	15.8%
600.6	616.0	597.0	610.7	0.9%
127.1	125.8	116.3	136.2	2.7%
77.1	72.5	75.8	83.4	14.7%
25.0	15.7	16.4	18.8	2.2%
9.8	16.0	14.4	12.8	−9.2%
511.0	499.4	566.1	583.5	4.1%
220.0	227.7	221.4	252.9	12.3%
35.7	37.6	38.2	38.0	7.6%
33.3	30.1	36.1	N/A	N/A
311.8	317.0	296.7	311.5	1.8%
130.1	134.6	131.6	136.9	6.1%
71.5	73.3	68.6	75.4	6.2%
73.8	72.2	73.6	78.9	4.8%
90.2	96.7	90.7	93.0	5.4%
79.9	77.5	82.8	84.4	1.8%
33.6	33.4	34.3	33.6	−0.9%
144.0	144.8	131.4	139.2	0.9%
146.3	149.8	140.9	142.8	3.3%
218.8	209.6	213.6	214.2	−0.5%
143.2	136.1	121.4	145.7	−0.6%
58.2	56.9	60.0	64.1	7.4%
144.2	140.5	142.4	143.0	0.6%
24.4	23.5	22.4	27.1	13.9%
41.1	39.2	33.7	48.1	0.2%
93.8	94.6	114.2	94.1	Unch
35.2	31.1	N/A	N/A	N/A
206.5	175.4	178.5	198.9	−0.6%

(Continued)

TABLE A.4   *(Continued)*

State	2002	2003	2004	2004.II
New Mexico	38.9	43.3	50.6	45.3
New York	290.4	282.6	307.5	274.7
North Carolina	142.1	156.3	192.6	175.7
North Dakota	12.3	12.9	14.5	17.3
Ohio	237.0	253.1	275.7	276.1
Oklahoma	79.5	85.1	93.6	91.3
Oregon	72.1	78.3	90.7	91.5
Pennsylvania	202.4	218.8	247.3	242.0
Rhode Island	17.1	16.9	19.2	19.5
South Carolina	72.7	83.0	99.3	98.3
South Dakota	14.9	15.6	17.3	16.3
Tennessee	112.0	128.8	156.1	153.9
Texas	412.4	425.4	485.5	482.6
Utah	40.9	43.9	43.6	46.2
Vermont	13.0	14.5	14.2	13.8
Virginia	150.1	158.3	186.0	182.8
Washington	116.3	132.3	147.6	139.0
West Virginia	28.1	28.9	36.0	33.6
Wisconsin	105.5	105.9	116.8	116.7
Wyoming	10.6	11.4	13.2	11.7

Source: National Association of REALTORS®.

2004.III	2004.IV	2005.I r	2005.II p	%Chya
	(Seasonally Adjusted Annual Rate, 000s)			
40.5	61.9	100.4	48.6	7.3%
334.7	296.4	335.6	293.4	6.81%
227.1	175.3	215.1	191.4	8.9%
15.0	15.2	11.5	18.6	7.5%
279.5	277.6	274.8	281.6	2.0%
95.8	93.7	98.1	99.9	9.4%
95.4	96.5	89.4	97.7	6.8%
247.9	250.3	239.5	247.4	2.2%
19.5	19.4	19.3	19.8	1.5%
102.1	104.2	102.5	112.5	14.4%
18.1	18.2	17.3	16.7	2.5%
159.0	162.0	158.3	167.8	9.0%
496.7	504.9	481.6	524.4	8.7%
43.6	43.7	47.1	50.7	9.7%
14.4	14.3	N/A	16.5	19.6%
191.9	195.9	179.6	187.7	2.7%
149.7	162.1	152.2	166.5	19.8%
37.5	39.4	36.6	40.9	21.7%
120.0	120.7	112.8	123.0	5.4%
13.7	15.7	15.1	13.3	13.7%

U.S. Economic Outlook: November 2005

Real estate is subject to the whims of the business cycle of the national economy, and Table A.5 provides a snapshot of overall economic activity.

Updated forecasts can be found at http://www.realtor.org/Research.nsf/files/currentforecast.pdf/$FILE/currentforecast.pdf.

TABLE A.5 U.S. Economic Outlook: November 2005

	2004	2005				2006				2007	2003	2004	2005	2006
	IV	I	II	III	IV	I	II	III	IV	I				
U.S. Economy														
Annual Growth Rate														
Real GDP	3.3	3.8	3.3	3.6	2.8	4.3	4.4	3.7	3.6	3.4	2.7	4.2	3.5	3.8
Nonfarm Payroll Employment	1.7	1.6	1.9	1.3	0.9	1.9	1.9	1.8	1.6	1.3	-0.3	1.1	1.6	1.6
Consumer Prices	3.6	2.4	4.2	5.1	4.3	0.7	2.4	2.2	2.3	2.1	2.3	2.7	3.4	2.7
Real Disposable Income	9.1	-3.4	1.5	-1.5	4.1	7.2	4.7	4.5	3.9	4.9	2.4	3.4	1.5	4.1
Consumer Confidence	96	104	102	99	98	99	101	104	105	106	80	96	101	102
Percent														
Unemployment	5.4	5.3	5.1	5.0	5.1	5.1	5.0	4.9	4.9	4.9	6.0	5.5	5.1	5.0
Interest Rates, Percent														
Fed Funds Rate	2.0	2.5	2.9	3.4	4.1	4.3	4.3	4.3	4.3	4.3	1.1	1.3	3.2	4.3
3-Month T-Bill Rate	2.0	2.5	2.9	3.4	4.0	4.1	4.1	4.1	4.1	4.1	1.0	1.4	3.2	4.1
Prime Rate	4.9	5.4	5.9	6.4	7.0	7.4	7.4	7.2	7.2	7.2	4.1	4.3	6.2	7.3
Corporate Aaa Bond Yield	5.5	5.3	5.1	5.1	5.6	5.8	6.0	6.1	6.1	6.2	5.7	5.6	5.3	6.0
10-Year Government Bond	4.2	4.3	4.2	4.2	4.6	4.8	4.9	5.0	5.0	5.1	4.0	4.3	4.3	4.9
30-Year Government Bond	4.9	4.7	4.5	4.4	4.9	5.1	5.2	5.3	5.3	5.4	5.1	5.1	4.6	5.2
Mortgage Rates, Percent														
30-Year Fixed Rate	5.7	5.8	5.7	5.8	6.2	6.4	6.5	6.6	6.7	6.8	5.8	5.8	5.9	6.5
1-Year Adjustable	4.1	4.2	4.3	4.5	4.9	5.1	5.2	5.2	5.2	5.3	3.8	3.9	4.5	5.2

Housing Indicators

Thousands														
Existing Home Sales*	6,877	6,837	7,223	7,237	7,057	6,897	6,853	6,883	6,842	6,875	6,183	6,784	7,108	6,860
New Single-Family Sales	1,243	1,249	1,297	1,333	1,318	1,297	1,267	1,212	1,179	1,208	1,086	1,203	1,299	1,241
Housing Starts	1,973	2,083	2,044	2,068	2,051	2,049	2,003	1,928	1,884	1,931	1,865	1,950	2,062	1,966
Single-Family Units	1,621	1,709	1,693	1,731	1,712	1,684	1,635	1,554	1,502	1,538	1,505	1,604	1,711	1,594
Multifamily Units	352	374	351	337	339	364	368	373	382	392	349	345	350	372
Residential Construction**	571	584	599	609	613	613	609	598	587	585	509	562	601	602
Percent Change—Year Ago														
Existing Home Sales	8.1	8.2	4.7	6.5	2.6	0.9	-5.1	-4.9	-3.0	-0.3	9.8	9.7	4.8	-3.5
New Single-Family Sales	10.8	5.0	7.8	14.5	6.1	3.8	-2.3	-9.0	-10.6	-6.9	11.9	10.8	8.0	-4.5
Housing Starts	-3.1	8.0	6.3	4.7	4.0	-1.7	-2.0	-6.8	-8.1	-5.8	8.4	5.2	5.7	-4.6
Single-Family Units	-2.2	9.4	5.9	5.9	5.6	-1.4	-3.5	-10.2	-12.3	-8.7	10.3	6.6	6.7	-6.9
Multifamily Units	-7.0	1.9	8.6	-0.7	-3.6	-2.6	4.8	10.8	12.7	7.7	0.6	-0.9	1.4	6.2
Residential Construction	6.6	7.7	6.1	7.0	7.4	4.9	1.6	-1.7	-4.3	-4.6	8.4	10.3	7.0	0.0
Median Home Prices														
Thousands of Dollars														
Existing Home Prices	190.3	190.3	209.3	216.0	211.8	202.4	220.7	227.3	221.5	211.1	169.5	185.2	208.1	219.2
New Home Prices	227.8	229.9	228.0	221.1	243.7	246.7	245.3	237.2	260.8	262.5	195.0	221.0	230.2	247.0
Percent Change—Year Ago														
Existing Home Prices	9.7	10.2	13.4	14.1	11.9	6.3	5.4	5.2	4.6	4.3	8.5	9.3	12.4	5.3
New Home Prices	14.4	8.0	5.3	3.3	7.0	7.3	7.6	7.3	7.0	6.4	3.9	13.3	4.1	7.3
Housing Affordability Index	132	133	121	118	118	120	111	108	110	113	138	133	123	112

Quarterly figures are seasonally adjusted annual rates.

*Existing home sales of single-family homes and condo/coops.

**Billion dollars.

Source: Forecast produced using Macroeconomic Advisers quarterly model of the U.S. economy. Assumptions and simulations by Dr. David Lereah and Dr. Lawrence Yun.

Measures of Real Estate Valuation

The two most fundamental measures of real estate valuation are the gross rent multiplier (GRM) and the capitalization rate (cap rate). Both are used and recognized by real estate professionals.

Gross Rent Multiplier (GRM)

The GRM relates the gross income from the operation of a parcel of real estate to the purchase price. The GRM is best understood by considering an example:

A strip center is 100 percent occupied and has four tenants, A, B, C, and, D. The scheduled monthly rent is:

Tenant A	$10,000
Tenant B	3,000
Tenant C	2,500
Tenant D	2,500
Total:	$18,000 × 12 months = $216,000 annual gross income

If the strip center is offered for sale for $1,600,000, the GRM would be 7.41:

$1,600,000/$216,000 annual gross income = 7.41 GRM

Therefore, both of the following equations are true:

$$\text{Annual Gross Income} \times \text{GRM} = \text{Purchase Price}$$
$$\text{Purchase Price}/\text{Annual Gross Income} = \text{GRM}$$

How to Apply the GRM.   In the preceding example, is a 7.41 GRM a good deal? It depends. This GRM should be compared to the GRM on other similar properties available for sale and, better still, compared to the GRM on other similar properties that have recently sold.

Capitalization Rate (Cap Rate)

The cap rate is a mechanism for relating anticipated *net operating income* (NOI) to the purchase price. To understand cap rates, you must first understand what is meant by net operating income. Net operating income is best defined by an equation:

$$\text{Gross Income} - \text{Operating Expenses} = \text{NOI}$$

Operating expenses are understood to include all costs of operating the property except mortgage interest and depreciation.

Therefore, the capitalization rate would be expressed by the following equation:

$$\text{NOI}/\text{Purchase Price} = \text{Cap Rate}$$

Both of the following equations are also true:

$$\text{Purchase Price} \times \text{Cap Rate} = \text{NOI}$$
$$\text{NOI}/\text{Cap Rate} = \text{Purchase Price}$$

Continuing the example of the strip shopping center, assume the center has operating expenses of $86,400. Therefore, the center would have net operating income as follows:

$$\text{Gross Income} - \text{Operating Expenses} = \text{NOI}$$
$$\$216,000 - \$86,400 = \$129,600$$

The NOI is $129,600.

Assuming the same purchase price of $1,600,000, the cap rate would be 8.1 percent:

$$\text{NOI/Purchase Price} = \text{Cap Rate}$$
$$\$129,600/\$1,600,000 = 8.1\%$$

How to Apply the Cap Rate.   In the example, is a cap rate of 8.1 percent a good deal? Again, it depends. Just like with the GRM, this cap rate should be compared to cap rates on other similar properties available for sale and compared to the cap rates on other similar properties that have recently sold.

Comparing GRMs and Cap Rates

Both measures are evaluating the ability of real estate to produce income. Both measures have strengths and weaknesses.

The GRM affords a quick value judgment based on facts (the gross income) that can be readily verified. The problem is the GRM does not consider operating expenses. Some similar properties can cost more to operate than others. For example, if two buildings have the same gross income but the landlord includes utilities in the rent in only one of the buildings, the building with utilities included in the rent probably costs more to operate.

In this way, the cap rates are superior to GRMs in that cap rates consider more information. Cap rates consider both gross income and operating expenses. The problem with cap rates is the quality of the information considered. What would constitute appropriate operating expenses is often a matter of debate. Sellers often under-report operating expenses.

Appraisers, lenders, and real estate agents can all be good sources of assistance in developing and understanding appropriate cap rates and GRMs.

NOTES

INTRODUCTION How to Make Real Estate Buying or Selling Decisions When a Crash May Be Imminent

1. As of September 15, 2005. *Source:* Bureau of the Public Debt, U.S. Treasury.
2. As of September 30, 2005. *Source:* U.S. Census Bureau.
3. From the Consumer Price Index of September 15, 2005, published by the Bureau of Labor Statistics, U.S. Department of Labor.
4. Mortgage Bankers Association, October 26, 2005.

CHAPTER 1 Do You Have a False Sense of Security? Why You Should Be Preparing for a Crash—Even If It Never Comes

1. Jill Stewart, *Los Angeles Times Magazine*, Los Angeles, March 21, 1993, page 14.

CHAPTER 2 What Caused the Real Estate Bubble, What Could Trigger a Crash, and Why the Crash Will Be Regional, Not National

1. *USA Today*, "Home Prices 'Extremely Overvalued' in 53 Cities," August 16, 2005, Money Section, page 1.
2. Wall Street Journal Online, September 19, 2005.
3. Greenspan made the comments in a speech to the American Bankers Association on September 26, 2005.
4. Kopin Tan, "Bubble Trouble," *Barron's*, March 21, 2005, page 18.
5. Comments from speech at the California Economic Forecast (CEF) presentation of the 2005 Real Estate and Economic Outlook, by CEF economist Mark Schniepp.
6. September 2005 comments to Dow Jones & Company subsidiary Market-Watch.
7. September 1, 2005, OFHEO report, "Largest U.S. House Price Increases in More Than 25 Years."
8. Comments from speech at the California Economic Forecast (CEF) presentation of the 2005 Real Estate and Economic Outlook, by CEF economist Mark Schniepp.

CHAPTER 3 History Lessons from Previous Real Estate Bubbles: Who Lost and Who Came Through Stronger

1. T.J. Collins in *Newsday* for Zeckendorf's obituary.
2. The *New York Times*, October 4, 2005, page 1.

CHAPTER 5 Should You Sell Now?

1. This simple example does not attempt to compute the impact of depreciation recapture. Consult a qualified accountant or CPA before making any assumptions about your own potential tax liability.

CHAPTER 10 Life After the Bust: How Homeowners, Investors, Landlords, Lenders, and the National Economy Will React—and How to Profit

1. The Northern Trust Company, *Daily Economic Comment*, May 23, 2005.

INDEX

Absolute auction, 224–225
Accommodation, 33
Accountant, functions of, 98, 101, 105, 173, 193
Acquisitions, 95, 97–100, 110, 173, 197–210, 223–227
Adjustable rate mortgages (ARMs), 18, 31, 37–38, 135, 167
Adjusted basis, 95
Advertising, 111, 148, 151, 178, 213
Affordability/affordable housing, 36–37, 62, 79, 177, 241
Affordable housing, 36–37
Age of property, 110, 112
Aggressive leasing, 147
Allen, Robert, 184
Alternative investment, 38
Alternative investor(s), selling strategies, 97–105
Ambassador apartment, 148
American Bankers Association (ABA), 35, 37
Amortization, 91, 186, 213
Annual growth rate (employment), 63
Apartment buildings/complex, 207, 220, 228
Apartments, 117–121, 123–124, 141–142, 145–147, 178, 192, 235–236
Appraisal, 20, 91, 218, 234
Appraisal theory, 110–115
Appraiser, functions of, 20, 111
Appreciation rates, 17–18, 23–28, 64, 74–75, 110, 133, 165, 208
As improved property, 234
As is property, 226, 234–235, 237
Asking price, REO properties, 236–237
Assemblage of parcels, 209
Assumable mortgages, 185, 230
Attorney, functions of, 98, 101, 105, 173, 186, 188, 193–194, 198, 206–207, 219–220, 224, 229, 238
Auction(s), 220–225, 227–228, 232

Back ratio, 133
Back taxes, 238
Balloon mortgage, 135, 189, 192
Bankruptcy, 8, 14, 138, 167, 187, 212, 218–219, 224
Bidding process, 171, 223–227, 229–230, 232–233
Black Monday, 44–45
Boom and bust cycles, 14, 32, 60–61, 63
Break-even prices, 10
Broker's price opinion (BPO), 218, 234
Bubble-bust market, 22, 29, 41–50, 90–105, 108, 244–245
Bubble measurements, 63–64
Budget/budgeting, 111, 138
Building inspector, 236
Bureau of Labor Statistics (BLS), 63
Business cycle, 29, 166–167
Business failure, 29, 63, 179, 182
Buying opportunities, identification of, 170
Buy strategies, 107–110, 170, 182, 244–245

California housing market, 8, 17, 19, 45, 61, 87, 89, 176–177, 239
Canada, real estate investments in, 44
Capital gains, 10, 95–97, 103, 142
Capital improvements, 95, 114
Capitalization rate (cap rate), 112, 265–266
Capital reserves, 182, 197
Cash cushion strategy, 130–132
Cash flow action strategies, 125–139, 141–151
Cash reserves, 172–173
Census Bureau, as information resource, 64, 81
Change of use, 116, 120–121
Chicago Title, 105
Ciccarelli, Scot, 12
Class A/Class B buildings, 117

Closing costs, 90–91, 94, 97, 115, 184, 218, 226
Co-ops, 258–260
Commercial leases, 143–145, 176
Commercial real estate, 56, 159–160, 178–180, 207
Commissions, 90–91, 94, 97, 192, 227
Commuters, 122, 245
Comparable sales, 110–114, 234–236
Competition, 170
Condominiums, 61, 78, 108, 121, 169, 240, 258–260
Construction, 51, 110, 181. *See also* New construction
Consumer Price Index (CPI), 4
Consumer spending, 51, 166
Contrarian investing, 170
Conventional financing, 189–190, 195
Converting existing space, 150
Corporate guaranty, 159
Cosmetic improvements/repairs, 116, 118, 191–192
Cost approach, valuation process, 112–113, 115
Counteroffers, 214
Creative borrowing, 192–193. *See also* Creative financing techniques
Creative financing techniques, 168, 170, 183–195
Credit cards, 134, 138–139
Credit check, 186
Credit report, 91, 217
Crivello, Frank, 48
Crowding out, 36
Custom housing, 181

Data compilation, 63–64, 74–81, 113–115
Days on the market (DOM), 58, 62, 78
Debt ratio, 133–134
Decker, Dave, 9–11
Deed in lieu of foreclosure, 232, 237
Deed preparation, 226
Default, 37, 160. *See also* Foreclosure
Defensive strategies:
  buy signals, 107–124
  cash flow action plans, 125–161
  crash assessment, 55–87
  sell signals, 89–105
Deferred maintenance, 142, 149, 173
Deficiency judgment, 217

DeKaser, Richard, 12
Delayed exchange, 101–102
Depreciation recapture, 95–96
Depression, 169
Desperate sellers, 182, 208, 212–213
Direct exchange, 100
Discount real estate brokerages, 90–91
Dispute resolution, 194
Distance investing, 157–161
Distressed properties, 170, 173
Do-it-yourself sales approach, 93, 114
Down cycle, 10
Down payment, 39, 109, 184–186, 189, 192, 221, 230, 238
Due-on-sale clause, 185, 188
Dukakis, Michael, 46
Duplexes, 99–100, 102, 104

Easy money environment/financing, 59, 167–168
Economic conditions, impact on real estate market, 5, 12, 29, 166–168
Economic stagnation, 166
Electrical system, 112, 215
Employment, 28–29, 39–40, 56, 58, 61, 63–64, 86, 129–130, 176, 239
Empty nesters, 93, 108
Energy audits, 150
Energy prices, 33–35, 50–51, 244–245
Environmental issues, 123–124, 129
Equipment leases, 151
Equitable interest, 206
Equity/equity position, 3, 98–100, 139, 142–143, 166, 219, 221, 226
Escrow, 189
Escrow intermediary, 101–104
Eviction process, 219
Exclusive rights, real estate options, 198, 205
Existing home sales, 62, 78, 247–249
Existing stock of real estate, 57
Exotic loans, 18

Fair market value, 20, 99, 110, 112, 116, 213–214
Fannie Mae, 167
Federal Deposit Insurance Corporation (FDIC), 17, 21–22, 64
Federal Housing Finance Agency, 167–168
Federal Reserve Bank, 33, 36, 51

Financial distress, foreclosure process, 214–217
Financial health, 133–139, 144
Financial instability, 134
Financial resources, 3, 59. *See also* Mortgage loans
First American Real Estate Solutions, 60–61
First-time home buyers, 108–109
Fixer-uppers, 109, 116–117, 235
Flat rent lease, 143
Flipping, 3, 10, 169, 188, 245
Florida, real estate market in, 4, 43–44, 51, 61, 63, 239–240
Foreclosure, 7–8, 37–38, 167, 183, 211–214, 223–224, 232
Freddie Mac, 32, 37, 167
Free rent deals, 142, 178
Friendly foreclosure, 232
Front ratio, 133
FSLIC, 37
Full-service brokers, 91

Garage, 119–120
Gentrification, 116, 121–122
Great Depression, 44, 49, 107
Greenspan, Alan, 11, 17–18, 36
Gross income, 134, 265–266
Gross rent multiplier (GRM), 112, 264–267
Growth in income, inflation-adjusted, 56
Gulf Coast, rebuilding expenses, 35, 50

Hard money loans, 192
Hardship letter, 218
Heating system, 215
Hedging positions, 155
Hindy, Tom and Jill, 7–8, 40
Historical cycles, 60–63
Historical data/prices, 21, 81–85
Hoenig, Thomas, 33
Home equity lines of credit (HELOC), 139
Home equity loans, 35
Homeowners:
  cash flow action plan, 125–139
  first contact, 116
  selling strategies, 90–94
Home ownership statistics, 168

Hot markets, 93
Household(s), number of, 64, 74–75, 86
House turnover, 18
Housing Affordability Index (HAI), 22, 57, 60, 62, 78–79, 81, 86, 177–178, 241
Housing and Urban Development (HUD), 218, 234
Housing debt-to-income ratio, 21
Housing inventory, 240
Housing ratio, 133–134
Housing starts, 8
HUD1 settlement statement, 218
Hurricanes Katrina/Rita/Wilma, 35–36, 50, 245

Illiquid property, 160
Improvements, 3, 142, 149, 160, 230
Income approach, valuation process, 111–114
Income growth, 56–58, 63–64
Industrial real estate, 56, 120, 161
Inflated real estate market, 29
Inflation, 10, 12–13, 30, 33–36, 51
Information resources, 113–115, 158, 209, 234
Infrastructure changes, 57, 116, 122–123, 209
Inner-city apartments, 156–157
Inside information, 209
Insurance, 90–91, 94, 111, 115, 134, 159, 186, 189
Insurance agents, functions, 193
Interest-only loans, 18, 37–39, 135, 167
Interest rates, 21–22, 28–31, 32, 35–39, 49, 56, 51, 59–62, 78–79, 91, 149–150, 167, 177, 186, 189
Internal Revenue Code (IRC), Section 1031, 97–98
Internal Revenue Service (IRS), 217, 227–228
Inventory of unsold houses, 58, 78
Investment analysis, 157
Investment properties, 94–97, 111–112

Japanese real estate market, 29, 48, 182
Junior liens, 237–238

Land, generally:
  contracts, 168, 188–190
  sale of, 96
  undeveloped, 122–123
LandAmerica Financial Group, Inc., 105
Las Vegas, real estate market, 89, 244
Laundry equipment, 151
Law of averages, 12–14
Lawler, Patrick, 18
Lawsuit/litigation, 212
Leading indicators, 62, 78–79, 179–180
Lease(s):
  commercial, 143–145
  equipment, 151
  extension of, 160
  long-term, 182
  market downturn, 175–176
  NNN, 159–161
  options, 198, 207
  purchase, 135
  renewal negotiation strategies, 100,
    143–144
  residential, 145–149
  undeveloped land, 123
Leasing agent, functions of, 142, 144, 160,
  180, 210
Leasing incentives, 178
Lenders/lending industry, 30–32, 38, 59,
  61, 133, 167–168, 192–193,
  212–220, 223–224, 231–234,
  236–238
Lereah, David, 11, 18
Leverage/leveraging, 50, 197, 215
Liens, foreclosure process, 214–217,
  226–227, 232
Lifestyle considerations, 90, 93
Like-kind exchange, see Section 1031
  exchange
Lines of credit, 139, 150
Liquidity, 37–38, 59–60, 171–172
Loan servicing company, functions of,
  187–188
Loan to value ratio, 160
Local economic conditions, 29
Local real estate market, 29, 49–50, 55–87,
  133
Location, significance of, 123
London, real estate investments, 44
Loopnet.com, 158
Loose money environment, 59

Maintenance, 3, 111, 142, 159, 215. See
  also Deferred maintenance; Repairs
Marginal properties, 149
Market approach, valuation process,
  110–113
Market conditions, 11, 38, 42–47, 49,
  50–51, 93
Market cooldown, indicators of, 58
Market correction, 49
Market downturn, 135, 141, 168–169, 172
Market expansion, 60
Market exuberance, 19–20
Market performance, 13
Market pressures, 33
Market recovery, 176–182, 208
Market research, importance of, 156–157
Market reversal, 49, 97, 142, 168, 170,
  172
Market stagnation, 49
Market timing, 91–93, 97, 142, 173, 182
Massachusetts, real estate bubble, 46–47,
  87
Mechanical defects, 116–117
Mechanic's liens, 214–216, 232, 237
Media, impact of, 5, 13, 81, 107–108, 151,
  153, 165, 170
Median home prices/sale prices, 21–22,
  56–57, 60, 252–257
Median income, 21–22, 57
Metropolitan Statistical Areas (MSAs), 18,
  21–22, 28, 64–77, 155, 158,
  240–243, 245
Michigan, real estate market, 61, 244
Midwest region, 24, 78, 81, 86
Minimum bid auction, 225
Ministorage facilities, 123
Model apartments, 147–148
Monetary policies, 168
Mortgage-backed securities, 167
Mortgage loans, 4, 11, 18, 21, 30–31, 36,
  57–58, 62, 70, 90–91, 94, 133–134,
  167, 185–189, 212–213, 219
Moskow, Michael, 33
Motivated buyers/sellers, 102–104,
  115–117, 168, 171, 182
Moving expenses, 90–91
Multi-family units, 207, 220, 228
Multiple Listing Service (MLS), 114
Municipal liens, 216, 237
Municipal water, 122, 216

National Association of REALTORS®
(NAR), 11, 18, 22, 78–79, 81, 223
National economy, impact of bust on, 4,
12, 166–168
National real estate market, 22, 50
Negative cash flow, 10, 182
Neighborhood, assessment strategies,
60–64, 74–81, 86–87
Net operating income (NOI), 265–266
Networking, benefits of, 111, 173,
193
New construction, 58, 63, 81, 112, 122,
124, 169, 180–181
New home sales, 62, 78
Newspaper, as information resource, 78
New York City, real estate investments,
41–43, 45–46, 87
No money down, 184–185
Nonperforming loans, 183
Nonrecourse debt, 160
Nontraditional financing, 35, 135,
192–193
Northeast, real estate market, 25, 61, 78,
81
Nothing Down (Allen), 184

Obsolete properties, 120–121, 142, 149
Offer(s), 102, 171, 191, 207, 214,
217–218, 236–237
Office building/space, 117–121, 124, 172,
176, 179
Office of Federal Housing Enterprise
Oversight (OFHEO), 18, 21, 45
Oil prices, 34, 37, 46, 51
Olympia & York, 44
Operating costs, 233
Operating expenses, 150, 265–266
Operating numbers, 157–158
Operating statements, 111–112, 114
Optimism, 12, 165, 169
Options, 4, 197–210
Origination fee, 90–91, 94
Overextension of credit, 50, 211
Overvalued property, 12, 240–241
Owner financing, 184

Panic, 20, 49, 169, 175
Parking, 117
Partnership(s), 101–102, 117, 173,
193–195

Pending home sales index, 250–252
Pennsylvania, real estate crash, 61
Percentage leases, 143–144
Permits, 119, 236
Personal finances, 12, 35
Pessimism, 166
Photographs, digital, 114
PITI (principal, interest, taxes, and
insurance), 134
Plumbing system, 215
Points, 91
Population statistics, 65–73, 76–77,
176–177
Post-bust:
auctions, 223–230
creative financing, 183–195
investment strategies, 165–173
overvalued properties, 239–241
preforeclosure properties, 211–221
profit opportunities, 169–170
REO (real estate owned) properties,
231–238
short sales, 211–220
undervalued properties, 239, 241–244
using options, 197–210
when to start buying, 175–181
Potential equity, 219
Preapproved financing, 237
Preforeclosure, 212, 214–221
Price bubbles, 61
Price correction, 12
Price pressure, 9, 64, 123
Price-to-income ratio, 21
Private lenders, 192–193
Private mortgage insurance (PMI),
134
Private well water, 122
Profit-taking, 94
Property damage, 219
Property inspections, 214–215,
237
Property management, long distance,
159–161, 191
Property owner, foreclosure process,
211–224, 232–233
Property search database, 114
Property taxes, 111, 151, 159, 189, 206,
216
Public auction, 227–228
Public sale, 224

Purchase agreement/contract, 103, 217–218
Purchase decisions, consumer-driven, 109–110

RBC Capital Markets, 12
Real estate agent, 78, 90–91, 94, 97, 113–115, 158, 192, 218, 227, 238
Real estate bubble, 5, 11, 17–19, 30–31, 33, 133
Real estate bust, 3–6, 7–15, 17–51, 166–173, 240–241
Real estate crash, 4, 8, 20, 22–28, 32–40, 141, 169, 176–178, 208–210
Real estate cycle, 8
Real estate deal makers, see Reichmann family; Trump, Donald; Zeckendorf, William
Real estate gurus, 184–185, 188, 197
Real estate investment trust (REIT), 99
Real estate investor(s), strategies for, 94–97, 141–151
Real estate limited partnerships, 37
Real estate market, 20–21, 41–50
Real estate owned (REO), 213–214, 219, 226
Real estate principles, 10
Real returns, 30, 32
Realtor.com, 158
Recession, 14, 47, 87, 144, 169, 177, 241
Recording fees, 226
Recourse loans, 160
Redeveloping, 57, 116, 119–120
Refinancing, 104, 139, 150, 220
Regional real estate, 22–28, 48–49
Register of Deeds, 113
Rehab properties, 207, 220, 235, 245
Reichmann family, 44
Remodeling costs, 235
Rental property, 59, 99–101, 104, 111–112, 119, 123, 141–142, 145–147, 148–149, 190–191, 209
Rent/rent survey, 111, 114, 117, 123
Rent with option to buy, 135, 190–191
Repairs, 111, 149, 215, 233, 237
Replacement property, 98–104
Repositioning, 116–118
Resale expenses, 219
Reserve auction, 225
Residential real estate, 56, 180

Retail industry, 56, 161
Revenue generation, 150
Reverse amortization loans, 32, 38
Reverse exchange, 104–105
Risk reduction strategies, 93, 141–143, 197

Sale of home, 90–105, 155–159
Sale proceeds, Section 1031 exchange, 101–103
Sales contract, 218
Savings and loan crisis, 37–38
Second mortgages, 32, 37, 167–168, 185, 220–221, 230, 232
Section 1031 exchange, 97–104
Security deposits, 192
Seizure of property, 227, 229
Seller behavior, influential factors, 168–169
Seller financing, 100, 168, 185–186, 188
Seller's market, 115, 170, 181
Sell-offs, 49, 62
Sell-rent-buy strategy, 90, 92–94, 97, 166
Septic system, 122
Sewer service, 122, 216
Shopping malls, 122
Short sales/short pay, 211–220, 232
Showing patterns, 149
Simultaneous exchange, 100
Single-family homes, 94, 122, 252–260
Snowbirds, 93
Snow removal, 151
Soft real estate markets, 141–142, 178, 181
South, real estate market, 26, 60, 74, 78, 81, 86
Spec housing, 181
Speculation, 5, 18, 47, 49, 108
Starker Exchange, 98, 101
Staying put, 154–155
Stock market, 13–14, 30, 44–45, 175
Structural defects, 116–117
Subleases, 179–180
Sub-markets, 29, 124
Sub-par credit, 30–31, 59, 167
Supply and demand, 11, 38, 49, 55–58, 243
Syron, Richard, 18

Tax assessor, as information resource, 64, 111, 113–114, 116
Taxation, 3, 10, 37, 90–91, 94–100, 103–104, 111, 142, 151, 194, 217, 233
Tax-deferred exchange, 98, 142, 156, 170
Tax liens, 227–228, 237
Telephone call patterns, 148–149
Tenancy in common, 102
Tenant improvements, 178
Tenant retention, residential, 145–149
Terrorism, economic impact of, 35, 50, 81
Texas, real estate market, 46, 244
Third-party buyer, 103–104
Third-party exchanges, 100–101
Tipping Point, The, 166
Title company, 101–105, 193
Title insurance, 90–91, 94, 101–102, 104–105, 186, 226
Title search, 227, 229, 232, 237–238
Total sales, 258–260
Townhouses, 124
Traditional financing, 183–184
Traffic patterns, 157
Transaction costs, 91–94, 96. See also Closing costs
Transaction volume, influential factors, 78, 168, 248–249
Transfer of real estate option, 206
Transfer tax, 90, 94, 226
Triple net lease (NNN) investments, 159–161
Trump, Donald, 14–15, 48
28/36 rule, 133–134, 138

Underperforming space, 150
Undervalued property, 155, 241–243, 245
Undeveloped land, 122–123
Unemployment, economic impact of, 7–8, 32, 46, 49, 51, 141, 145, 167, 182

Unique properties, 123–124, 142, 172
U.S. Department of Agriculture, 234
U.S. Department of Housing and Urban Development (HUD), 45
U.S. economic outlook, 260–263
U.S. government deficit, 4, 51
U.S. housing market, 11–12, 18
Unrecorded sales, 188
Upgrading properties, 149–151
Utilities, 111–112, 150, 159, 233, 266

Vacancies, 111, 118, 141–142, 145–147, 149, 169, 179–180, 182
Vacation homes, 108
Valuation measures, 264–267
Value investing, 10, 108–124, 171
Value judgments, 234
Value vision, 115–116
Vendors, lease negotiations, 151
Veterans Administration, 234
Virtual tours, 114
Volatile markets, 48, 50
Vulture fund, 172–173

War, economic impact of, 4, 35–36, 42, 50
Warehouse buildings, 99, 121, 141
Waste hauling, 151
Waterfront property, 123
Weather, economic impact, 4, 35–36, 43
Web sites, as information resource, 78–79, 116, 158, 228, 234, 247, 250, 252, 258, 260
Webb & Knapp, 41–42
West, real estate market in, 26, 74, 78, 81, 86
Wrap around mortgages, 186–189

Zeckendorf, William, 41–42
Zell, Sam, 172
Zoning, 119